Psychology and Systems at Work

Robert B. Lawson
E. Doris Anderson
Lawrence P. Rudiger
The University of Vermont, Burlington

Boston   Columbus   Indianapolis   New York   San Francisco   Upper Saddle River
Amsterdam   Cape Town   Dubai   London   Madrid   Milan   Munich   Paris   Montréal   Toronto
Delhi   Mexico City   São Paulo   Sydney   Hong Kong   Seoul   Singapore   Taipei   Tokyo

Editorial Director: Craig Campanella
Editor in Chief, Psychology: Jessica Mosher
Executive Editor, Psychology: Susan Hartman
Editorial Assistant: Shivangi Ramachandran
Director of Marketing: Brandy Dawson
Senior Marketing Manager: Wendy Albert
Managing Editor: Denise Forlow
Senior Production Project Manager: Donna Simons
Senior Operations Specialist: Diane Peirano
Digital Media Editor: Amy Trudell
Media Project Manager: Tina Rudowski
Cover Photo: © Berkut/Shutterstock
Project Coordination and Editorial Services: Electronic Publishing Services Inc., NYC
Art Rendering and Electronic Page Makeup: Jouve
Printer/Binder: Edwards Brothers Malloy
Cover Printer: Lehigh-Phoenix Color/Hagerstown
Text Font: Palatino

Library of Congress Cataloging-in-Publication Data
Lawson, Robert B.
    Psychology and systems at work / by Robert B. Lawson, E. Doris Anderson, and Lawrence P. Rudiger
Pearson Education.
      p. cm.
    Includes index.
    ISBN 978-0-205-73578-5
    1. Psychology, Industrial. 2. Organizational behavior. I. Anderson, E. Doris. II. Rudiger, Lawrence P.
III. Title.
    HF5548.8.L323 2013
    158.7—dc23   2012026353

10 9 8 7 6 5 4 3 2 1

Student Case
ISBN 10: 0-205-73578-9
ISBN 13: 978-0-205-73578-5

Instructor's Review Edition
ISBN 10: 0-205-95000-0
ISBN 13: 978-0-205-95000-3

BRIEF CONTENTS

CONTENTS

PREFACE

Organizations matter. Most people spend a third to a half of their lives working in organizations. Given the high rate of unemployment today, people are also spending more time looking for work. In addition, globalization and technological innovation will continue to profoundly shape organizational leadership, demography, and structure.

For these and many other reasons, it is important for individuals to understand the nature of contemporary organizations. How can you get in and stay in? What makes an organization thrive or flounder? And given the chance, how can you advance, succeed, and perhaps even lead?

Helping students meet these important goals inspired us to write this book. *Psychology and Systems at Work* is grounded in our own experiences as students, teachers, and researchers; as participants in organizations (academic and otherwise); and as consultants retained by organizations to identify problems and facilitate change.

Our outlook is based on the broad field known as industrial/organizational psychology, which has a long and colorful history that you will discover as you read. Throughout the text, our intent is to integrate traditional and contemporary research findings from psychology and beyond. In particular, we will draw on practices and theoretical perspectives that conceive of organizations as social systems.

This systems-thinking approach provides a useful and flexible framework, particularly needed to guide organizations through periods of stress and uncertainty. It will also help you understand behaviors that defy logic, such as transactional redundancy, or doing the same thing again and again but expecting different results.

Organizational life goes through times of relative harmony disrupted by periods of essential transition. It has always been this way, and, though the pace of change is increasing, we think it always will be this way. However, in our many decades of experience, we've been pleasantly surprised at how people face challenges, defy the odds, and triumph.

Success is always the result of many factors—including good luck. But we have noticed, as Louis Pasteur observed long ago, that chance favors the prepared mind. We hope that this book provides a useful and effective means of preparing you to make organizations a positive and productive part of a rewarding life.

Lastly, we offer our appreciation to the following people, who reviewed the manuscript in its early stages:

Anila Bhagavatula, California State University, Long Beach
John Binning, Illinois State University
Jennifer Bowler, East Carolina University
Alan Clardy, Towson University
David Devonis, Graceland University
Gayle Davidson-Shivers, University of South Alabama

Elisa Grant-Vallone, California State University, San Marcos
Don Hantula, Temple University
Linda Hoffman, McKendree University
Leona Johnson, Hampton University
Jeff Keil, Mary Baldwin College
Evan Kleiman, George Mason University
Laurel McNall, The College at Brockport, SUNY
Cindy Nordstrom, Southern Illinois University, Edwardsville
Nicholas Salter, Ramapo College of New Jersey
Holly Traver, Rensselaer Polytechnic Institute
Penny Willmering, Arkansas Tech University

SUPPLEMENTS

Pearson is pleased to offer the following supplements to qualified instructors:

Instructor's Manual with Tests (ISBN 0-205-73579-7): The Instructor's Manual is a wonderful tool for classroom preparation and management. Corresponding to the chapters in the text, each of the manual's chapters contains a brief overview of the chapter with suggestions on how to present the material, sample lecture outlines, classrooms activities and discussion topics, ideas for in-class and out-of-class projects, and recommended outside readings. The Test Bank contains multiple-choice, short-answer, and essay questions, each referencing the relevant page in the text.

PowerPoint™ Presentation (ISBN 0-205-73580-0): The PowerPoint Presentation is an exciting interactive tool for use in the classroom. Each chapter pairs key concepts with images from the textbook to reinforce student learning.

MySearchLab (ISBN 0-205-95063-9): MySearchLab provides engaging experiences that personalize learning, and comes from a trusted partner with educational expertise and a deep commitment to helping students and instructors achieve their goals. Features include the ability to highlight and add notes to the eText online or download changes straight to the iPad. Chapter quizzes and flashcards offer immediate feedback and report directly to the grade book. A wide range of writing, grammar, and research is included.

Organizations As Systems

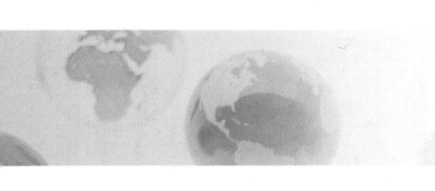

Introduction to Organizations and Systems

CHAPTER OVERVIEW

This chapter identifies some of the forces that shape the nature of work and organizations in the 21st century. We consider the psychological importance of work for the individual, family, and society and reflect on some consequences of unemployment. When studying organizations, *systems thinking* is a useful form of planning and problem solving that considers interdependence shared within and between organizations, the short-term and long-term consequences of individual and organizational actions, and the influences of society and the environment upon organizations. Because every organization is a system, no matter where you are working in the world, knowledge of systems thinking is an asset.

Maxstockphoto/Shutterstock

Changes in the global population as well as the demographics of that population afford better recruitment and retention of a diversified workforce reflective of the demographics of customers or clients. A brief overview of the history of industrial/organizational psychology promotes understanding of previous organizational actions and manipulations, as well as appreciation for suggestions about future treatment within and between organizations.

LEARNING OBJECTIVES

When you have finished reading this chapter, you will be prepared to do the following:

- Identify the importance of work in the 21st century for individuals, families, and society
- Describe organizations as systems and identify the core tendencies of social systems as they apply to organizations
- Define systems thinking and indicate the advantages this type of problem solving affords analytical thinking and the study of organizations

Moodboard/SuperStock

- Define a global organization and explain why it is critical to study these organizations
- Discuss the history of industrial/organizational psychology and specify some of the important topics being studied by I/O psychologists

WORK AND SYSTEMS IN THE 21ST CENTURY

Why study organizations? There are several reasons. First, organizations are a necessary and universal aspect of a person's life. No matter what type of work history you have experienced, you have learned and developed confidence while fulfilling goals through coordinated efforts with other individuals in school, the workplace, sports teams, fan clubs, and volunteer organizations. These varied organizational experiences can enrich your life and lead you to a rewarding career as you learn more about yourself and organizations. Second, as you are likely to soon embark on post-collegiate professional life, you may gain insight from looking back on these varied organizational experiences, and armed with this knowledge, you can select organizations offering multiple career development opportunities.

Third, life in this exciting, dynamic, and fast-changing era alters the operations of organizations and the way work is done in the 21st century. As more and more countries achieve access to the global marketplace, competition is on the rise at the organizational and individual levels—"with everyone, everywhere, and for everything" (Sirkin, Hemerling, & Bhattacharya, 2008). These forces add complexity and challenge to finding balance in work and personal life.

Work Matters

Work plays a central role in people's lives. When properly managed, work is important and essential for sound psychological health. For example, when people lose their jobs, they are at much greater risk for widespread disintegration in their overall quality of life, with corresponding uptakes in drug abuse, criminal activity, and violence. When individuals are fired, laid off, or *riffed* (the common term for a "reduction in force"; sometimes you will hear other jargon, such as *downsizing* or *right-sizing,* to describe layoffs), they often struggle with mental health problems, including lowered self-esteem, relational conflicts, substance abuse, and alcoholism (Blustein, 2008; De Meuse, Marks, & Dai, 2011; Rousseau, 2011). In addition, as Fouad and Bynner (2008) point out, work transitions of any kind are likely to be stressful and pose psychological challenges. This may be the case if you are a young person going from school to work, or if you are transitioning to different work, or from work to non-work, even by choice (staying at home with children or retiring).

People spend at least a third to a half of their lives working in organizations, which are embedded in an ever-changing world driven by economic, political, and technological forces (Erez, 2011; U.S. Department of Labor, 2009). Historically, individuals interacted most closely with others in their same community, but no more! Communication networks make individuals increasingly connected to each other so that we become more *a part of,* rather than *apart from,* the global system of human affairs. The interconnectedness of individuals and the convergence of people from diverse cultures and different parts of the globe in organizations are major hallmarks of work and organizations in the 21st century. A sense of being part of a bigger and more connected whole is intensified by the relentless changes brought about by information technology and the creation of virtual organizations that often pull together people across the globe.

In addition to these kinds of changes, the worldwide population continues to increase and is projected to reach nine billion by 2050, with a growing proportion of the population under 25 years of age, especially in the newly advanced BRIC countries—Brazil, Russia, India, and China. On the other hand, the so-called rich countries and regions—such as Canada, Japan, United States, and Western Europe—have populations that are comparatively older, coupled with slower population growth (Erez, 2011).

Organizations As Systems

Systems are everywhere. They are found in the physical, biological, and social worlds. Examples include the braking system in a car, the nervous system in the human body, and a customer relations department in an organization. Katz and Kahn (1978), in their classic book *The Social Psychology of Organizations*, advocate for thinking about organizations as systems, social systems that are alive, organic, dynamic, and complex. As systems, organizations make choices—for example, to expand business or hold steady for another year. The systems perspective was introduced by Ludwig von Bertalanffy (1956, 1968), who proposed that all systems—physical, biological, or social—have predictable tendencies or behaviors:

1. *Open/closed exchange*: high or low attention and responsiveness to information about the system that is internal or external to the system
2. *Interdependence*: members (subsystems) of the system influence each other simultaneously, and each part is affected by the actions of the other parts
3. *Homeostasis*: participation in maintaining system stability; parts of the system adjust their communications and other behaviors to achieve or retain equilibrium
4. *Nonsummativity*: the whole system equals more (is greater than) the sum of its parts

Meadows and Wright (2008) proposed a slightly different emphasis. They defined *system* as an organized collection of parts or subsystems that are integrated to accomplish an overall goal. An organization of even modest size is composed of many units or departments, such as personnel and payroll, customer service, or billing and shipping, and each of these units is a system. If one part of the system is changed, the overall system is likely to be influenced through the network of relationships between parts. For example, when a new employee is hired, her presence is likely to change the systems within the organization, especially within her own department. And if the marketing department doesn't effectively promote the organizational product or service, sales may tumble and employees will be laid off. In short, systems exist at many different levels in an organization, and the performance of one system influences the performance of the other systems.

To maintain the health of organizations of every kind, they must be receptive to fresh perspectives as exposure to negative entropy (the dissenting voice) builds *resilience*. Every system is dependent on a periodic infusion of opposing forces (*negative entropy*) to secure a reservoir of energy for future use (Flood, 1999; Meadows & Wright, 2008). Balancing the opposing forces that compose it are what makes the system possible. For example, a successful retail industry makes regular investments in the production of their products because they know that to make money (reap profit), it is important to spend money (make the product enticing to customers). This is an example of systems thinking. In a sagging economy, the retail industry must decide how best to remain solvent (alive)—is it wiser to be conservative and *cut costs* through a reduction in the workforce, or is it better to take risks, such as converting to online marketing, with the prospect of *growing revenue* by increasing the customer base? The industry will probably make this decision—shrink or expand—by consulting trusted members of the industry, by collecting data about conditions within the organizational walls (e.g., determining the human and financial capital available for expansion), and by assessing conditions outside the organizational walls (e.g., looking for signs of near-future economic growth or high product or service demand across regional, national, and international target demographic markets). Thus, diverse perspectives enrich an organization's pool of knowledge for information processing, which—when well managed—generates an electric, creative atmosphere that energizes and enhances group performance (Mannix & Neale, 2005; Zhou & Shalley, 2011).

Systems Thinking

According to systems thinking, the actions of organizations can be understood only when observed within the context in which these actions were generated. Systems thinking enriches and enlightens problem solving by tracing the origins (and perpetuation) of a problem and the surrounding context as well as by focusing on the problem itself, thus going beyond the linear or cause-and-effect that isolates organizational systems from each other and their context.

Although systems theory provides for the study of single parts of an organization (e.g., employees or customers, organizational functions such as marketing or manufacturing, and organizational structures such as division, departments, or teams), it stresses the need to study the multiple parts within their context and to examine the organization as a whole, particularly when embarking on change. The study of the organization as a whole means becoming familiar with the relationships between the discrete parts as well as the networking of partners, customers, and community.

Systems Applications

The application of systems thinking and related tools and skills are discussed and developed further throughout this text. We begin here by making plain from the outset that systems thinking sheds light on how to identify underlying problems, how to address ineffective practices, and how to accommodate the needs of unfulfilled stakeholder groups—all of which can give rise to a dysfunctional system if ignored. For example, unaddressed hurt feelings, unfair wages, or overlooked promotions—once identified—can be corrected by identifying the required solution, such as a conflict resolution system, adjustments to the reward system, or enhanced record keeping of employee productivity to assure a valid and fair performance review and promotion system, all of which will build loyalty to the organization and produce satisfaction. Throughout this text, we present the theoretical foundations of I/O psychology, including important and useful concepts and empirical findings, which we examine with systems thinking to provide a wider view of challenges and opportunities by merging the two "languages" or disciplines of psychology and systems. Our intent is to enrich your understanding of how organizations work as well as how individuals work in organizations, and to shed light on how best to promote individual and organizational lives.

A FRAMEWORK FOR UNDERSTANDING ORGANIZATIONS

The field of industrial/organizational psychology covers a wide range of topics, as presented in Table 1-1. There are four major domains in our framework for understanding organizations, beginning with **Part I: Organizations As Systems. Chapter 1: Introduction to Organizational Psychology and Systems** focuses on the nature of work, organizations as systems, global organizations, and challenges to individuals and organizations in the 21st century. **Chapter 2: Methods of Study** begins with a treatment of situational and dispositional variables and features of individuals that impact work performances and methods of study employed in I/O psychology. The chapter presents descriptive and inferential statistics as well as a discussion of meta-analysis for comparing and summarizing the findings across many studies in organizational psychology. Chapter 2 also describes the impact of moderator variables on the relationship between independent and dependent variables and suggests tools for getting a snapshot of an organization.

The second domain of our framework is covered in **Part II: Macrosystems.** These systems involve and influence all levels and all individuals in an organization. **Chapter 3: Organizational Culture** focuses on specific tools to identify, construct, or change organizational culture, and it explains how managing problems of external adaptation and internal integration promotes resilience

TABLE 1-1 A Framework for Understanding Organizations

Organizations As Systems	Macrosystems	Microsystems	Managing Change
Introduction to Organizations and Systems	Organizational Culture	Hiring and Performance Management	Individual and Organizational Change
Methods of Study	Leadership, Power, and Politics Workforce Diversity and Ethics	Group Dynamics and Teams	Organizational Change and Learning
		Motivation and Productivity at Work	
		Leadership, Power, and Politics	
		Organizational Decision Making Workplace Negotiation	
		Organizational Conflict Management	

or organizational health. **Chapter 4: Leadership, Power, and Politics** reviews different models of leadership, examines how leadership facilitates full-system potential, and explores the role of power and politics in leadership. **Chapter 5: Workforce Diversity and Ethics** identifies barriers as well as strategies to enhance the diversity and inclusion of persons from underrepresented groups, and also indicates how ethics and ethical practices can improve the well-being of all members of an organization.

Part III: Microsystems is the third major domain of the framework, and it focuses on organizational systems that have more limited influence on an organization compared to macrosystems. Microsystems are focused on doing things right and how management functions work, as compared to leadership, which is concerned with doing the right things for organizational members and the organization. Specifically, **Chapter 6: Hiring and Performance Management** treats the recruitment and hiring of organizational members, as well as training and performance evaluation systems, and discusses the impact of dispositional variables on work performances, contemporary issues in performance evaluation, and the hiring and retention of members of legally protected groups. **Chapter 7: Group Dynamics and Teams** focuses on the similarities and differences between groups and teams, reasons for joining groups, the stages of group-team development, the types of teams, team cognition, and self and collective efficacies. **Chapter 8: Motivation and Productivity at Work** begins with a definition of motivation, includes a review of major theories of motivation, looks at tools to enhance motivation, examines the relationship between extrinsic and intrinsic motivation, and covers dysfunctional motivation and work performance.

Chapter 9: Organizational Decision Making introduces decision-making models that promote inclusion, build ownership, and prevent common system dysfunctions such as groupthink and the Abilene Paradox. **Chapter 10: Workplace Negotiation** treats distributive and integrative negotiation in the workplace, and then looks at the harmonizing of these two approaches to negotiation to produce high-quality outcomes for all parties, as well as introducing best alternatives to negotiated agreements (BATNAs) and the six keys to quality negotiation. **Chapter 11: Organizational Conflict Management** begins with a definition of organizational conflict, reviews the major theories of the causes of conflict in the workplace, describes the management of workplace conflict, and presents specific tools for organizational conflict management systems.

The fourth and final domain of our framework, **Part IV: Managing Change,** is primarily concerned with openness to change at individual and organizational levels. **Chapter 12: Organizational Change and Learning** discusses the nature of change, receptivity to change, models of organizational learning essential for individual and organizational change, and specific tools and skill sets to guide self-organization and continuous improvement.

GLOBAL ORGANIZATIONS

You can find evidence of global organizations all over the Internet. Many of them are accessible to anyone from anywhere at almost any time. The customer or client in the global marketplace is a person or group of persons anywhere in the world that is willing and capable of purchasing a product or service regardless of its place of origin—providing it meets customer or client specifications of the highest quality, at the lowest possible price, delivered as quickly as possible. What counts in global organizations is *what* you do rather than *where* you do it. If you need an immediate image of the global marketplace, just go online to find a book, health professional, or the latest electronic gadget; tour the hotel room you plan on booking for your next business or vacation trip; or make flight reservations—the list goes on!

An important aspect of understanding global organizations is determining how leadership and operating principles are consistent across diverse cultures and how they can vary, depending on the global context. One major research initiative in this realm is the GLOBE Project. The GLOBE Project was created to determine if there are leader behaviors, attributes, and organizational practices that are acceptable and effective across cultures. The project also examined how features of the larger societal or contextual culture and the organizational culture affected leader behaviors and organizational practices (Chhokar, Brodbeck, & House, 2007; House & Global Leadership and Organizational Behavior Effectiveness Research Program, 2004).

In this study, 17,000 managers working in 951 organizations across 62 different countries respond to a survey questionnaire that included 112 leader attributes (for example, a good leader promotes participation in decision making). The results indicated that charismatic, team-oriented, and participative leaders are rated as the most effective. In particular, charismatic leadership (when promoting a shared vision of the organization's major goals, inspiring followers, valuing honesty, and being decisive and performance oriented) is rated as the most effective leadership style (House & Global Leadership and Organizational Behavior Effectiveness Research Program, 2006). Thus, there appears to be a uniform leadership style and associated behaviors that are effective in a wide variety of cultures and suitable in organizations across the globe.

It is nearly inevitable, given the global economy, for organizational members to be drawn from diverse cultures from around the world (Kitayama, 2002; Leung & Peterson, 2011; Markus & Kitayama, 1991; Triandis, 1994). Interestingly, research has identified some common needs that appear in both individualistic cultures like those of Western Europe and North America, where there is relatively more emphasis placed on individuals' personal satisfaction and fulfillment, and collectivistic cultures, like those seen in Asia, where the emphasis is on the stability of cultural groups, such as families, employers, and nations. Given the rich diversity across cultures, there appears to be a near-universal human psychological need for each of us to be a *good person* as defined by one's culture (Heine, Lehman, Markus, & Kitayama, 1999; Norenzayan & Heine, 2005). Although this need is quite pervasive, there is wide variation in how specific cultures define their model citizen. In Western individualistic cultures, the good or valued person is confident, self-sufficient, and focused on personal achievements, whereas in Eastern collectivistic cultures, the good person promotes harmonious functioning of the group, adopts flexible approaches to different situations, and pursues self-improvement almost exclusively as it benefits the group rather than the individual (Erez, 2011; Heine et al., 1999).

Researchers have found a universal interest in *autonomy*, which is the capacity to make choices about how to act and what to do, versus being controlled by other people. The value of autonomy has been widely endorsed in diverse nations, including Russia, China, and the United States (Chirkov, Ryan, Kim, & Kaplan, 2003; Sheldon et al., 2004). And finally, several researchers have proposed that *belonging to meaningful groups* is also a universal need (Aronson & Aronson, 2008; Baumeister & Leary, 1995; Deci & Ryan, 1985; Smith, Spillane, & Annus, 2006). This rather uniform pattern of basic psychological needs as observed across a variety of cultures indicates that perhaps people are more alike than different from each other.

The world in which we work and live is changing—and dramatically impacting organizational demography (the composition of the membership of an organization) as well as the customers or clients they serve. Today it has become commonplace for people to travel anywhere in the world in 24 hours or less, and global communication networks allow us to easily contact almost anyone, anywhere, at any time. Another term for these trends is *globalization*: the open exchange of goods, services, information, culture, sociopolitical systems, and religions, with people growing closer together while paradoxically growing farther apart as well. By this, we mean people appear to be more frequently in contact through electronic communication (cell phones, laptops), while passing up opportunities for face-to-face communication.

Table 1-2 shows world vital statistics per unit of time as of June 12, 2012. The global population has a natural estimated increase of 148 persons per minute. In the United States alone, as of June 12, 2012, the population was 313,726,294, with a net gain of one person every 13 seconds.

As Table 1-3 indicates, as of June 12, 2012, if we reduced the world's population to a village of 100 with all existing human ratios staying the same, we would find that, for example, 50 would be male and 50 female; 61 would be Asians, 13 Africans, and 12 Europeans; eight would have access to the Internet; and one would have a college education!

TABLE 1-2	World Vital Events per Time Unit as of June 12, 2012		
Time Unit	**Births**	**Deaths**	**Natural Increase**
Year	134,475,195	56,224,687	75,250,507
Month	11,206,256	4,685,391	6,520,876
Day	367,419	153,619	213,799
Minute	255	107	148
Second	4.3	1.8	2.5

Source: Timely updates available from U.S. Bureau of Census (2011); retrieved on June12, 2012, from http://www.census.gov/main/www/popclock.html

TABLE 1-3	If The World Were a Village of 100 People

The demographics of the world would appear as something like the following if we reduced the world's population to a village of just 100 people, with all existing human ratios remaining the same.

50 would be male, 50 would be female
61 would be Asian, 13 African, 12 European, 9 Latin American, 5 from the United States and Canada
75 would be non-white, 25 would be white
16 would be unable to read or write
8 people would have access to the Internet
1 would have a college education

Source: Adapted from Family Care Foundation (2012); retrieved on June 12, 2012 from http:// www.familycare.org/special-interest/if-the-world-were-a-village-of-100-people

A BRIEF HISTORY OF INDUSTRIAL/ORGANIZATIONAL PSYCHOLOGY

We conclude this chapter with a look at some of the important persons and events in the fascinating history of industrial/organizational psychology. Although the field itself is relatively new, its subject matter is ancient. The construction, management, and leadership of groups of people to accomplish work that no one person could do alone has been part of cultural groups for many millennia.

Pioneers in the Field

I/O psychology evolved into a specialization within general-experimental psychology in the latter half of the 19th century. It grew out of the pioneering work of Hugo Munsterberg (1863–1916), an experimental psychologist particularly interested in the selection of employees with the use of psychological tests (Hilgard, 1987). Munsterberg wrote the first I/O textbook, *Psychology and Industrial Efficiency,* which was published in 1913. Walter Dill Scott (1869–1955) shared Munsterberg's interests in I/O psychology and also studied advertising. He wrote *The Theory of Advertising* (1903), an influential book that continues to this day to move psychology into more applied directions (Vinchur & Koppes, 2011).

In the beginning of the 20th century, Frederick Winslow Taylor introduced what he called Scientific Management, also known as Taylorism, which was initially developed to increase productivity in factories. According to Taylor, each job should be carefully analyzed so that the optimal way of doing tasks can be specified, and then employees should be hired according to characteristics that are related to job performance (Taylor, 1911). The time-and-motion studies of Lillian Gilbreth and her husband Frank Gilbreth focused on measuring the time for doing specific tasks in order to improve productivity (Lawson, Graham, & Baker, 2007). The key points of Taylorism and the Gilbreth time-and-motion studies are that work behaviors can be measured and analyzed into components to promote a good fit between the capacities of the worker and the demands of the job (Vinchur & Koppes, 2011).

Another noteworthy pioneer of the field was Mary Parker Follett (1868–1933). Her work was grounded in the then-new field of empirical psychology. She is remembered for at least two lasting contributions. First, she resisted the cutthroat competition of 19th-century American industrialization (as well as the potentially dehumanizing implementation of Taylorism) with her *Principles of Coordination* (Follett, Fox, & Urwick, 1973). Instead of analyzing workers' actions and then giving highly detailed directions, Follett advocated for employee engagement at all levels of production, because she believed that this would lead to optimal organizational performance (Tonn, 2003). Her second major contribution was also influential, as it is the earliest psychological work on negotiation. In her essay "Constructive Conflict," she proposed that conflict—"the appearance of differences"—is neither good nor bad and can actually motivate people to strive for integrative solutions, so neither side has to sacrifice everything it seeks (Graham, 1995).

The Organizational Side Develops

The organizational side of I/O, with a focus on workplace interactions between people and groups, comes into focus in the early 1920s with the Hawthorne studies. These studies involved the Western Electric Company and researchers from Harvard University, who were interested in the impact of environmental or contextual variables such as lighting and wage incentives on productivity (Mayo, 1933; Whitehead, 1935; Whitehead, Mitchell, & Western Electric Company, 1938). The "Hawthorne effect" is a response by workers arising from any change to their work environment. Researchers find that productivity increases as the level of illumination *changes,* regardless of whether the illumination is increased or decreased. The initial interpretation of these studies' results is somewhat debatable, and there are credible alternative explanations. However, the basic finding has been reproduced (or replicated) many times. The overarching conclusion of the Hawthorne studies is that social context influences organizational behaviors (Vinchur & Koppes, 2011). Other important findings of the Hawthorne studies that have been confirmed in later research are that work groups establish and enforce production norms or rules and that employees respond differently to different leadership styles.

Other developments that indicate the importance of organizational systems for understanding organizational and individual behaviors include the growth of labor unions during the 1930s, which argued for participative decision making for quality-of-work-life issues, and workplace democracy gave employees a voice in collective bargaining agreements in unionized organizations. Kurt Lewin (1890–1947) arrived in the United States in 1933 to escape Nazi anti-Semitism. His single-minded drive to use research to solve practical organizational and community problems greatly contributed to the further development of organizational psychology (Marrow, 1984; Vinchur & Koppes, 2011). He is also considered a founding figure in social psychology (Fiske, 2010).

World War II spurred studies in morale and leadership, followed a number of years later by the publication of *Motivation and Morale in Industry* (Viteles, 1953). This text makes plain that it is important to research topics such as leadership, group dynamics, and motivation.

Morton Deutsch was a student of Kurt Lewin. Deutsch has conducted pioneering studies on cooperation and competition, intergroup relations, conflict resolution, social conformity, and the social psychology of justice (Frydenberg, 2005). In addition, the human relations movement arose during the 1950s, arguing for more opportunities to be creative and fulfilled at work (Hammer & Zimmerman, 2011). As the emphasis on conformity during the postwar era gave way to the transformational social movements of the 1960s, young persons in general not only protested against the Vietnam War and segregation, but many of them also developed a mistrust of authority. Many of the so-called Baby Boomers, born between 1944 and 1964, chose lifestyles that do not have work as a major focus.

These broad cultural shifts of the 20th century continue to have reverberations today. For example, the children and grandchildren of the Baby Boomers have been and still are exposed to a culture of individualism and distrust of established institutions. Some researchers propose that members of Generation X (born between 1965 and about 1982) and Generation Y (born between 1983–1995) are, overall, rather confident—which can be good—but also can have unrealistic expectations about the nature of organizational life and its capacity to provide personal fulfillment (Gentile, Twenge, & Campbell, 2010; Twenge & Campbell, 2008; Twenge, Zhang, & Im, 2004). This is a provocative hypothesis, and only time will tell how these workers of the early 21st century fare over the decades (Baumeister, Campbell, Krueger, & Vohs, 2003; Trzesniewski & Donnellan, 2010).

A Changing Field for Changing Times

Today and in the years ahead, we need industrial/organizational psychologists who study organizations as systems that operate in the global marketplace. There has been a significant increase in studying the impact of globalization on organizations, as reflected in the growing number of international students enrolled in business schools around the globe and the emphasis of globalization in the curriculum of master's degree programs in business administration (Schumpeter, 2011).

To appreciate the challenges that organizations face in the 21st century, consider the World Economic Forum's Global Competitiveness Index (available at http://gcr.weforum.org/gcr). This index scores countries on a number of dimensions, such as institutional environment (factors such as government attitudes about regulation, corruption, and lack of transparency) and infrastructure (things like the condition and presence of roads, railroads, and ports). From the ratings of these factors, U.S. organizations—and in fact organizations from every country—will not only be competing with European, Japanese, South Korean, and Chinese organizations but also with highly competitive organizations from every corner of the world that are not yet in the top 50 rankings of globally competitive countries but are clearly on the rise.

Questions for the Future

A number of pressing research areas and questions need to be addressed to narrow the gap between the research and applied sides of I/O psychology. These topics include assessment of the impacts on motivation and performance of flexible approaches to compensation (Martocchio, 2011), work/family issues (Hammer & Zimmerman, 2011; Kossek & Michel, 2011), productive and respectful interpersonal relations at work (Reich & Hershcovis, 2011), managing stress and promoting wellness (Griffin & Clarke, 2011), employee-employer commitment and loyalty to each other (Rousseau, 2011), justice in the workplace (Greenberg, 2011), sexual harassment (Berdahl & Raver, 2011), and gender-based compensation disparities (George & Ng, 2011; Kossek & Michel, 2011; Martocchio, 2011). In addition, other areas that need further study include leadership development for an increasingly diversified workforce, telecommuting or working from home or elsewhere away from the actual workplace (if one exists), educating people to embrace change, increasing attention to global events and their impact upon organizations, ethical conduct and values, and the need to build collaborative alliances between organizations in the context of highly competitive environments. We will address these topics and other timely issues throughout the rest of this text.

An excellent resource for contemporary topics, career paths, salary data, and a listing of I/O psychologists can be found at http://www.siop.org, the website of Division 14 of the American Psychological Association, the Society for Industrial and Organizational Psychology.

Chapter Summary

We began this chapter by describing some of the major global changes that are shaping the nature of work in the 21st century and requiring increased flexibility in the operations of organizations. It is critical to study organizations as systems and to focus on systems thinking given the diverse and sustained contact between individuals and organizations around the world, mediated by electronic communication systems. We identified important features of systems that apply to organizations, such as the interrelationship of all parts of a system and systems change in response to feedback. We distinguished between macro- and microsystems and presented our framework for understanding organizations.

In describing the 21st-century world, we made note of the ever-increasing world population that impacts all organizations and individuals. Thereafter, we turned to a brief history of industrial/organizational psychology and identified major questions that need to be addressed by I/O psychologists in the 21st century.

Chapter References

Aronson, E., & Aronson, J. (2008). *The social animal* (10th ed.). New York: Worth Publishers.

Baumeister, R. F., Campbell, J. D., Krueger, J. I., & Vohs, K. D. (2003). Does high self-esteem cause better performance, interpersonal success,

happiness, or healthier lifestyles? *Psychological Science in the Public Interest, 4*(1), 1–44. doi:10.1111/1529-1006.01431

Baumeister, R. F., & Leary, M. R. (1995). The need to belong: Desire for interpersonal attachments as a fundamental human motivation. *Psychological Bulletin, 117*(3), 497–529. doi:10.1037/0033-2909. 117.3.497

Berdahl, J. L., & Raver, J. L. (2011). Sexual harassment. In S. Zedeck (Ed.), *APA handbook of industrial and organizational psychology* (Vol. 3, pp. 641–669). Washington, DC: American Psychological Association.

Blustein, D. L. (2008). The role of work in psychological health and well-being: A conceptual, historical, and public policy perspective. *American Psychologist, 63*(4), 228–240. doi:10.1037/0003-066X.63.4.228

Chhokar, J. S., Brodbeck, F. C., & House, R. J. (2007). *Culture and leadership across the world: The GLOBE book of in-depth studies of 25 societies.* Mahwah, NJ: Lawrence Erlbaum.

Chirkov, V., Ryan, R. M., Kim, Y., & Kaplan, U. (2003). Differentiating autonomy from individualism and independence: A self-determination theory perspective on internalization of cultural orientations and well-being. *Journal of Personality and Social Psychology, 84*(1), 97–110. doi:10.1037/0022-3514.84.1.97

De Meuse, K. P., Marks, M. L., & Dai, G. (2011). Organizational downsizing, mergers and acquisitions, and strategic alliances: Using theory and research to enhance practice. In S. Zedeck (Ed.), *APA handbook of industrial and organizational psychology* (Vol. 3, pp. 729-768). Washington, DC: American Psychological Association.

Deci, E. L., & Ryan, R. M. (1985). *Intrinsic motivation and self-determination in human behavior.* New York: Plenum.

Erez, M. (2011). Cross-cultural and global issues in organizational psychology. In S. Zedeck (Ed.), *APA handbook of industrial and organizational psychology* (Vol. 3, pp. 807-854). Washington, DC: American Psychological Association.

Fiske, S. T. (2010). *Social beings: A core motives approach to social psychology* (2nd ed.). Hoboken, NJ: John Wiley.

Flood, R. L. (1999). *Rethinking the fifth discipline: Learning within the unknowable.* London: Routledge.

Follett, M. P., Fox, E. M., & Urwick, L. F. (1973). *Dynamic administration: The collected papers of Mary Parker Follett.* London: Pitman Publishing.

Fouad, N. A., & Bynner, J. (2008). Work transitions. *American Psychologist, 63*(4), 241–251. doi:2008-05553-003[pii]10.1037/0003-066X.63.4.241

Frydenberg, E. (2005). *Morton Deutsch: A life and legacy of mediation and conflict resolution.* Brisbane: Australian Academic Press.

Gentile, B., Twenge, J. M., & Campbell, W. K. (2010). Birth cohort differences in self-esteem, 1988–2008: A cross-temporal meta-analysis. *Review of General Psychology, 14*(3), 261–268. doi:10.1037/a0019919

George, E., & Ng, C. K. (2011). Nonstandard workers: Work arrangements and outcomes. In S. Zedeck (Ed.), *APA handbook of industrial and organizational psychology* (Vol. 1, pp. 573–596). Washington, DC: American Psychological Association.

Graham, P. (1995). *Mary Parker Follett: Prophet of management: A celebration of writings from the 1920s.* Boston: Harvard Business School Press.

Greenberg, J. (2011). Organizational justice: The dynamics of fairness in the workplace. In S. Zedeck (Ed.), *APA handbook of industrial and organizational psychology* (Vol. 3, pp. 271-327). Washington, DC: American Psychological Association.

Griffin, M. A., & Clarke, S. (2011). Stress and well-being at work. In S. Zedeck (Ed.), *APA handbook of industrial and organizational psychology* (Vol. 3, pp. 359-397). Washington, DC: American Psychological Association.

Hammer, L. B., & Zimmerman, K. L. (2011). Quality of work life. In S. Zedeck (Ed.), *APA handbook of industrial and organizational psychology* (Vol. 3, pp. 399-431). Washington, DC: American Psychological Association.

Heine, S. J., Lehman, D. R., Markus, H. R., & Kitayama, S. (1999). Is there a universal need for positive self-regard? *Psychological Review, 106*(4), 766–794.

Hilgard, E. R. (1987). *Psychology in America: A historical survey.* San Diego, CA: Harcourt Brace Jovanovich.

House, R. J., & Global Leadership and Organizational Behavior Effectiveness Research Program. (2004). *Culture, leadership, and organizations: The GLOBE study of 62 societies.* Thousand Oaks, CA: Sage Publications.

House, R. J., & Global Leadership and Organizational Behavior Effectiveness Research Program. (2006). *Culture, leadership, and organizations: The GLOBE study of 62 societies* (2nd ed.). Thousand Oaks, CA: Sage Publications.

Katz, D., & Kahn, R. L. (1978). *The social psychology of organizations* (2nd ed.). New York: John Wiley.

Kitayama, S. (2002). Culture and basic psychological processes—Toward a system view of culture: Comment on Oyserman et al. (2002). *Psychological Bulletin, 128*(1), 89–96. doi:10.1037/0033-2909.128.1.89

Kossek, E. E., & Michel, J. S. (2011). Flexible work schedules. In S. Zedeck (Ed.), *APA handbook of industrial and organizational psychology* (Vol. 1, pp. 535-572). Washington, DC: American Psychological Association.

Lawson, R. B., Graham, J. E., & Baker, K. M. (2007). *A history of psychology: Globalization, ideas, and applications.* Upper Saddle River, NJ: Pearson Prentice Hall.

Leung, K., & Peterson, M. F. (2011). Managing a globally distributed workforce: Social and interpersonal issues. In S. Zedeck (Ed.), *APA handbook of industrial and organizational psychology* (Vol. 3, pp. 771-805). Washington, DC: American Psychological Association.

Mannix, E., & Neale, M. A. (2005). What differences make a difference? The promise and reality of diverse teams in organizations. *Psychological Science in the Public Interest, 6*(2), 31–55.

Markus, H. R., & Kitayama, S. (1991). Culture and the self: Implications for cognition, emotion, and motivation. *Psychological Review, 98*(2), 224–253.

Marrow, A. J. (1984). *The practical theorist: The life and work of Kurt Lewin.* Annapolis, MD: BDR Learning Products.

Martocchio, J. J. (2011). Strategic reward and compensation plans. In S. Zedeck (Ed.), *APA handbook of industrial and organizational psychology* (Vol. 1, pp. 343–372). Washington, DC: American Psychological Association.

Mayo, E. (1933). *The human problems of an industrial civilization.* New York: Macmillan Co.

Meadows, D. H., & Wright, D. (2008). *Thinking in systems: A primer.* White River Junction, VT: Chelsea Green Publishing..

Munsterberg, H. (1913). *Psychology and industrial efficiency.* Boston: Houghton Mifflin.

Norenzayan, A., & Heine, S. J. (2005). Psychological universals: What are they and how can we know? *Psychological Bulletin, 131*(5), 763–784.

Reich, T. C., & Hershcovis, M. S. (2011). Interpersonal relationships at work. In S. Zedeck (Ed.), *APA handbook of industrial and organizational psychology* (Vol. 3, pp. 223-248). Washington, DC: American Psychological Association.

Rousseau, D. M. (2011). The individual-organization relationship: The psychological contract. In S. Zedeck (Ed.), *APA handbook of industrial and organizational psychology* (Vol. 3, pp. 191-220). Washington, DC: American Psychological Association.

Schumpeter, E. (2011). Tutors to the world: Business schools are globalising at a furious pace—which is largely a good thing. *The Economist, 399,* 74.

Scott, W. D. (1903). *The theory of advertising: A simple exposition of the principles of psychology in their relation to successful advertising.* Boston: Small, Maynard & Company.

Sheldon, K. M., Elliot, A. J., Ryan, R. M., Chirkov, V., Kim, Y., Wu, C., et al. (2004). Self-concordance and subjective well-being in four cultures. *Journal of Cross-Cultural Psychology, 35*(2), 209–223.

Sirkin, H. L., Hemerling, J. W., & Bhattacharya, A. K. (2008). *Globality: Competing with everyone from everywhere for everything.* New York, NY: Business Plus.

Smith, G. T., Spillane, N. S., & Annus, A. M. (2006). Implications of an emerging integration of universal and culturally specific psychologies. *Perspectives on Psychological Science, 1*(3), 211–233. doi:10.1111/j.1745-6916.2006.00013.x

Taylor, F. W. (1911). *The principles of scientific management.* New York: Harper & Brothers.

Tonn, J. (2003). *Mary Follett: Creating democracy, transforming management.* New Haven, CT: Yale University Press.

Triandis, H. C. (1994). *Culture and social behavior.* New York: McGraw-Hill.

Trzesniewski, K. H., & Donnellan, M. B. (2010). Rethinking "Generation Me." *Perspectives on Psychological Science, 5*(1), 58–75. doi:10.1177/1745691609356789

Twenge, J. M., & Campbell, S. M. (2008). Generational differences in psychological traits and their impact on the workplace. *Journal of Managerial Psychology, 23*(8), 862–877. doi:10.1108/02683940810904367

Twenge, J. M., Zhang, L., & Im, C. (2004). It's beyond my control: A cross-temporal meta-analysis of increasing externality in locus of control, 1960–2002. *Personality and Social Psychology Review, 8*(3), 308–319. doi:10.1207/s15327957pspr0803_5

U.S. Department of Labor (2009). American time use survey (ATUS), 2008. doi:10.3886/ICPSR26149

Vinchur, A. J., & Koppes, L. L. (2011). A historical survey of research and practice in industrial and organizational psychology. In S. Zedeck (Ed.), *APA handbook of industrial and organizational psychology* (Vol. 1, pp. 193–208). Washington, DC: American Psychological Association.

Viteles, M. S. (1953). *Motivation and morale in industry* (1st ed.). New York: Norton.

von Bertalanffy, L. (1956). General systems theory. In F. E. Emery (Ed.), *General systems: Yearbook of the Society for the Advancement of General Systems Theory* (Vol. 1, pp. 1–10). Washington, DC: Society for General Systems Research.

von Bertalanffy, L. (1968). *General system theory: Foundations, development, applications*. New York: George Braziller.

Whitehead, T. N. (1935). Social relationships in the factory: A study of an industrial group. *Human Factors (London), 9*, 381–382.

Whitehead, T. N., Mitchell, H., & Western Electric Company. (1938). *The industrial worker: A statistical study of human relations in a group of manual workers*. Cambridge, MA: Harvard University Press.

Zhou, J., & Shalley, C. E. (2011). Deepening our understanding of creativity in the workplace: A review of different approaches to creativity research. In S. Zedeck (Ed.), *APA handbook of industrial and organizational psychology* (Vol. 2, pp. 275–302). Washington, DC: American Psychological Association.

CHAPTER

2

Methods of Study

CHAPTER OVERVIEW

As indicated in Chapter 1, to work effectively and efficiently in the 21st century, it is important to see organizations as systems, engage in systems thinking, and continuously assess the impact of globalization on organizations and individuals. Three tool sets presented in this chapter help to identify individual and organizational functioning levels.

    The first tool set, *instrumental forces,* assesses the impact of dispositional and situational variables, individual learning, and rationality-emotionality on work performances. The second tool set includes five *methods of study* commonly

Spaxiax/Shutterstock

employed in the study of organizations. These five methods are the case study, archival research, field experiment, the questionnaire-survey, and laboratory experiment. Knowledge of the methods of study coupled with knowledge of statistical tools can assist you in evaluating the findings of the many studies presented in subsequent chapters and in industrial/ organizational psychology. The third tool set encompasses the means to create an *organizational snapshot*—a broad-based initial assessment of an organization constructed from collected information about organizational structure, demography, power and politics, and networks.

LEARNING OBJECTIVES

When you have finished reading this chapter, you will be prepared to do the following:

- Describe the first tool set, instrumental forces, which assess the impact of key dispositional and contextual variables and rationality-emotionality on work performances

- Identify and distinguish between independent and frequently measured dependent variables in the study of organizations

- Describe the second tool set, methods of study, which includes five frequently employed techniques to study organizations

- Define *measurement* and distinguish between descriptive (shrinking data chunks into meaningful wholes) and inferential statistics (reaching beyond limited observations to larger groupings or populations)

Radius Images/Alamy

- Describe the third tool set, which generates an organizational snapshot, constructed by the systematic collection of data of four key domains of organizations—organizational structure, demography, power and politics, and networks—to produce a preliminary assessment of the organization

INSTRUMENTAL FORCES

Imagine that you are an organizational consultant hired by the leadership team of a troubled start-up firm called Great Grow. The company's main product speeds up crop growth and yields abundant harvests just about anywhere around the globe, so it has an impressive potential market. But there are problems, particularly in the company's manufacturing and distribution departments. Nobody inside the company can quite figure out the causes of these problems; that's why they have hired you to analyze the situation and (quickly!) develop some recommendations. How will you do this? You arrive at Great Grow with limited knowledge of the company, but you have a deep understanding of several tools that you will use to give you a sense of the people in the organization, their relationships, and areas for improvement.

Table 2-1 lists some prominent *instrumental forces* that shape developments within an organization. The first one is grounded in contemporary theories of

TABLE 2-1 Instrumental Forces
Individual actions and experiences arise from dispositional and situational forces
Individuals have the capacity to learn, and to share their learning
Individuals behave rationally and emotionally, and both are essential for effective work performances

personality, which seek to understand the relative potency of dispositional and situational forces that influence behavior. The second force derives from the fact that people are capable of learning. And finally, this "mental" work is influenced by our basic human nature, which has rational and emotional elements.

You can collect data for all three forces influencing work performances by several methods. In any organization, it is wise to conduct structured interviews of leaders and key managers. In bigger organizations, you may find it most efficient to survey large numbers of employees using computer-scored questionnaires. (More detailed information about structured interviews and questionnaires is presented later in this chapter.)

Dispositional and Situational Variables

Through your interviews and survey of the people who work at Great Grow, you find that most individuals believe that job performance is influenced primarily by dispositional traits—in other words, by personality or each person's relatively stable pattern of behavior in various situations. Thus, the organization tends to select members who exhibit a pattern of personality traits associated with workplace productivity. As a consequence, although the organization might be highly productive, it takes on the same "personality" seen in most of the individual members. In short, people are making the place rather than the place making the people. This is known as the attraction-selection-attrition or ASA model of organizational demography (Schneider, 1987; Schneider, Smith, Taylor, & Fleenor, 1998). Looking at this model more broadly, the psychological literature tends to support a dispositional approach for hiring individuals with a particular personality profile (Barrick & Mount, 1993; Barrick, Mount, & Judge, 2001; Wildman, Bedwell, Salas, & Smith-Jentsch, 2011).

According to the current consensus among personality theorists, a list of five personality traits, known as the *Big Five*, does the best job of explaining variations in personality among individuals (see Table 2-2). The first trait in the list, conscientiousness, is the best predictor of job performance across all types of work and occupations (Barrick, Mount, & Gupta, 2003; Barrick et al., 2001). Zhao and Seibert (2006) found that the two personality traits with the strongest relationship to entrepreneurship were conscientiousness—an individual's penchant for organizational persistence, hard work, motivation, and pursuit of goal

---

TABLE 2-2   The Big Five Personality Factors

Conscientiousness—responsible, dependable, persistent, organized, achievement oriented

Extraversion—sociable, assertive, ambitious, and active

Agreeableness—good-natured, cooperative, and trusting

Emotional Stability—calm, secure, at ease

Openness to Experience—imaginative, sensitive

accomplishments—and openness to experience or being intellectually curious and drawn to new experiences and novel ideas. Thus, to enhance the entrepreneurial activities of Great Grow or almost any organization, you will recommend that they hire people who score high on these personality traits.

Learning

Learning is a relatively permanent change in behavior and cognitive operations as a result of the past experience of the individual or the organization (Bouton, 2007). Learning is a dynamic process—what is learned can be replaced by new learning, which makes individuals and organizations flexible and adaptable (Nystrom & Starbuck, 1984). Organizational learning arises from learning by individual members (Martins, 2011) and is expressed in revised organizational policies, standard operating procedures, cultural norms, and organizational stories and ceremonies (Argyris & Schön, 1978; Fiol & Lyles, 1985; Jelinek, 1979; Martins, 2011). Lower-level organizational learning is based on repetition and routine; it takes place "in organizational contexts that are well understood and in which management thinks it can control situations" (Fiol & Lyles, 1985, p. 807). For example, if some members of an organization attend a week-long seminar on innovative management practices or technologies and then return to the organization, where they implement what they have learned, other members may put into practice the newly acquired, individually based learning as well. The new practices or technologies eventually become embedded in operating manuals and other organizational memory systems. It is at this point that we have organizational learning.

If the new material is focused on making current organizational operations or systems more efficient, then this is an example of single-loop organizational learning—doing the same operation, but doing it better now (Argyris & Schön, 1978). However, if the new material requires changing to different organizational norms, products, or services, for example, if an organization transforms from toy maker to software manufacturer, then this is an example of double-loop organizational learning, in which the focus is on doing the right thing (market-wise) or becoming more effective (Argyris & Schön, 1978; Lawson & Ventriss, 1992). After the newly learned material is deposited and encoded in the organizational memory systems (through computerized manuals, procedural guidelines, and mission statements), even if the original learners leave the organization, the organization will still benefit from the new knowledge because it has learned the new practices or norms. They will endure as part of the memory system of the organization, rather than being restricted to the knowledge of an individual or a small band of individuals who first learned the material (George, 1990; George & Brief, 1992; Lawson & Ventriss, 1992).

At Great Grow, you also want to understand how the organization learns. You can do this by a careful audit of documents, looking for evidence that truly critical individual learning is routinely stored for later use. In addition, you want to look for evidence that the organization is engaged in both single-loop and double-loop learning. Deficits in any of these areas can be explored and corrected.

Rationality-Emotionality

The final components in forces impacting work performances are rationality and emotionality. Individuals are not governed strictly by rational decision making and actions; they are influenced by emotions as well. This affective, emotional, or non-rational cluster of influences is a fact of individual and organizational life (George, 1990; George & Brief, 1992; Schleicher, Hansen, & Fox, 2011).

All of us, everywhere, learn through our emotions as well as through our conscious thoughts, and to ignore one kind of learning at the expense of the other fails to recognize the fundamental nature of humans and organizations (Bouton, 2007). Members of organizations experience anger, anxiety, fear, belonging, identity, joy, sadness—the full range of emotions—and we all use these experiences as a baseline for guiding our interactions as well as learning about the organizations.

METHODS OF STUDY

Quantitative and qualitative data of individual and organizational actions or behaviors and experiences can be collected at the individual (*micro*) level, the work-team or small-group (*meso*) level, and the organizational (*macro*) level of an organization. Some quantitative measurements include absenteeism rates, number of projects completed successfully on time, and instances and frequency of conflict, as well as a range of financial measures. In addition to data that can be expressed quantitatively, qualitative data are also useful. Examples include organizational stories about critical incidents and shared beliefs about key members of the organization, such as the founder or current leader of the organization. It also includes member descriptions of shared assumptions, beliefs, and values of the organizational culture, as well as members' responses to questions about what it is like to work there.

Table 2-3 presents some of the frequently studied dispositional and situational independent (the manipulated) variables and dependent (the measured) variables within industrial/organizational psychology.

Regardless of the method you use to study an organization, your focus when collecting data may vary. In some cases, you will gather information from individuals (e.g., searching for the dispositional variable that is the best predictor of job performance), small groups (e.g., the quality of decisions made by a small group of five to seven knowledgeable persons as reflected in resources saved, compared to decisions made by an expert), or the entire organization (e.g., turnover rates for members of an organization in response to a substantial pay cut of 20% for all employees).

Ideally, there should be the tightest possible control over the independent and dependent variables. Then you will have confidence in the findings of the relationship between variables, for example, between a pay cut (an independent variable) and the turnover rate or actual departure from the organization (a dependent variable). Almost all of the standard research methods in industrial/organizational psychology study a relationship such

TABLE 2-3	Examples of Independent (Manipulated) and Dependent (Measured) Variables in Industrial/Organizational Psychology	

Independent Variables	Dependent Variables
Dispositional	*Dispositional*
Motivation	Job performance
Educational level	Production or service output
Age	Job satisfaction
Sex	Stress and wellness
Race	Absenteeism
Ethnicity	Turnover
Interpersonal skills	Organizational citizenship
Coping skills	
Contextual	*Contextual*
Open and communicative organizational environment	Frequency, quality, and consequences of individual and work team communications performances and outputs
Compensation: Salary, wages, benefits program	Organizational competitiveness, productivity, and/or quality of product or service
Opportunities for promotion	Financial indices of profitability and community development
Respectful, challenging, safe, and clean work environment	Organizational innovation
Job security	
Functional systems such as financing, marketing, and production	

as this example (pay cuts and turnover). Each method of study available has advantages and disadvantages (Chan, 2011; Stone-Romero, 2011).

Table 2-4 presents the five primary methods for studying organizations. In general, as we move from case study to laboratory experiment, we gain increasing control over the measurement of the independent and dependent variables at the expense of losing touch with the realities of actual organizations, members, or events within and outside an organization.

Case Study

The *case study* research strategy provides a detailed description of a single or multiple organizations based on records kept by the organization (Stone-Romero, 2011). The researcher seeks measures from organizational records such as the change in the composition of the organizational workforce in terms of size, diversity, tenure, patterns of changes in leadership or services, and/or products

TABLE 2-4	Methods of Study	
Method	**Plusses**	**Minuses**
Case Study	Allows for new topic areas	Little control of variables
	Provides insights	Difficult to discern determinants of actions and experiences
	Suggests hypotheses	
Archival Research	Unobtrusive	Limited to using available data relevant to the topic of interest
		Correlational data
Field Experiment	Permits causal inferences	Limited degree of control
	Easier to generalize results	Employees are not randomly selected
	Permits enhanced realism and precision	
Survey-Questionnaire	Collects data from members and others (customers, etc.)	Low return rates
	Protects anonymity	Limited ability to generalize the results
Laboratory Experiment	Allows a high degree of control	Often artificial and unrealistic
	Permits strong causal inferences	Limited ability to generalize the results
	Random assignment to treatment groups	Arouses participant suspicion

over time, without any direct manipulation of independent variables. You can use case studies to provide rich or detailed descriptions of organizations in general or to examine a genre of organizations, as well as to generate theoretical propositions for further testing (Lee, Mitchell, & Harman, 2011). For example, you could use a case study design to determine if there has been a significant change in the diversity of organizational members over a 10- or 20-year period, based on organizational records. From these data, you could propose a hypothesis that could be tested in a field or laboratory experiment (e.g., Do leadership changes enhance the diversity of an organization?). The limitations of the case study method include a lack of control over independent—and to lesser extent dependent—variables and the difficulty of determining which independent variables are responsible for whatever dependent measures are part of the study (Howell, 2008; Lee et al., 2011; Stone-Romero, 2011).

Archival Research

When using *archival research* to collect information about an organization, the data are limited to whatever is available from the organization, including records of absenteeism, turnover, sales performance, team performance, and so on. Archival research is a relatively unobtrusive procedure that will not impact the current behavior of organizational members. Unlike case studies, which are primarily focused on providing a detailed description of an organization, archival methods can produce data that can then be used to test hypotheses.

An example of archival research would be a study designed to determine accident rates among different types of employees (new workers versus those with three or more years experience in the organization) at different times of the day, or as a function of the amount of work required in a fixed period of time. The archival method can be employed to test a hypothesis—more accidents arise late in the day shift than in the early part of the day shift because of fatigue, for example.

Field Experiment

The *field experiment* method involves systematic observations of events in organizations where it is possible to manipulate and measure some independent and dependent variables. In addition, when conducting a field experiment, you can achieve random assignment of participants to treatment conditions. Compared to the laboratory experiment, the field experiment is more realistic, but it gives less control over other factors that may influence the outcome(s) you are observing.

Examples of field experiments include determining the effects of procedural justice or the explanation by management for a pay cut on employee job satisfaction and turnover or voluntary departure from the organization. You may not be able to control independent variables, however—such as the magnitude of the pay cut—so you must contend with whatever happens in the field. Likewise, this method may offer you limited opportunities to select dependent variables; in the example experiment, employees might be resentful and overworked and could refuse to cooperate or attempt to sabotage any data collection processes (Stone-Romero, 2011).

Survey-Questionnaire

The *survey-questionnaire* is the most widely used method of collecting data in industrial/organizational psychology (Stone-Romero, 2011). Surveys involve selecting a sample of respondents and administering some type of questionnaire. They can be a useful method for collecting data from members of an organization (about job satisfaction, for example) as well as from customers or clients (measuring their opinions on the quality of a product or service). Questionnaires can be created as paper-and-pencil forms or in a computer-based format, both of which can assure the confidentiality of the respondent, which is especially important for sensitive topics. In general, the return rate for a computer-based questionnaire is higher than for the paper-and-pencil version.

Surveys can contain open-ended questions, which respondents answer in their own words—similar to an essay examination question—or they can be fixed-alternative (multiple-choice) questions, such as "This organization should do which one of the following options?" Telephone surveys may also be an appropriate method of conducting a survey or a structured interview. They are generally cost effective because of the low cost per interview, and a large number of people can be surveyed by one person or a team. However, several factors may reduce telephone-survey response rates, including the widespread use of answering machines and caller identification (so incoming calls can be screened). In addition, the growing trend of individuals having only a mobile or cellular telephone can have an impact on a survey, because certain groups will be less well represented in a survey using only conventional phone numbers to contact participants (Kempf & Remington, 2007).

Laboratory Experiment

Conducting *laboratory experiments* allows controlled observations in response to manipulations of the independent variable(s) and measurement of the dependent variable(s). In general, laboratory experiments involve highly controlled and artificial environments. Laboratory experiments can involve a systematic study of any aspect of an organization, such as organizational decision making or conflict resolution, as the experiment usually involves the simulation or creation of testing conditions by the researcher. Although the results of a laboratory experiment may have a limited ability to be generalized, the trade-off is that there is a high degree of control and precision over the major variables (Howell, 2008).

MEASUREMENT

Regardless of the method of study utilized, *measurement*, or the assignment of numbers to people, actions, or things, is inevitable. It serves to distinguish quantitative methods from qualitative methods; the former represents empirical data and the latter involves recorded observations in narrative form (Howell, 2008). It is important to establish that all data collected is reliable and valid. Reliability focuses on the consistence of a measurement of the same thing over time or across subjects, whereas validity refers to finding a meaningful relationship between what is being counted (the predictor or test) and what the information is assumed to mean (the criterion). For example, if a person scores high in conscientiousness on a personality instrument and her subsequent job performance gives clear evidence of this trait, it is concluded that this particular measurement or assessment of personality has high predictive validity.

Descriptive Statistics

In almost all instances, collected data are subject to some kind of statistical treatment for analysis. In general, descriptive statistics takes large quantities of data and summarizes them into measures of central tendency, such as the mean (average value) or median (middle score when all scores are rank-ordered). Statistics also compute the statistical variance, which is a measure of dispersion around the central tendency. If the variance in the measurements of the dependent variable is broad or high, you will probably conclude that the independent variable (or other factor) did not have a powerful and predictable influence over a particular dependent variable.

Correlation is another descriptive statistic that summarizes the degree (magnitude) and direction (positive or negative) of a relationship between two variables. Correlations range from +1 to –1, with a correlation of zero indicating no relationship between the variables. A correlation of –1 indicates a perfect negative correlation, meaning that as one variable goes up, the other goes down. A correlation of +1 indicates a perfect positive correlation, meaning that both variables move together in the same direction, up or down. Thus, if increasing or decreasing pay is associated with higher or lower productivity, respectively, then the correlation is positive. On the other hand, if increasing pay is associated with lower productivity, then the correlation is negative. If level of pay does not influence productivity, there is a zero correlation between the two variables. It is not always possible to determine with certainty the correlation between two variables; for example, to establish that level of pay influences level of productivity would require a systematic study in which pay for some subjects was decreased, for others there was no change, and still others were given varying degrees of increase.

Correlation analysis focuses on the relationship between only two variables, but in some cases you may be interested in the relationship among three or more variables. For example, you might want to examine the extent to which pay, length of employment, and age all contribute to absenteeism. Multiple linear regression analysis is a related statistical technique that allows you to estimate the impact of more than one variable (predictor variables) on a criterion or outcome variable. Furthermore, multiple linear regressions allow you to assess the relative impact of each predictor variable on the criterion. With this technique, you might find that age has the greatest impact on absenteeism, with older workers having significantly lower absenteeism rates than younger employees (Howell, 2008).

Inferential Statistics

Inferential statistics generalize findings beyond the sample and express confidence that the actual measures from a limited sample of participants (such as a group of 1,000 21-year-old women) would apply to larger groupings or populations of subjects (*all* 21-year-old women in China or *all* 21-year-old women). To make such generalizations requires tests that are based on probabilities and widely shared conventions about the cutoff points that distinguish statistically reliable differences from random variance. For example, let us assume that in a study of the relationship of pay and productivity, you have controlled all or almost all other influential independent variables, varying only the level of pay, and you find a substantial mean difference in productivity levels between high and low pay conditions. You can statistically establish the probability of finding such a mean difference. When an analysis reveals a mean difference, happening by chance less than 5% of the time, you can conclude that the difference in productivity levels is due to the treatment conditions, and in this case the change in productivity is probably due to pay (the independent variable) rather than chance. Such an outcome has statistical significance because the probability of finding the observed value of the statistical test is less than 0.05, or 1 in 20, or 5 in 100 (Howell, 2008).

An important feature of hypothesis testing is establishing the confidence level that an investigator wants in order to reject the null hypothesis—that there is no statistical difference between the control or no-treatment group and the treatment or intervention group. A Type I error arises when the null hypothesis is rejected but it should not have been. In other words, a Type I error occurs when the null hypothesis is rejected although it is true. A Type II error arises when the null hypothesis is accepted although it is false. These two errors most often result from sample sizes that are too small. Given the underlying assumptions of inferential statistics, average differences between small groups must be quite large to cross the threshold of significance (Howell, 2008).

Meta-Analysis

Meta-analysis is an increasingly important statistical tool because it allows for a highly structured ordering of the findings derived from many studies on a related theme (Chan, 2011; Hedges & Olkin, 2002). Techniques for meta-analysis employ a hybrid of qualitative and quantitative methodologies. The qualitative aspect is seen in the rules researchers develop to determine which studies will be analyzed (and which will not). There is also sometimes a set of judgments made about how the source studies will be weighted. Often, larger studies are given more weight than smaller ones. Or there may also be weights for study quality, so that more tightly controlled designs (experiments) are given more credence than case-control studies. When these judgments have been made, then each study will have one or more standardized values or numbers. These numbers are the basis for the quantitative aspect of meta-analysis, and they are analyzed using variations on the sort of statistical techniques used to analyze the results of individual research events. For example, you might select 50 studies from a body of 300 potentially relevant publications. These 50 studies enrolled a total of 10,000 participants. Most of the studies reported a high positive correlation score between level of pay and productivity. If you calculate a mean or average of the reported correlations across these 50 studies, you will be in a stronger position to report that the literature suggests that pay and productivity are correlated and most likely causally related.

Moderator Variables

The final concept affecting measurement is moderator variables, which are any factors that influence the relationship between two other variables. The relationship between two variables usually changes at different levels of the moderator variable (Baron & Kenny, 1986). For example, the relationship between absenteeism and hourly pay level is influenced by age. With increasing age, absenteeism decreases even when hourly pay level is low, whereas absentee rates are much higher for younger employees regardless of hourly pay level.

The organizational studies presented in subsequent chapters involve one of the five methods of study, as well as some type of statistical treatment presented in this chapter. In addition, many of the topics that are important for understanding organizations can only be understood by looking at sets of variables or factors that interact in complex ways. If you understand the methods of study and the tools of measurement introduced here, you will have a better sense of the value and limitations of each study you encounter.

ORGANIZATIONAL SNAPSHOT

To understand an organization requires several skills: listening, observing, and inquiring respectfully about organizational experiences that occur frequently, are laced with feelings, and may appear surprising or confusing to an outsider yet are readily accepted by organizational members. Table 2-5 presents a brief definition of the four domains or areas of organizational knowledge that, when pieced together, can provide a picture of an organization—a snapshot of where the organization is at a particular moment in time. Collecting the qualitative and quantitative data sets required to create such a snapshot can be relatively unobtrusive (Webb, 2000). Most of the data are available from organizational websites, public relations materials, and personnel department publications, and this information can be enriched by moving throughout the organization and listening with an open mind to identify functional as well as dysfunctional systems across all levels of the organization.

Organizational Structure

To piece together an initial portrait and an initial assessment of the organization's systems, you need to know the structure (divisions, departments, units, and work teams), demography (workforce mix), power and politics (influence relationships), and networks (how members communicate with each other, as well as how they communicate with people and systems inside and outside the organization). Table 2-6 presents a summary of key informational items about organizational structure that give a sense of whether an organization is big and bulky or small and nimble.

TABLE 2-5 Data Sets for an Organizational Snapshot
Organizational structure—structural patterns of the arrangement of people into units within the organization and for interaction with the external environment
Organizational demography—defining features of organizational members and client or customer clusters
Organizational power and politics—authority and functional-influence relationships in the internal and external organizational environments
Organizational networks—communication patterns within the organization and for interaction with the external environment

TABLE 2-6   Organizational Structure

Focus on the structural patterns of organizing people and activities within the organization and with the external environment.

- How many divisions, departments, or units exist?
- How long has each existed and what is the size of the budgets and number of employees per unit?
- How and why are units created, merged, and eliminated?
- What are the units and the positions within the units that interact systematically with the external environment?
- What are the patterns of interaction and how is the externally collected information then dispersed within the organization?

Information about these structural patterns can provide some preliminary indices of the *relative* power and influence of the different units within an organization. In general, the larger the budget and number of employees in a unit, the more the influence potential of that unit. The rationale for creating, modifying, and eliminating units provides some preliminary indices of the forces that shape the organization, such as a customer focus or a technical focus. The structural patterns of interaction with the external environment can provide useful information about the relationship(s) between the organization and the external environment.

Organizational Demography

Table 2-7 outlines some suggested demographic factors that can help you define an organizational workforce as well as the customer or client base and potential clients. In general, diversity or variation along a variety of dimensions can enhance the possibilities of cultivating and strengthening a nimble organization and global marketplace presence because variation is inherent in all systems.

TABLE 2-7   Organizational Demography

Focus on the composition and distribution of the organizational members and clients or customer clusters and any noteworthy changes in them over the past three to five years.

- What are the average age, education, length of employment, and salary and/or wage features that describe the overall organization and the members of each of the major structural units (divisions or departments) within the organization?
- What are the major or noteworthy differences between managers and non-managers or between levels of management in reference to gender, race, ethnicity, or any other definable attribute?
- What common features, if any, are shared among members of the highest and lowest levels of the organization? What is the income or overall compensation ratio between the highest paid and lowest paid employees in the organization?
- What features define and distinguish the customer or clientele base in terms of age, education, gender, race, ethnicity, educational level, or any other feature, and have there been any major changes in these features over the past three to five years?

Information about organizational demography can provide an initial sense of the membership and some of the major forces, such as age, race, gender, and educational level, that may be shaping organizational actions and experiences. Also, such information can be useful in constructing the membership of an intervention or leadership team.

| TABLE 2-8 | Organizational Power and Politics |

Focus on the physical arrangement of the organization as a reflection of authority as well as influence patterns expressed in nonverbal behaviors, gestures, and who gets invited and who participates in key meetings or other key organizational functions.

- What is the overall quality of the organizational facilities, cleanliness, and orderliness, as well as the relative size of space(s) assigned to different managers and organizational functions?
- What are the policies (written guidelines) and/or practices governing the assignment and use of physical facilities from offices to equipment of all kinds?
- What are the symbols of influence and specific guidelines or policies governing the exercise of authority (legitimate organizational influence)?

Information about organizational power and politics can suggest possible questions or hypotheses to identify more clearly organizational loci of power and influence. It is important to remember that physical structures and distances between persons or groups have social meaning (e.g., bigger physical structures often suggest more power than smaller ones, or members in a group may defer to or respectfully recognize a particular group member). Also, it is important to remember that influence lines may not be as visible as or similar to reporting lines in the organization.

Organizational Power and Politics

This domain provides a sense of influence relationships, affords a perspective on the non-rational or emotional side of the organization, and can provide suggestions of possible levers for organizational change. Information about politics within an organization is difficult to ascertain—although authority (legitimate power inherent to a position in an organization) is usually expressed publicly, power relationships based on politics are seldom directly expressed, especially to organizational outsiders. Table 2-8 provides a guide to important features of organizational power and politics.

Organizational Networks

Lastly, Table 2-9 provides a guide for obtaining overarching information about communication networks within an organization and also about the processes an organization employs to communicate with components of the external environment. Do members communicate primarily face to face, by phone and/or voice mail, through email, or by texting or social media? Is it a real organization or a virtual organization, in which informational nodes rather than people communicate with each other and exchange or hide data sets? Do people get back to each other in a timely fashion or leave communication loops open and hanging? How and what does the organization communicate to customers and clients, and, if appropriate, how does the organization work with the press—both traditional media representatives, and increasingly, so-called citizen journalists who can freely express their opinions on the Internet (Miller, 2009)?

Information in these domains will give you a starting point—a way to form some initial assumptions about organizational systems. Then you can test and

TABLE 2-9   Organizational Networks

Focus on who communicates with whom, how they communicate, the frequency and content of communication, and the outcome of communications both within and outside the organization.

- What are the methods of communication between members of the organization, such as electronic systems, social media, and sharing of critical financial and other organizational data about organizational performances?
- How are positive and negative emotions expressed? Are they valued or avoided by organizational members?
- How and what does the organization communicate with customers or clients? Does the organization solicit regular feedback from customers, and what happens as a result of customer or client feedback?
- What does the community know about the organization, and how is that information acquired?

Information about organizational networks can provide insight into the level of awareness of members and customers about important and emotionally charged organizational activities and functions.

refine those ideas through continued data collection as well as through genuine, open-minded interactions with organizational members and constituents.

Finally, when discussing ethics later in this text, you are invited to think about how the study of organizations can guide one's own moral and ethical framework. An appealing individual-level ethical framework is the American Psychological Association Ethical Principles and Code of Conduct (2010), although most professional associations also publish similar codes. Given the explosive growth of easily accessible information along with the potential for negative fallout when misbehavior is brought to light, many large organizations are now expressing their commitment to ethical behavior by hiring a chief ethics officer (Aguinis, 2011). This is a trend we applaud.

Chapter Summary

This chapter focused on tool sets to promote understanding of individuals and organizations as systems. The first tool set, instrumental forces, allows us to see individuals and organizations as systems and promotes systems thinking. We defined and then examined dispositional (trait) and situational (contextual) forces that powerfully influence individual and organizational actions and experiences. We also noted that organizations exhibit and require variation, that organizations, like individuals, have problems that provide a platform for organizational learning. We also examined rationality and emotionality as components of organizations as systems. Organizational learning arises from learning by individual members, but is also much more, because it is shared learning with other members

that becomes embedded in the organization by inclusion in standard operating manuals and procedures as well as through other forms of organizational documentation.

The second tool set, methods of study, includes five specific techniques used in industrial/organizational psychology: the case study, archival research, the field experiment, the survey-questionnaire, and the laboratory experiment. The third set of tools, used to prepare an organizational snapshot, includes a preliminary portrait of an organization constructed from collected information about organizational structure, demography, power and politics, and networks. The systematic use of all three of these tool sets can help us better understand and manage organizations.

Chapter References

Aguinis, H., & Vaschetto, S. J. (2011). Editorial responsibility: Managing the publishing process to do good and do well. *Management and Organization Review, 7*(3), 407–422.

American Psychological Association, Amendments to the 2002 Ethical Principles of Psychologists and Code of Conduct. (2010). *American Psychologist, 65*(5), 493. doi:10.1037/a0020168

Argyris, C., & Schön, D. A. (1978). *Organizational learning*. Reading, MA: Addison-Wesley.

Baron, R. M., & Kenny, D. A. (1986). The moderator–mediator variable distinction in social psychological research: Conceptual, strategic, and statistical considerations. *Journal of Personality and Social Psychology, 51*(6), 1173–1182. doi:10.1037/0022-3514.51.6.1173

Barrick, M. R., & Mount, M. K. (1993). Autonomy as a moderator of the relationships between the Big Five personality dimensions and job performance. *Journal of Applied Psychology, 78*(1), 111–118. doi:10.1037/0021-9010.78.1.111

Barrick, M. R., Mount, M. K., & Gupta, R. (2003). Meta-analysis of the relationship between the five-factor model of personality and Holland's occupational types. *Personnel Psychology, 56*(1), 45–74. doi:10.1111/j.1744-6570.2003.tb00143.x

Barrick, M. R., Mount, M. K., & Judge, T. A. (2001). Personality and performance at the beginning of the new millennium: What do we know and where do we go next? *International Journal of Selection and Assessment, 9,* 9–30. doi:10.1111/1468-2389.00160

Bouton, M. E. (2007). *Learning and behavior: A contemporary synthesis*. Sunderland, MA: Sinauer Associates, Publishers.

Brannick, M. T., Michaels, C. E., & Baker, D. P. (1989). Construct validity of in-basket scores. *Journal of Applied Psychology, 74*(6), 957–963. doi:10.1037/0021-9010.74.6.957

Chan, D. (2011). Advances in analytical strategies. In S. Zedeck (Ed.), *APA handbook of industrial and organizational psychology* (Vol. 1, pp. 85–113). Washington, DC: American Psychological Association. doi:10.1037/12169-004

Ethical Principles of Psychologists and Code of Conduct. (2002). *American Psychologist, 57*(12), 1060–1073. doi:10.1037/0003-066X.57.12.1060

Fiol, C. M., & Lyles, M. A., (1985). *Organizational learning*. The Academy of Management Review, 10(4), 803–813.

George, J. M. (1990). Personality, affect, and behavior in groups. *Journal of Applied Psychology, 75*(2), 107–116. doi:10.1037/0021-9010.75.2.107

George, J. M., & Brief, A. P. (1992). Feeling good—doing good: A conceptual analysis of the mood at work-organizational spontaneity relationship. *Psychological Bulletin, 112*(2), 310–329. doi:10.1037/0033-2909.112.2.310

Hedges, L. V., & Olkin, I. (1985). *Statistical methods for meta-analysis* San Diego, CA: Academic Press.

Howell, D. C. (2008). *Fundamental statistics for the behavioral sciences* (6th ed.). Belmont, CA: Thomson/Wadsworth.

Jelinek, M. (1979). *Institutionalizing innovation: A study of organizational learning systems*. New York: Praeger.

Kempf, A. M., & Remington, P. L. (2007). New challenges for telephone survey research in the twenty-first century. *Annual Review of Public Health, 28*(1), 113–126. doi:10.1146/annurev.publhealth.28.021406.144059

Lawson, R. B., & Ventriss, C. L. (1992). Organizational change: The role of organizational culture and organizational learning. *Psychological Record, 42*(2), 205–219.

Lee, T. W., Mitchell, T. R., & Harman, W. S. (2011). Qualitative research strategies in industrial and organizational psychology. In S. Zedeck (Ed.), *APA handbook of industrial and organizational psychology* (Vol. 1, pp. 73–83). Washington, DC: American Psychological Association.

Martins, L. L. (2011). Organizational change and development. In S. Zedeck (Ed.), *APA handbook of industrial and organizational psychology* (Vol. 3, pp. 691–728). Washington, DC: American Psychological Association.

Miller, C. C. (2009). The review site Yelp draws some outcries of its own. *The New York Times*. Retrieved from http://www.nytimes.com/2009/03/03/technology/start-ups/03yelp.html

Nystrom, P. C., & Starbuck, W. H. (1984). To avoid organizational crises, unlearn. *Organizational Dynamics, 12*(4), 53–65. doi:10.1016/0090-2616(84)90011-1

Schleicher, D. J., Hansen, S. D., & Fox, K. E. (2011). Job attitudes and work values. In S. Zedeck (Ed.), *APA handbook of industrial and organizational psychology* (Vol. 3, pp. 137–190). Washington, DC: American Psychological Association.

Schneider, B., Smith, D. B., Taylor, S., & Fleenor, J. (1998). Personality and organizations: A test of the homogeneity of personality hypothesis. *Journal of Applied Psychology, 83,* 462–470.

Stone-Romero, E. F. (2011). Research strategies in industrial and organizational psychology: Nonexperimental, quasi-experimental, and randomized experimental research in special purpose and nonspecial purpose settings. In S. Zedeck (Ed.), *APA handbook of industrial and organizational psychology* (Vol. 1, pp. 37–72). Washington, DC: American Psychological Association.

Webb, E. J. (2000). *Unobtrusive measures* (Rev. ed.). Thousand Oaks, CA: Sage Publications.

Wildman, J. L., Bedwell, W. L., Salas, E., & Smith-Jentsch, K. A. (2011). Performance measurement at work: A multilevel perspective. In S. Zedeck (Ed.), *APA handbook of industrial and organizational psychology* (Vol. 1, pp. 303–342). Washington, DC: American Psychological Association.

Zhao, H., & Seibert, S. E. (2006). The Big Five personality dimensions and entrepreneurial status: A meta-analytical review. *Journal of Applied Psychology, 91*(2), 259–271. doi:10.1037/0021-9010.91.2.259

Macrosystems

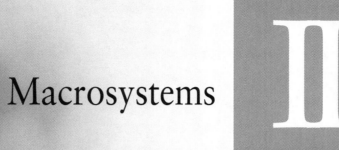

PART

II

CHAPTER

3

Organizational Culture

CHAPTER OVERVIEW

Organizational culture is a macro-level variable because it impacts all members of an organization in one way or another. Organizational culture is found in families and schools, in for-profit and nonprofit companies, in local, state, regional, and national governmental bodies and nongovernment organizations, as well as in social and friendship groups. Wherever there is an organization, there is an organizational culture. In most instances, there is an organization-wide culture that also includes a series of subcultures.

To get a feel for the organizational culture of a group, take a minute to focus on your family of origin—think about your family values, practices, and basic assumptions about human nature (people are basically good), the nature of your family's relationship with the biological world (contributing time and energy to protect animals and other living creatures) and the physical world (it is critical to recycle and reuse things). Also, think about how your family is different from other families

Alx/Fotolia

(for example, you may celebrate certain holidays and not others) and consider how these differences came about to make your family unique.

Understanding organizational culture includes studying the origins of the culture, the contributions it brings to the workplace, and the importance it holds for membership in the organization. An explanation of how a learning culture retains organizational hierarchy through an open feedback loop and healthy debate, thus combating system inertia or self-elimination, is supported by tools used to retain organizational resilience. The chapter concludes with a brief discussion of how changing an organizational culture is supported by individual and organizational learning.

LEARNING OBJECTIVES

When you have finished reading this chapter, you will be prepared to do the following:

- Define organizational culture and distinguish it from organizational climate
- Identify the three levels of organizational culture: artifacts, values, and basic assumptions

Radius/SuperStock

- Understand the relationship between individual and organizational learning and organizational culture
- Identify the origins of organizational culture
- Understand the function of organizational culture in addressing the problems of external adaptation and internal integration
- Use a directory of organizational culture derived from organizational documents, manuals, ceremonies, rites, rituals, and stories to describe an organizational culture
- Explain how a learning culture orchestrates organizational resilience, strengthing relationships between individual and organizational learning
- Learn specific applied strategies to change an organizational culture

ORGANIZATIONAL CULTURE

Organizational culture is a hypothetical construct rather than a thing that can be directly observed, measured, and manipulated, and it must be inferred from the shared feelings, actions, and thoughts of organizational members (Schneider, Ehrhart, & Macey, 2011). Following are some definitions of organizational culture:

> The shared values of organizational members (Peters & Waterman, 1982)
> The way we do things around here (Bower, 1966)
> The shared and relatively enduring pattern of basic values, beliefs, and assumptions in an organization (Sethia & Von Glino, 1985)

Edgar Schein (1992, p. 12) defined organizational culture as "a pattern of shared basic assumptions that the group learned as it solved its problems of external adaptation and internal integration, that has worked well enough to be considered valid, and, therefore, to be taught to new members as the correct way to perceive, think, and feel in relation to those problems." Schein's definition of organizational culture is used throughout the remainder of this chapter.

Organizational culture and climate are sometimes used interchangeably because they both refer to the awareness of the overall context, environment, or situation of the organization. Organizational climate usually focuses on an individual's perception or awareness of events, practices, procedures, and behaviors that are rewarded, supported, and expected in a given organization or unit within the organization (Schneider, Ehrhart, & Macey, 2011). Organizational culture, however, goes beyond individual awareness of organizational events and ambience. Organizational culture focuses on the shared meanings of events, procedures, and behaviors by members of the organization rather than individual perceptions. In short, climate is an individual's awareness while culture embraces *shared* awareness by members coupled with shared meaning or interpretations of organizational events, practices, and actions.

Organizational culture distinguishes members from non-members of an organization although both may be aware of the climate. By fostering a sense of true organizational membership, the culture strengthens the basic forces of group identity and cohesion (Bauer & Erdogan, 2011; Cannon-Bowers & Bowers, 2011; Ferris & Hochwarter, 2011; Fiske, 2010; Rousseau, 2011; Schneider et al., 2011). A strong culture does this through ceremonies, stories, rituals, and artifacts.

Organizations are located everywhere around the globe. Obviously there is cultural variation among the broader social cultures of nations as well as within each national culture, depending on the geographic region within which a particular organization is located (Triandis, 1995). A question then arises: does an organizational culture arise primarily from the broader social culture within which the organization is nested, or are there other factors at play (Schneider et al., 1987)? In general, almost regardless of where an organization is geographically located, organizational culture arises from three primary sources: (1) the broader culture in which an organization is nested; (2) the type of business or the business environment of the organization; and (3) the beliefs, values, and basic assumptions about the nature of reality and human nature held by the founder(s) or first-generation leadership of the organization.

G. H. Hofstede (1980, 2001) identified four interpersonal dimensions that differentiate managers drawn from 40 different countries, based on his study of thousands of managers employed by a large transnational business organization. These dimensions—which some researchers believe are related to organizational design and culture—are as follows:

> *Power distance.* The degree of power inequities or differences between two individuals. High power distance signals that the power holders or authority figures are entitled to privileges framed within strong and clear superior–subordinate relationships among organizational members.

Uncertainty avoidance. The degree of organizational stability and predictability preferred by members. High uncertainty avoidance reflects strong preferences for written rules and regulations, the desire for consensus, and susceptibility to high levels of anxiety and stress.

Individualism. The preference for collective or individual action. High individualism is characterized by less emotional dependence on the organization, preference for individual rather than group decisions, and high value placed on individual initiative.

Masculinity. The dominant sex role pattern. Usually, male roles are assertive and female roles are nurturing, and high masculinity favors larger organizations and intense achievement motivation.

Hofstede, Neuijen, Ohayv, and Sanders (1990) studied 10 organizations based in several countries. They conducted 180 in-depth interviews and also collected surveys from 1,295 respondents who were asked about organizational values and practices. The researchers concluded that the *values* of the organizational members are determined primarily by the larger culture in which the organization is nested. However, members learn *practices* while being socialized into the distinctive culture of the organization of which they are a member. Organizational values are shaped by the broader social culture, whereas organizational behaviors are shaped by the organizational culture.

Recently, Taras, Kirkman, and Steel (2010) reported a meta-analysis of 508 studies involving over 20,000 individuals. They examined the relationships among Hofstede's original four cultural value dimensions and a variety of organizational outcomes such as job performance, absenteeism, organizational commitment, citizenship behavior, and team-related attitudes. They found that individual adherence to the cultural values of the employee's organization were less reliable predictors than personality traits and demographics for job performance and absenteeism. Another noteworthy finding was that the broader social cultural values were most strongly related to emotions, attitudes, behaviors, and, lastly, job performance. Some moderators of these associations include age (the associations were stronger in older members), gender (stronger in men), and education (stronger in people with relatively more years of formal schooling).

Some researchers have proposed that organizational culture is most strongly determined by the organization's industry and its general business environment (Deal & Kennedy, 1982). Other researchers suggest that particular professions selectively attract people who already hold (or are very open to) its beliefs, values, and actions (Schein, 1990). In explaining how an organization's cultural path is set, others stress the importance of the basic assumptions, beliefs, and values of the founder, or of leadership in place during organizational crises (Schein, 2010). The influence of the founder may be especially important when trying to understand unique features of a specific culture. For example, research on sales-oriented organizations suggests that charismatic founders use their emotional expressiveness, linguistic ability, confidence, and vision to inspire their followers and build a culture that suits their own values and inclinations (Biggart, 1989).

LEVELS OF ORGANIZATIONAL CULTURE

According to Schein (1990), organizational culture is discernible at three levels, which are examined in more detail in the following sections.

Cultural Artifacts

The most readily observable—although the least exact—expression of the organizational culture is represented by *cultural artifacts,* which include things such as furnishings and their arrangement; observable behaviors; organizational stories and jokes; ceremonies such as annual meetings, graduation, or promotion exercises; rites and rituals that are habitual activities, such as weekly or monthly departmental meetings or presentations; and norms, which are the unwritten rules for appropriate and inappropriate behaviors. Artifacts of a culture are quickly detected, although their underlying meaning may be rather difficult for new members to decipher and understand. It is not the artifact or thing in itself, but rather the shared meanings of the artifacts, that is key to becoming deeply aware of the organizational culture.

Values

In Schein's (2010) analysis, the second level of organizational culture consists of values that define a culturally appropriate sense of what *ought to be* as distinct from what *is.* Suppose a company experiences a sudden and inexplicable drop in sales. In response, the organization decides to do more advertising. If that appears to restore and increase sales, and if this pattern is repeated with similar results, the organizational members who shared in the experiences will come to think of advertising as a sound investment. As members begin to explain, mostly to themselves, why advertising worked and is therefore valued, they will develop focused and strongly held beliefs associated with particular values.

No matter how they came about, however, values can be espoused (the talk), enacted (the walk), or both (talk the talk *and* walk the walk). People tend to pay more attention to enacted values and respond by bringing their own values in line. In general, a single enactment of a core organizational value is many times more powerful than a thousand espousals of that value.

Basic Assumptions

According to Schein (1990, 2010), as the initial preferences for organizational problem solving continue to be successful, organizational members increasingly take the originally tentative solutions for granted and believe that they uniquely and accurately reflect reality because they have continued to prove successful; that is, if it works repeatedly, it *must* be true.

During an organization's formative stages, culture is likely to be consciously recognized and actively debated. As the members act on their fundamental beliefs and the organization endures, the fundamental beliefs are taken

TABLE 3-1	Examples of Basic Assumptions Carried by an Organizational Culture

Relationship to the environment
- Earthly resources are infinite or can be replaced and should be developed for profit.
- Earthly resources are finite and should be protected or developed sparingly.

Nature of reality, time, and space
- Reality is based on social consensus rather than absolute truths.
- Time is money.
- Small is better than big.

Nature of human nature
- People are basically honest, trustworthy, realistic, and enjoyable.
- People are lazy, greedy, only interested in self, and cynical.

Nature of human activity
- If you do what you love for a living, you will never have to work again.

Nature of human relationships
- Never mix business and friendship.
- People interact only for self-interest.

for granted, and eventually the organization's members simply act on these beliefs without further reflection or regard. When these fundamental beliefs are shared, taken for granted, and closed to further debate, we have—according to Schein (1990) and others (Ott, 1989)—reached the level of basic assumptions of the culture. Table 3-1 presents some examples of basic assumptions that might be part of an organizational culture.

In fact, Schein (1992, p. 26) asserted that "the essence of a culture lies in the pattern of basic underlying assumptions, and once one understands those, one can easily understand the other more surface levels and deal appropriately with them." According to Argyris (1976), Argyris and Schon (1974), Schneider et al. (2011), and many others, to change an organization's culture, you must first change its basic assumptions. This is usually a difficult and anxiety-provoking process. It requires what is known as *double-loop organizational learning*, changing the important things you have done and still do, rather than *single-loop learning*, which involves getting more efficient at what you are already doing (Argyris, Putnam, & Smith, 1985).

FUNCTIONS OF ORGANIZATIONAL CULTURE

The primary functions of an organizational culture are to enhance the organization's responsiveness to the problems of external adaptation and internal integration (Frost, 1991; Schein, 2010). All organizations confront these two broad categories of problems. As a result, they remain engaged in ongoing learning and change. Table 3-2 presents some of the specific issues of external adaptation and internal integration that must be handled by organizational leaders and members.

TABLE 3-2	Problems of External Adaptation and Internal Integration

Problems of External Adaptation and Survival

Mission and Strategy. Obtain a shared understanding of core mission, primary task, manifest and latent functions.

Goals. Develop consensus on goals, as derived from the core mission.

Means. Develop consensus on the means to be used to attain the goals, such as the organization structure, division of labor, reward system, and authority system.

Measurement. Develop consensus on the criteria to be used in measuring how well the group is doing in fulfilling its goals, such as the information and control system.

Correction. Develop consensus on the appropriate remedial or repair strategies to be used if goals are not being met.

Problems of Internal Integration

Common Language and Conceptual Categories. If members cannot communicate with and understand each other, a group is impossible by definition.

Group Boundaries and Criteria for Inclusion and Exclusion. One of the most important areas of culture is the shared consensus on who is in and who is out and by what criteria one determines membership.

Power and Status. Every organization must work out its pecking order, its criteria and rules for how one gets, maintains, and loses power; consensus in this area is crucial to help members manage feelings of aggression.

Intimacy, Friendship, and Love. Every organization must work out its rules of the game for peer relationships, for relationships between the sexes, and for the manner in which openness and intimacy are to be handled in the context of managing the organization's tasks.

Rewards and Punishments. Every group must know what its heroic and sinful behaviors are; what gets rewarded with property, status, and power; and what gets punished in the form of withdrawal of the rewards and, ultimately, excommunication.

Ideology and "Religion." Every organization, like every society, faces unexplainable and inexplicable events, which must be given meaning so that members can respond to them and avoid the anxiety of dealing with the unexplainable and uncontrollable.

Source: Adapted from E. H. Schein (1985). *Organizational Culture and Leadership.* San Francisco, CA: Jossey-Bass, pp. 52 and 66. Copyright © 1985 by Jossey-Bass. Used with permission.

External Adaptation

The most condensed expression of an organization's culture and values is a *mission statement* which represents the *raison d'être*—its purpose for being. In general, a short overarching mission statement is sound if it can be expressed readily by members of the organization as well as appearing prominently in a variety of organizational communications. Also, a broad but short mission statement makes it simpler to develop more tailored mission statements to suit the main units or subcultures within an organization. A mission statement provides focus, gives a sense of grounding, and can evoke deep passions and tireless effort. Table 3-3 presents some guidelines for constructing a mission statement.

| **TABLE 3-3** | Guidelines for Constructing a Mission Statement |

- Ask if the mission statement reinforces the organization as something one should identify with and which deserves respect from employees, customers, vendors, and the community.
- Ask if the mission statement provides a rallying point, uniting people so they can feel satisfaction in working toward a common goal.
- Ask if the mission statement focuses on quality, cost effectiveness, continuous improvement, and customer satisfaction.
- Avoid managerial zeal to complete the mission statement.
- Do not behave as if the mission statement is a "done deal" before it is even begun. Writing the statement requires attention and consideration. If you get stuck writing the mission statement, you may not yet have all the information you need to complete it.
- Do not consider the mission statement to be "cast in stone," because it will need frequent revisiting and updating.
- Do not forget about the mission statement after it is written.
- Do not fall into the trap of believing that the mission statement will tell you how to behave in specific situations.

An organization's goals arise from its mission statement, and specific statements of actions are derived from the goals. The goal-setting process affords the ability to align organizational capacity—as reflected by cultural, human, financial, and physical resources—with organizational aspiration (Locke, Latham, Smith, & Wood, 1990). Goals also assist response and adaptation to external forces. By routinely measuring and monitoring progress on their goals, organizational members can better determine which actions to continue and which actions to modify or drop. To do this effectively, members must have a strong understanding of the relevant external societal, cultural, global, regional, and domestic markets, as well as knowledge of the most pressing issues for their particular type of business. Knowledge about the functioning of groups, organizations, governments, and larger societal cultures is necessary for effective external adaptation.

Internal Integration

Organizational boundaries influence disclosure and trust levels. They are usually higher among organizational members than with outsiders, especially around important organizational issues and challenges (Schneider et al., 2011). For example, several noteworthy corporations, such as Apple and IBM, are famous for their discipline regarding their own business plans, and they seek to maintain total control over such knowledge (McGrath, 2010). In addition, every organization develops its own specialized language, rich with unique terms, in-jokes, and obscure references to important events. While learning and adopting other culturally appropriate behaviors and attitudes, a failure (or unwillingness) to employ an organization's language may signal that a new member is not fitting in (Bauer & Erdogan, 2011). For this reason, learning the language of an organization is often a strong mechanism for achieving internal integration, which is the coordination of internal organizational systems by regularly and openly sharing achievements as well as barriers in order to enhance the functioning of internal systems and the relationships among such systems.

In most organizations, internal integration will also place a new member at the level of power that is consistent with his or her new position—usually relatively low (thus the term *entry level*).

Cultural Directory

Table 3-4 presents a directory of sources that are focused on the problems of external adaptation and internal integration. The timeliness, content, and distribution of the documents identified in Table 3-4 are all sources of information about the organizational culture. For example, if an organization's mission statement is

TABLE 3-4 Directory of Organizational Culture	
External Adaptation	**Organizational Loci of Information**
Mission	The charter, mission/vision statements, annual reports, founder's documents and biographies, accreditation reports, recruitment materials, and minutes of board meetings
Goals	Strategic planning documents, annual budget reports, and public relations materials
Means	Technological reports, standard operating procedures, manuals, and organizational charts
Performance Measures	Management information systems, personnel documents and performance appraisal forms, and financial statements
Correction Mechanisms	Strategic planning documents, personnel records, internal management documents, and records of retreats
Internal Integration	**Organizational Loci of Information**
Language	Internal memoranda, email, records of management meetings, and public relations materials
Boundaries	Recruitment and employee selection materials, orientation materials, organizational stories, and personnel management systems
Power and Status	Organizational structures, annual budget reports, physical plant documents, space and equipment budgets, strategic planning documents, and minutes of board meetings
Peer Relationships and Intimacy	Personnel records and management systems, human resource materials, employee assistance program materials, informal memoranda, public bulletin boards, and email
Reward System	Personnel records, performance appraisal system, unit or departmental budgets, space and equipment inventories, and employee development programs
Ideology	Organizational charter, biographies of the founder, annual reports, organizational stories, strategic planning documents, and public relations materials

not revisited and updated about every five years, or if very few members can briefly (and readily) state the organization's mission, then leadership needs to pay closer attention to updating the mission statement and making sure members are knowledgeable about it. If the problems of external adaptation and internal integration are denied or ignored by organizational members, it is most likely that the organization will be ineffective and dysfunctional (Schneider et al., 2011).

To get a clear view of an organizational culture, you must collect the kinds of documents and other sources of information about the culture presented in Table 3-4. In addition, if it is possible, you should observe organizational rites, ceremonies, and rituals to obtain a richer description and appreciation of the organizational culture. According to Trice and Beyer (1993), an organizational rite is a fairly elaborate, carefully planned, and dramatic set of activities that consolidate various forms of cultural expression into one event, which is usually presented before an audience.

An organizational ceremony is a system of collected rites, such as the annual meeting of shareholders or annual budget and planning sessions. Organizational rituals involve a standardized set of behaviors used to manage anxieties. They often include departmental or unit meetings that may not yield specific decisions or action outcomes but reduce the anxiety of members who attend the meetings. It is informative to look for themes, patterns, trends, idiosyncrasies, or any pattern of information across the printed and electronic organizational information as well as the rites, ceremonies, rituals, and stories that almost inevitably provide direction for further inquiry into the organizational culture.

ORGANIZATIONAL CULTURE CHANGE

In general, there are three indicators that will tell you when it is wise to modify an organization's culture rather than change programs focused on specific individual units, departments, or groups of individuals. The three presenting symptoms are as follow:

- The problem is widespread throughout the organization, rather than limited, to a particular department or unit of the organization.
- The problem has resisted prior focused interventions to address the problem.
- The problem has existed for at least two to three years.

Cultural change in an organization is structural, requires time (approximately three to five years), and is usually resisted because it is perceived initially as a loss at some level by almost all organizational members (Schein, 2010). Organizational culture change involves changes in the way members feel, act, and think in regard to critical issues, problems, and challenges facing their organization. Cultural change is initially experienced as difficult, because it is perceived as a loss, usually of stability, clarity, and predictability; it appears as inevitable; and it impacts almost all organizational members.

The first step in effectively changing organizational culture is to recognize that initially, members will have a sense of loss when they realize (or are told) that the culture needs to evolve. The sense of loss is often most apparent in people who are highly socialized in the current culture and those in the most powerful organizational positions, perhaps because they sense that they have the most to lose by accepting that the old ways no longer work.

The second step to cultural change is to foster belief that the organization can be strengthened and enhanced through cooperative change efforts. Individual and organizational change involving the adoption of a fundamental and unifying new pattern of feelings, actions, and thoughts can appear to members as both a threat and an opportunity. Organizations that are open to individual and corporate learning may be predisposed to focus on opportunity (Mowday & Sutton, 1993). The key to understanding and modifying the relationship between organizational culture and individual members is the process of organizational learning.

Lastly, it is important to appreciate that organizational culture is ultimately *internalized*. As members become more socialized in a given organizational culture, they tend to make sense, attribute meaning, and understand organizational events in a similar fashion; this connection among members serves to unify them as well as creating cognitive and emotional boundaries between themselves as insiders and non-members as outsiders.

ORGANIZATIONAL CULTURE AND LEARNING

Edgar Schein (2010) believes that organizational learning is initiated by the founder of the organization by articulating the overall rules and norms for the organization rather than by focusing on specific activities or behaviors. In this view, leader-initiated organizational learning serves as the mechanism for spreading and connecting the shared patterns of thoughts, feelings, values, and actions of members, thus creating new insights, knowledge, skill development, and cultural norms. According to Schein (2010), organizational values are shaped by culture, and if organizational problem solving meets the needs for external adaptation (dealing with changes outside the organization) and internal integration (coordinating activities inside the organization), members of the organization come to share the beliefs in the efficacy of those problem solving practices.

Classic *organizational learning,* as explained by Chris Argyris and David Schön (1978), occurs when individual employees inquire about "how things are done around here," and the answers to their questions are discussed with other employees. The employees use these shared descriptions of methods and practices to form a map of "how things are done around here," which employees have jointly constructed and which will guide future actions.

Organizational learning occurs when individual learning, having been shared with the other members of the organization, is adopted by the group as the correct way to solve a problem or complete a task, or when it is captured in organizational policies, standard operating procedures, cultural norms, and organizational stories and ceremonies. Organizational learning can shape standard operating procedures as well as future policy (Argyris & Schön, 1978, 2011; Jelinek, 1979; Schneider et al., 2011)).

Lower-level organizational learning is based on repetition and routine; it takes place "in organizational contexts that are well understood and in which management thinks it can control situations" (Fiol & Lyles, 1985, p. 807). In other words, lower-level or single-loop organizational learning involves the restructuring of practices and procedures without fundamentally changing existing cultural norms. Single-loop learning is the detection of errors in processes that results in changes in practices and procedures but not in the fundamental norms or assumptions of the group or organization (Argyris et al., 1985). As a result of single-loop organizational learning, the organization gets better and better at doing the same thing. In short, single-loop learning changes the way an organization manufactures or delivers a product or service, whereas double-loop (higher-level) learning changes what the organization does.

Organizational cultural change arises only when change reflects a shift in basic organizational assumptions brought about by double-loop learning. Double-loop learning gives rise to cultural change because the basic norms or assumptions are changed as values are changed. Successful organizational learning is enhanced when the organizational vision, organizational practice, and goals are all aligned. Higher-level organizational learning (double-loop learning) "aims at adjusting overall rules and norms rather than specific activities or behavior" (Fiol & Lyles, 1985, p. 808). This kind of organizational learning specifically tries to create new skill development, new knowledge, new cultural norms, and new insights. Moreover, a key characteristic of higher-level organizational learning is that an organization can *unlearn* previous behaviors and beliefs coupled with the development of *new* cognitive frameworks or interpretive schemes that its members use to confront ambiguous or ill-defined problems (Nystrom & Starbuck, 1984; Ventriss & Luke, 1988).

Organizational learning serves as the mechanism for spreading and connecting the shared patterns of thoughts, feelings, values, and actions of members. Thus, when a member learns a better way to think, feel, or act, relative to a given organizational problem, and then that individual-based learning is shared systematically with other members by behavioral modeling and inclusion in written operating procedures, manuals, policy statements, and other key organization documents or videotapes (employed, for example, for the socialization of new members), the result is organizational learning—because other members now have the opportunity to think, feel, and act like the original learner. Interestingly, even if the original learner and all her or his colleagues have left the organization, current members may still use the newer methods when dealing with the original organizational issue or similar challenges, because the manuals and policy statements still reflect the organizational learning that resulted from the earlier individual-based learning. This kind of behavior indicates that organizational learning transcends individuals even as it derives from individual learning that was shared with other organizational members.

There are innumerable applied strategies for changing organizational culture (Martins, 2011). Schein's (2010) leader-centered change strategy is perhaps the most fully articulated and considers the change strategy as a clinical (or helping) relationship between outside consultant(s) and informed and cooperative insider(s) whose primary joint task is to identify and then change basic assumptions about the organizational culture, primarily by leadership changes.

Schein (2010) has identified specific primary strategies to change an organizational culture, all of which focus on the formal (and optimistically, the informal as well) organization leader or leadership team. These include the following strategies:

- What leaders pay attention to, measure, and control
- How leaders react to critical incidents and organizational crises
- Observed criteria by which leaders allocate scarce resources
- Deliberate role modeling, teaching, and coaching
- Observed criteria by which leaders recruit, select, promote, retire, and excommunicate organizational members

In addition, Schein (2010) identifies secondary strategies and reinforcement mechanisms to change organizational culture, including modifying organizational rites, rituals, and stories; structuring reward systems to promote change; and revising formal statements such as organizational mission (what we do) and vision (what we aspire to be) statements, value statements, and recruitment materials. Schein's cultural change process focuses on the leader or leadership team; in this process, the consultant works closely with organizational insiders who are committed to organizational change and who have sufficient influence to impact many members of the organization (Schein, 2010).

Cultural transformation requires time, and if the leadership is not prepared for a sustained campaign, then the focus will be lost and the transformation effort will dwindle and die (Stahl & Bounds, 1991). Organizational culture transmits what is permissible and what is not allowed in an organization, and it sends a clear message to all members that those who do not adjust to the culture will not succeed, regardless of their competencies or achievements (Barney, 1986, 1992; Kets de Vries, 2010; Kets de Vries & Tromp, 1993; Ott, 1989).

Barney (1986, 1992) has suggested that organizational culture can be a source of competitive advantage if the culture is valuable. It creates this advantage by fostering actions by members that yield high sales, low costs, and high margins, or in other ways add financial value to the organization. In addition, to be competitively advantageous, the organizational culture must be rare—that is, it must have features that are not common to the cultures of a large number of organizations—and the culture must be *imperfectly imitable* so that other organizations cannot copy the unique features of the culture.

Chapter Summary

This chapter introduced organizational culture as the unifying and shared pattern of feelings, actions, and thoughts that bind together organizational members and distinguish them from non-members. Organizational culture determines the responses of organizational members to problems of external adaptation and internal integration that confront all organizations around the globe.

Organizational learning and organizational culture are intimately linked to each other, and this linkage provides the bases for instituting organizational cultural change. The chapter presented a specific change strategy with detailed steps for implementing the strategy, which can be applied in a wide variety of organizations. Workplace culture influences the financial and productivity outcomes of an organization, which means that organizational culture is an important factor for companies participating in the global marketplace.

A solid understanding of organizational culture yields many dividends for the individual member, department, or unit within an organization, as well as for the overarching organization, by making plain what is acceptable and what is unacceptable in the organization. This understanding minimizes the unnecessary expenditure of attention and emotions about what, how, when, and why individual members should do, think, value, feel, and act in the workplace.

Chapter References

Argyris, C. (1976). *Increasing leadership effectiveness.* New York: Wiley.

Argyris, C., Putnam, R., & Smith, D. M. (1985). *Action science* (1st ed.). San Francisco: Jossey-Bass.

Argyris, C., & Schön, D. A. (1974). *Theory in practice: Increasing professional effectiveness* (1st ed.). San Francisco: Jossey-Bass.

Argyris, C., & Schön, D. A. (1978). *Organizational learning.* Reading, MA: Addison-Wesley.

Barney, J. B. (1986). Organizational culture: Can it be a source of sustained competitive advantage? *The Academy of Management Review, 11*(3), 656–665.

Barney, J. B. (1992). Integrating organizational behavior and strategy formulation research: A resource-based analysis. *Advances in Strategic Management, 8,* 39–61.

Bauer, T. N., & Erdogan, B. (2011). Organizational socialization: The effective onboarding of new employees. In S. Zedeck (Ed.), *APA handbook of industrial and organizational psychology* (Vol. 3, pp. 707–721). Washington, DC: American Psychological Association.

Biggart, N. W. (1989). *Charismatic capitalism: Direct selling organizations in America.* Chicago: University of Chicago Press.

Bower, M. (1966). *The will to manage.* New York: McGraw-Hill.

Cannon-Bowers, J. A., & Bowers, C. (2011). Team development and functioning. In S. Zedeck (Ed.), *APA handbook of industrial and organizational psychology* (Vol. 1, pp. 597–650). Washington, DC: American Psychological Association.

Deal, T. E., & Kennedy, A. A. (1982). *Corporate cultures: The rites and rituals of corporate life.* Reading, MA: Addison-Wesley.

Ferris, G. R., & Hochwarter, W. A. (2011). Organizational politics. In S. Zedeck (Ed.), *APA handbook of industrial and organizational psychology* (Vol. 3, pp. 435–459). Washington, DC: American Psychological Association.

Fiol, C. M., & Lyles, M. A. (1985). Organizational learning. *The Academy of Management Review, 10*(4), 803–813.

Fiske, S. T. (2010). *Social beings: A core motives approach to social psychology* (2nd ed.). Hoboken, NJ: John Wiley & Sons.

Frost, P. J. (1991). *Reframing organizational culture.* Newbury Park, CA: Sage Publications.

Greenberg, J. (2011a). Organizational justice: The dynamics of fairness in the workplace. In S. Zedeck (Ed.), *APA handbook of industrial and organizational psychology* (Vol. 3, pp. 271–327). Washington, DC: American Psychological Association.

Hofstede, G. H. (1980). *Culture's consequences: International differences in work-related values.* Beverly Hills, CA: Sage Publications.

Hofstede, G. H. (2001). *Culture's consequences: Comparing values, behaviors, institutions, and organizations across nations* (2nd ed.). Thousand Oaks, CA: Sage Publications.

Hofstede, G. H., Neuijen, B., Ohayv, D. D., & Sanders, G. (1990). Measuring organizational cultures: A qualitative and quantitative study across twenty cases. *Administrative Science Quarterly, 35*(2), 286–316.

Jelinek, M. (1979). *Institutionalizing innovation: A study of organizational learning systems.* New York: Praeger.

Kets de Vries, M. F. R. (2010). *Reflections on leadership and career development.* San Francisco, CA: John Wiley & Sons.

Kets de Vries, M. F. R., & Tromp, T. H. J. (1993). *Organisaties op de divan: Gedrag en verandering van organisaties in klinisch perspectief.* Schiedam, Netherlands: Scriptum.

Locke, E. A., Latham, G. P., Smith, K. J., & Wood, R. E. (1990). *A theory of goal setting & task performance.* Englewood Cliffs, NJ: Prentice Hall College Div.

Martins, L. L. (2011). Organizational change and development. In S. Zedeck (Ed.), *APA handbook of industrial and organizational psychology* (Vol. 3, pp. 691–728). Washington, DC: American Psychological Association.

McGrath, B. (2010). Search and destroy: Nick Denton's blog empire. *The New Yorker, 86,* 50–61.

Mowday, R. T., & Sutton, R. I. (1993). Organizational behavior: Linking individuals and groups to organizational contexts. *Annual Review of Psychology, 44*(1), 195–229. doi:10.1146/annurev.ps.44.020193.001211

Nystrom, P. C., & Starbuck, W. H. (1984). To avoid organizational crises, unlearn. *Organizational Dynamics, 12*(4), 53–65. doi: 10.1016/0090-2616(84)90011-1

Ott, J. S. (1989). *The organizational culture perspective.* Chicago, IL: Dorsey Press.

Peters, T. J., & Waterman, R. H. (1982). *In search of excellence: Lessons from America's best-run companies* (1st ed.). New York: Harper & Row.

Rousseau, D. M. (2011). The individual-organization relationship: The psychological contract. In S. Zedeck (Ed.), *APA handbook of industrial and organizational psychology* (Vol. 3, pp. 191–220). Washington, DC: American Psychological Association.

Schein, E. H. (1985). *Organizational culture and leadership.* San Francisco: Jossey-Bass.

Schein, E. H. (1990). Organizational culture. *American Psychologist, 45*(2), 109–119. doi:10.1037/0003-066X.45.2.109

Schein, E. H. (1992). *Organizational culture and leadership* (2nd ed.). San Francisco: Jossey-Bass.

Schein, E. H. (2010). *Organizational culture and leadership* (4th ed.). San Francisco: Jossey-Bass.

Schneider, B. (1987). The people make the place. *Personnel Psychology, 40*(3), 437–453.

Schneider, B., Ehrhart, M. G., & Macey, W. H. (2011). Perspectives on organizational climate and culture. In S. Zedeck (Ed.), *APA handbook of industrial and organizational psychology* (Vol. 1, pp. 373–407). Washington, DC: American Psychological Association.

Sethia, N. K., & Von Glino, M. A. (1985). Arriving at four cultures by managing the reward system. In R. H. Kilmann (Ed.), *Gaining control of the corporate culture.* San Francisco: Jossey-Bass, pp. 400–420.

Stahl, M. J., & Bounds, G. M. (1991). *Competing globally through customer value: The management of strategic suprasystems.* New York: Quorum Books.

Taras, V., Kirkman, B. L., & Steel, P. (2010). Examining the impact of culture's consequences: A three-decade, multilevel, meta-analytic review of Hofstede's cultural value dimensions: Correction to Taras, Kirkman, and Steel (2010). *Journal of Applied Psychology, 95*(5), 405–439. doi:10.1037/a0020939

Tosi, H. L., Rizzo, J. R., & Carroll, S. J. (1990). *Managing organizational behavior.* New York: Harper & Row.

Triandis, H. C. (1995). *Individualism and collectivism.* Boulder, CO: Westview Press.

Trice, H. M., & Beyer, J. M. (1993). *The cultures of work organizations.* Englewood Cliffs, NJ: Prentice Hall.

Ventriss, C., & Luke, J. (1988). Organizational learning and public policy: Towards a substantive perspective. *The American Review of Public Administration, 18*(4), 337–357. doi:10.1177/027507408801800402

Leadership, Power, and Politics

CHAPTER OVERVIEW

Leadership is a mix of traits, behaviors, and situations influencing the relationship between leaders and followers and involving the use of power and politics to achieve a goal or set of goals. In this chapter, we define *power* and *politics* and examine their role in leadership along with the relationship between managers and leaders. We present three models of leadership, followed by a review of charismatic leaders. The chapter also looks at transformational leadership and the effects and

EDHAR/Shutterstock

consequences that result when, by carefully delegating power to followers, a leader can unleash the capacity of those followers to be highly productive and effective.

   We identify the sources of power and the relationship between power and politics, and we examine Machiavellianism as a strategic source of power, identifying some influence tactics used by leaders. Lastly, we present a brief treatment of empowerment and collective efficacies and leadership issues that challenge all organizations around the world, including the differences and similarities between female and male leaders, and servant and narcissistic leadership.

LEARNING OBJECTIVES

When you have finished reading this chapter, you will be prepared to do the following:

- Define leadership as a relational process and a mix of forces of traits, behaviors, and situations
- Differentiate between leaders and managers
- Describe the trait, behavior, and situational models of leadership and discuss empirical findings associated with each model

Maxstockphoto/Shutterstock

- Define and distinguish between charismatic and transformational leaders
- Define and identify sources of power in organizations
- Learn the organizational political strategies of coalition building and establishing control over important decision processes
- Define *Machiavellianism* and learn a variety of influence tactics for effective leadership in dynamic environments
- Define empowerment and identify the role of individual and collective efficacies for empowering followers
- Understand the issues, dynamics, and strategies arising from issues of leadership and gender, and servant and narcissistic leadership

LEADERSHIP

Imagine that you're on an airplane and the captain has just warned passengers of rough air. This was the situation as US Airways flight 1549 got under way on January 15, 2009. The flight ended abruptly when the captain landed the plane in the freezing cold Hudson River near New York City just a few minutes after taking off from LaGuardia Airport. During this true worst-case scenario, the passengers remained calm as the plane headed for the water and then landed in it. They followed the concise directives of the fully coordinated crew and the result was that there were no casualties. This landing has been hailed as a testament to Captain Chesley B. Sullenberger III's skill and experience, but it is also a vivid example of how—when it matters the most—our survival may depend on the performance of a well-honed leadership team.

Definition of Leadership

In spite of mythic stories that suggest that leaders are born, not made, and that "being in charge" is a position ordained at birth, research clearly shows that leadership is not simply a matter of some rare and special talent, personal quality, or knowledge—it is not something that people either have or do not have. Although behavioral genetic research suggests that heritability may play a minor role in determining who becomes a leader (Nicolaou, Shane, Cherkas, Hunkin, & Spector, 2008), it is apparent that life experience also matters. As a result, effective leadership derives from a mix of dispositional features (traits), behavioral patterns, and contextual settings (Avolio & Bass, 2002).

To get a feel for what leadership means and to develop a workable definition of the term, think about leadership as stewardship: the cultivation and enhancement of people, ideas, technology, the organization, and the environment. Although there are many definitions of leadership, the following definition captures the essence of the concept: "a process whereby intentional influence is exerted over other people to guide, structure, and facilitate activities and relationships in a group or organization" (Yukl, 2010, p. 3).

Leaders cannot do everything without help. They must share power and engage their followers' skills by directing them to pursue the appropriate goals that are necessary to address the situations that confront the organization. Although leaders usually are granted a large measure of formal power and influence, at the same time, they are heavily dependent on others to realize their plans and achieve success (Barling, Christie, & Hoption, 2011; Bass & Riggio, 2006).

Power and Politics

Power is always a factor in human relationships. It is everywhere. Yukl (2010) defines *power* as "an agent's potential influence over the attitudes and behavior of one or more designated target persons." The agent with power has influence not only over people but also over decisions, events, and resources.

Power is a necessary part of leadership; however, it is important to keep in mind that almost all organizational members are interested in power, and they use it in the pursuit of a variety of personal and organizational goals (Maner & Mead, 2010). Many times those with the most power in an organization exercise it in subtle and shielded expressions. This elusive quality of power makes it difficult to observe and study. Those who have power may not be obvious about using it. Later in this chapter we will look at different types of power, how leaders acquire and lose power, and influence tactics that are employed by leaders and followers as they interact with each other.

Organizational politics exists in every organization, and thrives in cultures lacking shared goals, clear guidelines, or consensus about decision making. It involves the acquisition, development, and use of power and resources to influence outcomes for particular individuals or groups. Organizational politics is the use of power to get things done. There are many sources of power. It can arise from one's talents and skills; from one's position in the organization; through access to scarce resources like money, physical space, or equipment; from control over valued information; and finally, through the use of persuasion, particularly by means of the capacity to build coalitions of influential people.

Leaders and Managers

Researchers have examined the relationship between *leaders* and *managers*: managers implement the leader's directions and supervise the people who do the bulk of organizational work. Leaders have a vision for their organization or department; managers follow through with the vision. Leaders dream; mangers translate the dream into reality. The leader-manager distinction can involve some overlap as people in both roles often do similar tasks, but in different proportions, or they serve in these two roles at different times in their careers (Brousseau, Driver, Hourihan, & Larsson, 2006; Sutton, 2010).

In general, managers have limited authority or position power over a limited set of persons, and they are focused on the present: they deal with "what is happening now." Managers tend to fix problems while leaders explore opportunities for organizational development (Pattison, 2010). Bennis and Nanus (1985, p. 21) famously proposed that "managers are people who do things right and leaders are people who do the right thing." Zaleznik (1992) suggests that managers are concerned about how things get done and that leaders focus on vision fulfillment, measuring and directing how people feel about and interpret organizational actions.

In summary, leaders broadly influence commitment to the organization whereas managers execute position responsibilities and exercise limited or focal authority that is usually confined to their group or unit (Yukl, 2010).

MODELS OF LEADERSHIP

Just as there are many definitions of leadership, we also find that there are numerous models of leadership. There is overlap among the different models, reflecting the complex pattern of traits, behaviors, and situations from which leadership arises. *Trait models* focus on what the person brings to his or her leadership activities, *behavioral models* examine the actions or behaviors of the leader, and *situational models* are concerned with identifying the environmental or contextual forces that shape and determine leadership. It is beyond the scope of this text to cover most of the models of leadership, and therefore we will focus primarily on the models for which there are substantial and recent empirical findings. Gary Yukl's book *Leadership in Organizations* (2010) provides a detailed review of the history and research findings of the three types of models of leadership identified previously and others as well.

Trait Models

In a pair of studies, Bono, Judge, and colleagues (Bono & Judge, 2004; Bono & Vey, 2007) found that of the "Big Five" personality factors, extraversion was generally correlated with successful leadership. Bauer and colleagues (Bauer, Erdogan, Liden, & Wayne, 2006) found that extraversion was especially helpful to new executives. In a review of personnel records over a 3.5-year period, junior executives scoring low on extraversion were less likely to be promoted through the ranks.

Beyond the "Big Five," the trait profile of effective leaders includes high energy level, stress tolerance, integrity, emotional maturity, and self-confidence (Yukl, 2010). Cho and Ringquist (2010) looked at data on more than 150,000 federal government employees. These researchers identified a composite trait that they called *trustworthiness of managerial leadership* (TWML). It is composed of three individual traits: competence, integrity, and benevolence. Leaders with high levels of TWML were generally more successful, particularly in settings that were otherwise doing poorly and when they were leading units that were experiencing uncertainty because of structural changes dictated at higher levels of government.

Although trait-based approaches have been popular, some leadership studies propose that they have limited utility (Zaccaro, 2007). By looking at individual traits or attempting to estimate how much a desired trait would be expected to add to a leader's effectiveness, trait models may fail to capture the ways that unique and uniquely effective combinations of traits are more strongly predictive of success.

Effective leaders generally possess strong technical, conceptual, and interpersonal skills (Barling et al., 2011; Yukl, 2010). *Technical skills* include knowledge about processes and methods for executing specific activities (such as finance). *Conceptual skills* include the abilities to develop ideas, reason, and interpret meaningfully ambiguous events or data. Finally, *interpersonal skills* focus on understanding interpersonal and group processes, sensitivity to ideas and feeling of others, and verbal fluency and expressiveness. In general, the higher the level of authority, the greater the need for conceptual skills.

To measure individuals on all these factors, potential and current leaders may be evaluated in leadership-assessment centers (Vinchur & Koppes, 2011). There, they will undergo a series of interviews, written personality and aptitude questionnaires, and situational exercises. Typically, the range of activities will then be reduced to a single score, or an overall assessment-center rating, sometimes called an OAR.

In a meta-analysis on assessment-center research, Arthur, Day, McNelly, and Edens (2003) summarized 34 studies that looked at 168 different labels for different aspects of effective leadership. Their analysis yielded six largely distinct dimensions: consideration, communication, drive, influence over others, planning and organizational skill, and problem-solving ability. In addition, the researchers concluded that the diverse nature of leadership positions means that different assessment centers may use different measurements and criteria, and a wide range of assessment-center ratings for effective leaders is understandable, although this makes it quite difficult to compare OAR score results from different centers.

Zaccaro, Foti, and Kenny (1991) reported that social perceptiveness (the capacity to recognize different group requirements) and behavioral flexibility (the ability to respond appropriately to a particular situation) are important personal attributes for effective leadership. More recently, flexibility and adaptability have emerged as definitive characteristics for some leadership researchers (Kaiser, 2010; Kaiser & Overfield, 2010; Yukl & Mahsud, 2010). Thus, multiple traits rather than a single trait or domain of traits best describe effective leaders.

Behavioral Models

A look at behavioral models reveals some of the most important research on leadership conduct and activities, with a focus on what leaders and managers *do*. Leaders operate in dynamic and often turbulent environments. They must deal with conflicts between people, problems with productivity, complex status reports, and unanticipated developments, all of which converge on the leader on a constant basis. Leaders routinely make decisions with incomplete and ambiguous information, and they often must rely on others to execute their plans. In many instances, decision processes are highly political rather than rational and will be made in response to external, unanticipated events. Even though it may seem wiser to plan ahead, little time is devoted to careful planning and proactive or anticipatory behaviors. What's more, a leader's decisions almost inevitably impact many people across an organization. Given this high decision dispersion, leaders who seek to be effective must develop coalitions of support so their decisions can be implemented.

Beginning in the 1950s, the Ohio State University Leadership Studies (OSU) Project has worked to develop a more tightly focused taxonomy of leadership behaviors based on their Leadership Behavior Description Questionnaire (LBDQ). This survey consists of 150 items that were whittled down from an initial list of 1,800 examples of leadership behavior (Fleishman, 1953; Halpin & Winer, 1957). Using *factor analysis,* which is a statistical technique that is intended to reduce a relatively large set of questions (or factors) to the smallest possible number of independent constructs, two major behavioral categories emerged. The first, *consideration,* involves how a leader shows support, exhibits concern for subordinates, and looks out for the well-being of her or his group or unit members. The second major category of leadership behaviors is known as *initiating structure* or *task-oriented* behaviors. This factor reflects the degree to which a leader defines a task or task roles, assigns subordinates to different task roles, monitors performance, and provides task-related performance feedback.

Table 4-1 presents a more refined taxonomy of most of the leadership behaviors that are measured by means of the Managerial Practices Survey (Yukl, 2010). In general, this taxonomy of leadership behaviors grew out of the earlier leadership behavior studies begun in the 1950s, and it involves a wide variety of laboratory- and field-based data. The categories in this taxonomy are sufficiently generic to encompass the behaviors of a wide variety of managers while specific enough to relate to specific situations and managerial task demands (Yukl, 2010).

TABLE 4-1	Taxonomy of Leadership Behaviors
Planning & Organizing	Determining long-term objectives and strategies, allocating resources according to priorities, and determining how to improve coordination, productivity, and the effectiveness of the organization or unit
Problem Solving	Identifying work-related problems, analyzing problems in a timely but systematic manner to find solutions, and acting decisively to implement solutions
Clarifying Roles & Objectives	Assigning tasks and communicating a clear understanding of job responsibilities, deadlines, and performance expectations
Informing	Disseminating relevant information about decisions, plans, and activities to people who need the information to do their work
Motivating & Inspiring	Using influence that appeals to emotion or logic to generate enthusiasm for work, commitment to task objectives, and compliance with requests for cooperation, assistance, support, or resources
Consulting	Checking with people before making changes that affect them and inviting participation in decision making
Delegating	Allowing subordinates to have substantial responsibility and discretion in handling problems and making important decisions
Supporting	Acting friendly and considerate, being patient and helpful, showing sympathy and support when someone is upset or anxious, and listening to complaints and problems
Developing & Mentoring	Providing coaching and doing things to facilitate a person's professional development and career advancement
Managing Conflict & Team Building	Facilitating the constructive resolution of conflict and encouraging cooperation, teamwork, and identification with the work unit
Networking	Socializing informally, developing contacts with people who are a source of information and support, and maintaining contacts through periodic interaction and attendance at meetings and social events
Recognizing	Providing praise and recognition for effective performance, significant achievements, and special contributions
Rewarding	Providing or recommending tangible rewards such as a pay increase or promotion for effective performance, significant achievements, and demonstrated competence

Source: From Yukl, Gary A., *Leadership in Organizations*, 3rd Ed., © 1994, p. 69. Reprinted and Electronically reproduced by permission of Pearson Education, Inc., Upper Saddle River, New Jersey.

Like trait models, behavioral models focus on what the person brings to the situation in terms of acquired behaviors and personal attributes, and they provide a framework for identifying and cultivating leaders within organizations. Likewise, both types of models recognize the importance of the situation or context that can shape and, in some cases, determine leadership effectiveness.

Situational Models

Situational models of leadership focus on either how the organizational situation shapes the leader's thoughts, feelings, and actions or how situational variables moderate the relationship between leader attributes and behaviors and the effectiveness of the leader. The former approach considers situational forces as the primary determinant of leadership, whereas leadership actions are contingent on and moderated by certain factors that may or may not emerge from a given situation in the latter approach (Davis-Blake & Pfeffer, 1989). In either approach, what is important is that the leader must focus her energies on reading the situation to determine what can be done and how, and then she must implement action or jettison out of the situation.

There are several situational models of leadership. They seek to explain how leader traits, behaviors, or both are influenced by situational factors with measurable results on outcomes. According to the path-goal model of leadership (House, 1977; House & Mitchell, 1974), the primary job of the leader is to enhance employee job satisfaction and to increase their productivity. To achieve these objectives, the leader must accurately discern two critical situational variables— employee needs and task demands—and then elect one of four possible categories of leadership. The four categories of leadership behaviors include supportive (similar to the OSU consideration style), directive (similar to the OSU initiating structure style), participative (shared decision making), or achievement-oriented (setting high goals and expressing confidence that employees can achieve such goals). Employees with strong needs for encouragement and affiliation are most responsive to a supportive leadership style; on the other hand, a mix of participative and achievement-oriented leadership is most appropriate for employees with strong needs for autonomy and responsibility. Also, the leader must assess the tasks or job demands that their employees confront and are most effective as leaders if they elect a supportive style of behaviors when the task is tedious and routine, such as collecting tolls or tickets, and a directive style when the job is unstructured, complex, and non-routine—at least until employees have experienced enough appropriate job-related activities.

Obviously, no one leadership style fits the employees' needs and job characteristics in every situation. You will most likely find that some mix or blend of the four styles, with perhaps one or two as most prominent, is the most appropriate leadership model in many situations. Although some studies report different results (Indvik, 1986), much of the research suggests that employees who perform highly routine or tedious tasks describe higher job satisfaction when their leader uses a supportive leadership style. For unstructured tasks, employees preferred and were more productive when their leader elected a more directive leadership style (Keller, 1989; Yukl, 1989).

The Hersey and Blanchard Situational Leadership Theory (SLT) (Hersey & Blanchard, 1969; 1988) identifies four leadership styles: telling, selling, participating, and delegating. An effective and flexible leader will choose a style that is the best fit for the situation at hand. Each of these four leadership styles is a mix of task behaviors (similar to the OSU initiating structure style) or relationship behaviors (similar to the OSU consideration style). If the follower readiness is low (as is often the case with new employees), then the telling leadership style would be most appropriate because it is relatively high on task emphasis but is low in relationship behaviors.

In general, the SLT model is more widely employed by organizations than it is supported by empirical research findings (Blank, Weitzel, & Green, 1990; Vecchio, 1987). It has enjoyed a lot of popularity in leader training, in part because it predicts what a leader *does* rather than describing who she *is* in terms of necessary personal characteristics or traits.

The final situational model of leadership we consider is known as *cognitive resources theory* of leadership, or CRT (Fielder, 1986; Fielder & Garcia, 1987). This model focuses on the leader's cognitive resources, such as intelligence and experience, directive leadership style, and the two situational variables of interpersonal stress and the nature of the group's task. Basically, when subordinates require guidance or direction to perform effectively and perceived stress is low, then superior intelligence is associated with productive plans and wise decisions. When perceived stress is high, however, leaders who offer merely cognitive resources don't appear as likely to make good decisions. This may be because emotional interference gets in the way of leaders' information gathering, processing, and decision making. Finally, in very stressful situations, experienced leaders are likely to make high-quality decisions, probably because they draw on their memory of what was effective in the past. The CRT model of leadership is worth considering if only because organizations tend to look for experienced leaders with a wealth of cognitive resources. Research findings to date generally support this model of leadership (Murphy, Blyth, & Fielder, 1992; Vecchio, 1990).

In general, situational models of leadership are fairly complex and receive moderate support from empirical studies (Yukl, 2010).

CHARISMATIC LEADERSHIP

Charisma is a Greek word meaning "special or divine gift." It wasn't a topic for leadership research until the early 1980s. Before that time, it was believed to be only relevant in religious communities where charismatic leaders usually presented a radical vision of a new world and often led their followers out of a crisis.

Charismatic leaders are thought to have extraordinary gifts or talents. They arouse strong emotions and are often trusted completely, even when they provide only a very general framework for action. Contemporary leadership research has shown that the impact of these factors is not limited to faith-based organizations and is at play in many organizations.

The Gifts of Charisma

According to House (1977), charismatic leaders have a strong need for power, are self-confident, and hold very strong beliefs. In addition, charismatic leaders articulate a compelling vision in which organizational goals are expressed in ideological rather than functional language. These leaders are also likely to communicate ambitious yet reachable expectations and set examples by their own behavior. Finally, they express confidence in the followers' capacities to achieve their daunting and alluring vision. Charismatic leadership is likely to be most effective under certain conditions, particularly when there is a profound sense of organizational discouragement or retreat from proactive organizational actions and when the tasks of the group or unit are fairly complex and non-routine. In other words, it may be most successful when "business as usual" has, for whatever reasons, led an organization to near-total failure.

The Consequences of Charisma

Under charismatic leadership, followers experience enhanced self-confidence and find their work meaningful (Smith, 1982). Research has shown that when a leader articulates a vision, models desirable behavior, and communicates high performance expectations, followers are more trusting of the leader, are more loyal, and exhibit more organizational spontaneity (Podsakoff, Mackenzie, Morrman, & Fetter, 1990). In a laboratory study, Kirkpatrick and Locke (1996) reported that by presenting a high-quality vision, charismatic leaders influence their followers' attitudes in several domains, such as trust and feeling inspired.

Conger and Kanungo (1987) and Conger (1989) proposed that followers consider a leader to be charismatic when he or she exhibits the following behaviors:

- Advocates a vision that is unlike the status quo but is still believable
- Employs innovative actions to achieve goals
- Appears confident and enthusiastic about the vision but is not overbearing
- Employs personal power and persuasive appeals rather than authority and participative decision making

Conger (1989) concluded that personal identification is the primary mechanism by which charismatic leadership is translated into follower commitment and extraordinary attachment and productivity. Followers internalize the charismatic leader's beliefs and values—imitating the leader, essentially—which bolsters the followers' own self-esteem.

TRANSFORMATIONAL LEADERSHIP

Unlike charismatic leadership, which focuses on the individual leader, transformational leaders build and strengthen commitment to organizational goals and empower followers to achieve them. Transactional leadership uses contingent rewards, the exchange of rewards for effort or solid performance—a quid pro quo or exchange of one thing for another. Bass and Reggio (2006) indicate that transactional leadership can complement transformational leadership, but transformational leadership takes followers beyond levels of performance and productivity arising from transactional leadership as a result of the following features of transformational leadership:

- Focus on long-term (3-5 year) goals
- Develop and inspire followers to pursue an articulated vision

- Change or reconfigure organizational systems to advance the vision rather than working within existing systems
- Coach followers to assure greater responsibility for their own development
- At the appropriate time, develop a leader succession plan so that the transformational activities continue within the organizational systems rather than within particular individuals

What Transformational Leaders Do

According to Bass and Riggio (2006), transformational leadership inspires employee loyalty, empowerment, and self-efficacy by modeling four separate behaviors. First, they infuse *idealized influence* as their actions are motivated by what is best for the organization and its members, rather than what is easy and expedient; these behaviors include providing a vision for the future and creating a collective sense of mission. Second, they provide *inspirational motivation* by encouraging their employees to achieve more than what was thought possible, either by themselves or by those around them. Third, they offer *intellectual stimulation* by encouraging employees to think for themselves, question their own commonly held assumptions, reframe problems, and approach matters in innovative ways. Fourth, they offer *individualized consideration* by paying special attention to employees' personal needs for achievement and development and by acting as mentors (Barling et al., 2011).

In summary, transformational leaders are transparent, accountable, inclusive, and continuously learning. They influence followers by arousing strong emotions and promoting identification with the leader. However, unlike charismatic leaders, they transform followers by serving as a coach, teacher, and mentor. They empower followers to promote their personal competencies and commitment to ideals. In contrast, the strictly charismatic leader seeks to foster dependence and loyalty. Transactional leaders rely on rewards as the mainstay of their leadership practices.

The Consequences of Transformational Leadership

Tichy and Devanna (1986) studied 12 chief executive officers, using extensive interviews of the leaders and followers in a variety of large organizations. In general, they found that the transformational process began with the organizational members' recognition that change was needed. This led them to construct a new shared vision for the organization. To realize this vision, they embedded change into the systems and processes, which inevitably involved changing the organizational culture. The shared vision was developed in a variety of ways, including encouraging a variety of organizational members to share aspirational statements and other input.

Bennis and Nanus (1985) interviewed 60 top-level corporate leaders and 30 leaders of public sector organizations. They found that transformational leaders develop a vision of a desirable yet reasonable future for their organization and then harness the collective energies of the organizational members in pursuit of the common vision. The organizational vision is usually a clear, appealing, and concise statement of future goals of the organization formed by listening to the aspirations of organizational members and stakeholders and then synthesizing the various statements into a unifying vision.

A vision statement, which provides an organization with a declaration—"this is what we aspire to do"—gives meaning to work, allows identification with a worthwhile enterprise, and serves as a guideline or internal compass for all members to shape decision making and elected courses of action. The vision statement is aspirational and enriched by construction or revision of the mission statement—"this is what we do." Then it is made more specific and operational by a patterned series of tactical plans, which leads to a plan that explains "this is how we do it" to realize the vision. Bennis and Nanus (1985), Deming (1986), and Senge (1990) all stress individual and organizational learning as essential for effective leadership and the creation of competitive world-class business and public service organizations.

Quantitative research strongly supports transformational leadership because it is most successful in inspiring employee job satisfaction and approval of the leader's effective leadership. Research indicates that transformational leaders exhibit both enhanced leader performance and group-organizational performance (Barling et al., 2011; Judge & Piccolo, 2004). Transformational leadership wins employee trust (Burke, Sims, Lazzara, & Salas, 2007) and commitment to the organization (Barling, Weber, & Kelloway, 1996); it provides the organization members with responsiveness to change initiatives (Herold, Fedor, Caldwell, & Lui, 2008) and psychological safety (Detert & Burris, 2007) as well as identification with the leader, group, and organization (Epitropaki & Martin, 2005a; Kark, Shamir, & Chen, 2003).

Indirect performance effects of transformational leadership include playing a more central role in advice and influence networks (Bono & Anderson, 2005), inspiring organizational citizenship behaviors (Piccolo & Colquitt, 2006), enhancing intrinsic motivation, sparking intellectual stimulation, and energizing followers (Shin & Zhou, 2003), as well as developing follower morality, motivation, and empowerment (Dvir, Eden, Avolio, & Shamir, 2002).

Leaders are learners, teachers, and stewards whose primary responsibility is to promote individual and organizational learning. For example, when an organizational member learns a new insight, technology, or practice as a result of experimenting or attending a conference, that new learning is shared with, used by, and—if it proves valuable—may be internalized by other members of the organization. When that new way of doing something is ultimately infused into organizational handbooks and policy and procedural manuals, then organizational learning has taken place. A leader, in cooperation with followers, produces a creative tension by telling "what is" or accurately describing the current state of the organization and then generates a compelling vision of "what we can be."

POWER AND INFLUENCE

Now we turn to an examination of the sources of power and how power is used by leaders—power and politics, strategic power, Machiavellianism, influence tactics, and empowerment—because regardless of the model of leadership, power is always a vital part of any leadership position.

Sources of Power

Power arises from a number of sources. It may flow from a person's position within the organization. Other sources of power are brought by the individual to the organization. Table 4-2 presents French and Raven's (1959) taxonomy of power sources. The first three kinds of power listed in the table are coupled to the organizational position of the person with power. In general, the higher a person's rank, the more formal and overt the power exerted. Reward and coercive power usually involve positive and negative consequences associated with an organizational position that an agent (the boss or supervisor) can use to influence the behaviors, thoughts, and feelings of a target person or group within the organization. Examples of reward power include compensation, promotion, larger or better office space, flexible work scheduling—whatever the target wants and the agent can deliver. Expressions of coercive power include failing to get pay increases or promotions, formal and informal warnings, and exclusion from the flow of information or appropriate decision-making situations (being kept "out of the loop"). Legitimate power or formal authority represents the institutionalized or contractual power between agent and target, which the latter believes the former has as a result of her or his position in the organization.

An agent may have a great deal of legitimate power because of her or his position, but may have little, if any, expert power, or the capacity to attain goals through skill and ability. Referent power arises from the attraction of followers to some behavioral or personality attribute possessed by a particular person.

Expert and referent power sources are grounded in the individual. The French and Raven (1959) taxonomy clearly indicates that the sources of power are from the position and the person, and some believe that most power wielded in organizations is primarily position-based rather than person-based power. In fact, Bass (1960), in his early and influential work on leadership, proposed that there are two fundamental power sources: position power arising from attributes

TABLE 4-2 French and Raven's Power Sources	
Reward	The target person complies in order to obtain rewards he or she believes are controlled by the agent.
Coercive power	The target person complies in order to avoid punishments he or she believes are controlled by the agent.
Legitimate power	The target person complies because he or she believes the agent has the right to make the request and the target person has the obligation to comply.
Expert power	The target person complies because he or she believes that the agent has special knowledge about the best way to do something.
Referent power	The target person complies because he or she admires or identifies with the agent and wants to gain the agent's approval.

Source: From Yukl, Gary A., *Leadership in Organizations*, 3rd Ed., © 1994, p. 197. Reprinted and Electronically reproduced by permission of Pearson Education, Inc., Upper Saddle River, New Jersey.

of the organizational position and personal power arising from attributes of the person. Yukl and Falbe (1991) proposed two other sources of power beyond the five-tier French and Raven (1959) taxonomy; these are persuasiveness and control over information.

Yukl and Falbe (1991) reported that for daily routine tasks, the primary source of power motivating subordinates to comply with their bosses' requests is legitimate power. Even though subordinates may not have been committed to getting the task finished, legitimate power provided enough of a push to complete what the boss wanted done. According to the leader member exchange theory (LMX) of power acquisition and use, leaders develop special relationships with a small group of subordinate advisors or lieutenants and primarily employ reward power with them and legitimate power with all other subordinates to harness their compliance with task demands (Dansereau, Graen, Haga, 1975; Graen & Cashman, 1975).

In general, a mix of power sources is usually most effective. As task complexity increases, the importance of expert power ascends in the mix. For routine tasks, legitimate power coupled with a dose of reward or coercive power is most appropriate. Refer to Table 4-3 for a summary of how to acquire, maintain, and use the five primary types of power (Yukl, 2010).

Power and Politics

As indicated earlier in this chapter, organizational politics represents actions to acquire, cultivate, and deploy power and related resources to secure preferred outcomes, particularly in ambiguous or uncertain contexts where there is not consensus about choices (Pfeffer, 1981, 1992a, 1992b). Political power is grounded in authority, control over resources, and access to information, although there are political processes to amplify and secure these power bases. Such a political process is coalition building, which creates alliances or alignments of people in the organization to support or oppose a particular policy, program, or decision and control over important decisions.

Control over decision making takes several forms. It can be acquired by shaping the agenda of an important meeting, by controlling what data and information are available and sanctioned for decision making, by determining decision criteria, or by influencing and selecting who attends critical decision-making meetings.

Another important political process to enhance power involves the politics of budgets to create resource dependency. Budget politics usually involves money, but it can also include equipment, space, or any other desirable resource. In almost all organizations, approximately 75% to 90% of the annual total budget represents encumbered resources, which are designated for specific expenses— with the biggest component most always for salaries, wages, and benefits. What's left is known as a *slack resource*: it is not committed to a particular expense and is comparable to finding an extra fifty dollar bill in your pocket or purse. Such unencumbered funds in an organization can be used to start a new program or project, coupled with the expectation that the recipient of such funds will seek outside funding and pay back the initial investment made by the organization. This use of unencumbered or slack resources allows for innovation and creativity, which is vital to the health of the organization (Pfeffer, 1981, 1992a, 1992b).

TABLE 4-3	Guidelines for Acquiring, Maintaining, and Using Power
Acquiring and Maintaining Power	**Using Power**
Legitimate power	
Gain more formal authority.	Explain the reasons for a request.
Exercise authority regularly.	Don't exceed your scope of authority.
Back up authority with reward and coercive power.	Follow up to verify compliance.
Reward power	
Discover what people need and want.	Offer fair and ethical rewards.
Don't promise more than you can deliver.	Explain criteria for giving rewards.
Don't use rewards for personal benefit.	Provide rewards as promised.
Expert power	
Gain more relevant knowledge.	Explain the reasons for a request or proposal.
Demonstrate competency by solving difficult problems.	Listen seriously to concerns.
Don't lie or misrepresent the facts.	Act confidently and decisively in a crisis.
Referent power	
Show acceptance and positive regard.	Use personal appeals when necessary.
Act supportively and helpfully.	Indicate that a request is important to you.
Keep promises.	Provide an example of proper behavior (role modeling).
Coercive power	
Identify credible penalties to deter unacceptable behavior.	Inform colleagues of rules and penalties.
Don't make rash threats.	Understand a situation before disciplining.
Don't use coercion for personal benefit.	Administer discipline in private.

Source: Adapted from G. Yukl (1994). *Leadership in organizations* (3rd ed.). Englewood Cliffs, NJ: Prentice Hall, p. 243.

Strategic Power: Machiavellianism

The pursuit of power was a topic of great interest for Niccolo Machiavelli (1469–1527), a 16th-century Florentine diplomat who wrote *The Prince* to explain how to acquire and use power by manipulating people and situations. His book is famously silent on virtues such as trust, honor, and decency. Machiavelli's writings serve as the basis for the personality trait of *Machiavellianism* (Dahling, Whitaker, & Levy, 2009)—a strategy of social conduct designed to manipulate others for personal gain. Individuals who fit this description are known as "Machs" or "high Machs." Dahling and colleagues (2009) reviewed research on Machiavellianism with an emphasis on leadership. They concluded that high

Mach leadership outcomes are unpredictable. Some studies suggest that they are effective and charismatic, but others found them to be unsupportive of their subordinates. They are likely to exploit their financial partners, and given the chance, they may even steal. They tend to gain influence by various means, including selective self-disclosure and ingratiation. Interestingly, high Machs tend to report low levels of career satisfaction (Dahling et al., 2009).

Influence Tactics

Influence is the impact of one party (the agent, which can refer to one person or a group of people) on another party (the target, which also can be a person a group). Influence tactics may lead to commitment (when a person internalizes a request from an agent and vigorously pursues the requested goal or objective), compliance (unenthusiastic acceptance of the request with only minimal effort expended to accomplish a requested goal or objective), or resistance (active avoidance of a requested task or assignment). Table 4-4 presents a list of influence tactics that are employed by leaders and other members of a wide variety of organizations.

Based on questionnaire results and analyses of critical incidents (crises or major problems), it appears that the influence tactics of rational

TABLE 4-4	Influence Tactics
Legitimating tactics	The agent seeks to establish the legitimacy of a request by claiming the authority or right to make it or by verifying that it is consistent with organizational policies, practices, or traditions.
Rational persuasion	The agent uses logical arguments and factual evidence to persuade the target that a proposal is practical and likely to result in the attainment of task objectives.
Inspirational appeals	The agent makes a request by appealing to the target's values, ideas, and aspirations, or by increasing the target's confidence that he or she can successfully complete the request.
Consultation	The agent seeks the target's participation in planning a strategy, activity, or change, or is willing to modify a proposal to deal with the target's concerns and suggestions.
Exchange	The agent offers an exchange of factors, indicates willingness to reciprocate at a later time, or promises the target a share of the benefits if the target helps to accomplish a task.
Pressure	The agent uses demands, threats, or persistent reminders to influence the target to do what the agent wants.
Ingratiation	The agent seeks to get the target in a good mood or to think favorably of the agent who is making the request.
Coalition tactics	The agent seeks the aid of others to persuade the target to do something or uses the support of others as a reason for the agent to agree.

Source: Adapted from G. Yukl & D. Van Fleet (1992). Theory and Research on Leadership in Organizations. In M. D. Dunnette & L. M. Hough (Eds.), *Handbook of Industrial and Organizational Psychology.* Palo Alto, CA: Consulting Psychologists Press, p. 165.

persuasion, consultation, and inspirational appeals are most effective for sustained commitment, whereas pressure, coalition tactics, and legitimizing tactics are least effective (Yukl & Van Fleet, 1992).

In general, effective leaders use a mix of political and influence tactics, selecting the most appropriate tactics to use for a given situation (Howell & Higgins, 1990; Kotter, 1985; Yukl & Van Fleet, 1992).

Empowerment

Conger and Kanungo (1988) and Conger (1990, 1993) explain that delegation is not to be confused with empowerment. Delegation refers to granting authority for fulfillment of task-specific, time-sensitive orders, whereas empowerment, a motivational process that enhances self-efficacy, is more permanent and pervasive in nature. The empowerment process involves strengthening individual efficacy at the employee level while establishing collective efficacy at the team or organizational level—a group sense of having what it takes to achieve success (Bandura, 1982). Stajkovic, Lee, and Nyberg (2009) conducted a meta-analysis of nearly 100 studies with more than 30,000 total participants. They found that collective efficacy is significantly related to performance, especially when group members are given a chance to discuss the problem at hand (versus what is known as *aggregation,* in which each person assesses the situation individually and those analyses are collected and combined).

Leaders and managers who are attentive to employee initiatives inspire psychological empowerment, which is positively related to affective commitment, innovation, and teamwork, while being negatively related to employee turnover (Gelfand, Fulmer, & Severance, 2011). In many respects, empowerment or the enhancement of individual and collective efficacies is a timely leadership development, given the pace of change, global competition, and diversification of the workforce. Inasmuch as no single person has a monopoly on good ideas, strategies, or tactics, empowerment enables all members of an organization to contribute, and it enhances the probability that the needed organizational strategy will emerge from a diverse, competent, and committed mix of members.

EMERGING TRENDS IN LEADERSHIP STUDIES

The majority of leadership studies have been based primarily on white male leaders in monochromatic or non-diversified workplaces, in which the forces of global competition were just beginning to have substantial and dramatic impacts on organizational performances (Eagly & Karau, 1991; Eagly, Karau, & Makhijani, 1995; Eagly, Makhijani, & Klonsky, 1992; Heilman, Block, Martell, & Simon, 1989; Hollander & Offermann, 1990; Morrison & Von Glinow, 1990; Offerman & Gowing, 1990; Powell, 1988, 1990; Ragnis & Sundstrom, 1989). Accordingly, there are many as yet unanswered questions about leadership and gender, leadership in different cultures, the impact of workforce diversification on leadership style, and the role of leadership in learning organizations that promote empowerment and shared power.

Leadership and Gender

Quantitative review of gender-based leadership studies indicates that the *perception* of leadership effectiveness is not dependent on leadership gender, but on men and women performing differentially—better or worse—under certain circumstances. Research by Eagly et al. (1995) finds that male leaders are considered more effective when assuming roles regarded as "more masculine" and when the majority of their subordinates are also male, as in a military setting. In contrast, women are given superior ratings when their leadership role is defined as "more feminine"—that is, when it requires interpersonal abilities. The percentage of favorability between women and men—one gender assumed to be "better" than the other—is not significant unless women use stereotypically "masculine" leadership styles (e.g., autocratic leadership), are in male-dominated positions, or were evaluated by men (Barling et al., 2011, p. 199). The paucity of women at higher leadership and managerial levels of organizations raises the issue of why women have limited access to some leadership roles (Eagly et al., 1992, 1995; Powell, 1988, 1990).

One important preventive strategy to moderate potential devaluation of women leaders in leadership studies is to include specific and individualized information about performance, especially outcome measures related to subordinate ratings and group or organizational level performances (Eagly & Karau, 1991). Murphy (1994) conducted a self-report survey of 60 women leaders in business firms (CEOs, presidents, and vice presidents) and found that they employed a more task-oriented leadership style than their male counterparts. In addition, both male and female leaders reported higher levels of perceived self-efficacy than middle-level managers, while there were no differences in efficacy levels between women and men in leadership positions.

Gender and Transformational Leadership

The transformational style of leadership has emerged as a contemporary ideal for which women may be at a slight but real advantage. Eagly, Johannensen-Schmidt, and van Engen (2003) conducted a meta-analysis of 45 studies that compared men and women on leadership styles. In addition to the transformational approach, research also looked at transactional leaders, who make it clear to subordinates that good performance is rewarded and poor work will be sanctioned, as well as *laissez-faire leaders*, who use an "anything goes" style and essentially shirk their responsibilities, allowing subordinates to do as they please.

Eagly and her colleagues (2003) found that men were more likely to use laissez-faire and transactional leadership strategies, whereas women tended to be more transformational in their approach. Although the difference was small, Bass and Riggio, in their influential book on the subject of transformational leadership, considered the findings of a gender difference favoring women to be "robust" (Bass & Riggio, 2006, p. 122). In fact, effective leaders will employ each strategy at different times. But as evidence continues to mount that a predominantly transformational approach is strongly associated with positive organizational outcomes, it will be interesting to see if women come to be more widely regarded as "natural" leaders.

Although transformational leadership has emerged as an important trend (as well as an influential model of effectiveness that may also help ease gender disparities in high-level organizational positions), researchers are identifying additional distinctive facets of leadership that appear to hold promise for empirical study and validation.

Servant Leadership

Servant leadership is a term that has been in use since the early 1970's. The initial definition of the term by Greenleaf (1973) places a premium on the notion that a leader should serve followers. There is no consensus about how this style can be operationally defined to allow researchers to measure servant leadership behaviors and attitudes and to distinguish them from similar conceptualizations, such as the transformational style. In a recent review of the literature, van Dierendonck (2010) summarized the available research to offer a definition of servant leader attributes. He analyzed the most widely researched models and identified six traits that were found in most of them: empowerment and development of subordinates; humility; authenticity; interpersonal acceptance; providing direction; and stewardship, or responsible morality. Of the several models, only the one developed by van Dierendonck and Nuijten (2010) has been tested with factor-analytic methodologies that can confirm that a set of proposed attributes are largely independent of each other. The availability of an empirically sound way to measure servant leadership will determine how this form of leadership is uniquely distinct from other approaches.

Narcissistic Leadership

Leaders influence their organizations—for good and for ill. Although some unsuccessful leaders are surely the victims of bad luck, there are several aspects of leadership style that researchers have found to be strongly correlated with poor organizational outcomes. One especially problematic type of leader is the narcissistic personality. Narcissists have extreme needs for attention, admiration, and power. They also have weak self-control and appear to have indifference to the needs and welfare of others (Twenge & Campbell, 2009). Kets de Vries and colleagues found that these leaders set up organizations that are very prone to fail because they seek out subordinates who are loyal and uncritical (Kets de Vries, 2001, 2009; Kets de Vries & Miller, 1984; Kets de Vries & Perzow, 1991). Such leaders also ignore or dismiss objective and impartial advice, and they monopolize decision making. In addition, this type of leader is likely to launch (yet seldom monitor or follow up on) grandiose organizational projects that seem to be mostly aimed at their own glorification. Unlike emotionally mature leaders, narcissistic leaders cling to power and seldom step aside gracefully in the face of mounting negative evidence and the clear organizational sense that new leadership is required to meet dynamic changes arising from within and outside the organization (Golec de Zavala, Cichocka, Eidelson, & Jayawickreme, 2009).

Chapter Summary

Effective leadership involves a mix of three features: traits, behaviors, and situations. Key traits include high energy, stress tolerance, integrity, and emotional maturity. These traits are coupled with strong social rather than personal power orientation and sound technical, conceptual, and interpersonal skills in successful leaders. Leadership behaviors include the broad domains of consideration (or people-oriented behaviors) and initiating structure (or task-oriented behaviors). Situational or contingency models of leadership include the path-goal, situational leadership theory and the cognitive resources theory, each of which emphasizes different situational features that moderate leadership behaviors.

We examined empirical findings of leadership, all of which indicate that leadership is a mix of traits, behaviors, and learning that leaders use to read distinctive situations in organizations. We examined the models and strategies of charismatic and transformational leadership and evaluated their effectiveness on follower and organizational performances.

Leaders wield power in an organization, and we looked at the types and sources of this power. Power arises from the organizational position held by a member as well as from unique features of the individual, including expert and referent (personal traits) power sources. We examined the relationship between authority and power and between power and organizational politics. We also examined a variety of influence tactics, some of which were identified hundreds of years ago by Niccolo Machiavelli and are still highly applicable in contemporary organizations around the world. We briefly considered the relationship between empowering followers and the centrality of individual and collective efficacies to empowerment. Lastly, we examined a variety of leadership issues including empowerment, and leadership stereotyping, and we reflected on servant leadership and signs of narcissistic leadership.

Chapter References

Arthur, W., Day, E. A., McNelly, T. L., & Edens, P. S. (2003). A meta-analysis of the criterion-related validity of assessment center dimensions. *Personnel Psychology, 56*(1), 125–153. doi:10.1111/j.1744-6570.2003.tb00146.x

Avolio, B. J., & Bass, B. M. (2002). *Developing potential across a full range of leadership: Cases on transactional and transformational leadership.* Mahwah, NJ: Lawrence Erlbaum Associates.

Bandura, A. (1982). Self-efficacy mechanism in human agency. *American Psychologist, 37*(2), 122–147. doi:10.1037/0003-066X.37.2.122

Barling, J., Christie, A., & Hoption, C. (2011). Building and developing the organization. In S. Zedeck (Ed.), *APA handbook of industrial and organizational psychology* (Vol. 1, pp. 183–240). Washington, DC: American Psychological Association.

Barling, J., Weber, T., & Kelloway, E. K. (1996). Effects of transformational leadership training on attitudinal and financial outcomes: A field experiment. *Journal of Applied Psycholgy, 81*, 827–832.

Bass, B. M. (1960). *Leadership, psychology, and organizational behavior.* New York: Harper.

Bass, B. M., & Riggio, R. E. (2006). *Transformational leadership* (2nd ed.). Mahwah, NJ: Lawrence Erlbaum Associates.

Bauer, T. N., Erdogan, B., Liden, R. C., & Wayne, S. J. (2006). A longitudinal study of the moderating role of extraversion: Leader-member exchange, performance, and turnover during new executive development. *Journal of Applied Psychology, 91*(2), 298–310. doi:10.1037/0021-9010.91.2.298

Bennis, W. G., & Nanus, B. (1985). *Leaders: The strategies for taking charge* (1st ed.). New York: Harper & Row.

Blank, W., Weitzel, J. R., & Green, S. G. (1990). Test of situational leadership theory. *Personnel Psychology, 43*, 579–597.

Bommer, W. H., Rich, G. A., & Rubin, R. S. (2005). Changing attitudes about change: Longitudinal effects of transformational leader behavior on employee cynicism about organizational change. *Journal of Organizational Behavior, 26*, 733–753.

Bono, J. E., & Anderson, M. H. (2005). The advice and influence networks of transformational leaders. *Journal of Applied Psychology, 90,* 1306–1314.

Bono, J. E., & Judge, T. A. (2004). Personality and transformational and transactional leadership: A meta-analysis. *Journal of Applied Psychology, 89*(5), 901–910. doi:10.1037/0021-9010.89.5.901

Bono, J. E., & Vey, M. A. (2007). Personality and emotional performance: Extraversion, neuroticism, and self-monitoring. *Journal of Occupational Health Psychology, 12*(2), 177–192. doi:10.1037/1076-8998.12.2.177

Brousseau, K. R., Driver, M. J., Hourihan, G., & Larsson, R. (2006). The seasoned executive's decision-making style. *Harvard Business Review, 84*(2), 110–121, 165.

Burke, C. S., Sims, D. E., Lazzara, E. H., & Salas, E. (2007). Trust in leadership: A multi-level review and integration. *Leadership Quarterly, 18,* 606–632.

Cho, Y. J., & Ringquist, E. J. (2010). Managerial trustworthiness and organizational outcomes. *Journal of Public Administration Research and Theory, 21*(1), 53–86. doi:10.1093/jopart/muq015

Conger, J. A. (1989). *The charismatic leader: Behind the mystique of exceptional leadership.* San Francisco, CA: Jossey-Bass.

Conger, J. A. (1990). The dark side of leadership. *Organizational Dynamics, 19*(2), 44–55.

Conger, J. A. (1993). The brave new world of leadership training. *Organizational Dynamics, 21*(3), 46–58.

Conger, J. A., & Kanungo, R. (1987). Toward a behavioral theory of charismatic leadership in organizational settings. *Academy of Management Review, 12,* 637–647.

Conger, J. A., & Kanungo, R. N. (1988). The empowerment process: Integrating theory and practice. *Academy of Management Review, 13,* 471–482.

Dahling, J. J., Whitaker, B. G., & Levy, P. E. (2009). The development and validation of a new Machiavellianism scale. *Journal of Management, 35*(2), 219–257. doi:10.1177/0149206308318618

Dansereau, F. Jr., Graen, G., & Haga, W. J. (1975). A vertical dyad linkages approach to leadership within formal organizations: A longitudinal investigation of the role making process. *Organizational Behavior and Human Performance, 13,* 46–78.

Davis-Blake, A., & Pfeffer, J. (1989). Just a mirage: The search for dispositional effects in organizational research. *Academy of Management Review, 14,* 385–400.

Deming, W. E. (1986). *Out of the crisis.* Cambridge, MA: MIT Center for Advanced Engineering Study.

Detert, J. R., & Burris, E. R. (2007).Leadership behavior and employee voice: Is the door really open? *Academy of Management Journal, 50,* 869–884.

Dvir, T., Eden, D., Avolio, B. J., & Shamir, B. (2002). Impact of transformational leadership on follower development and performance: A field experiment. *Academy of Management Journal, 45,* 735–744.

Eagly, A. H., Johannesen-Schmidt, M. C., & van Engen, M. L. (2003). Transformational, transactional, and laissez-faire leadership styles: A meta-analysis comparing women and men. *Psychological Bulletin, 129*(4), 569–591. doi:10.1037/0033-2909.129.4.569

Eagly, A. H., & Karau, S. J. (1991). Gender and emergence of leaders: A meta-analysis. *Journal of Personality and Social Psychology, 60,* 685–710.

Eagly, A. H., Karau, S. J., & Makhijani, M. G. (1995). Gender and the evaluation of leaders: A meta-analysis. *Psychological Bulletin, 111,* 3–22.

Eagly, A. H., Makhijani, M. G., & Klonsky, B. G. (1992). Gender and the evaluation of leaders: A meta-analysis. *Psychological Bulletin, 111*(1), 3–22. doi:10.1037/0033-2909.111.1.3

Epitropaki, O., & Martin, R. (2005). The moderating role of individual differences in the relation between transformational/transactional leadership perceptions and organizational identification. *Leadership Quarterly, 16,* 569–589.

Fielder, F. E. (1986). The contribution of cognitive resources to leadership performance. *Journal of Applied Social Psychology, 16,* 532–548.

Fielder, F. E., & Garcia, J. E. (1987). *New approaches to leadership: Cognitive resources and organizational performance.* New York: John Wiley.

Fleishman, E. A. (1953). The description of supervisory behavior. *Personnel Psychology, 37,* 1–6.

French, J. R. P., & Raven, B. H. (1959). The bases of social power. In D. Cartwright (Ed.), *Studies of social power* (pp. 150–167). Ann Arbor, MI: Institute for Social Research.

Gelfand, M. J., Fulmer, C. A., & Severance, L. (2011). The psychology of negotiation and mediation. In S. Zedeck (Ed.), *APA handbook of industrial and organizational psychology* (Vol. 3, pp. 495–554).

Golec de Zavala, A., & Cichocka, A., Eidelson, R., & Jayawickreme, N. (2009). Collective narcissism and its social consequences. *Journal of Personality and Social Psychology, 97*(6), 1074–1096.

Graen, G., & Cashman, J. F. (1975). A role making model of leadership in formal organizations: A developmental approach. In J. G. Hunt & L. L. Larson (Eds.), *Leadership frontiers* (pp. 46–62). Kent, OH: Kent State University Press.

Greenleaf, R. K. (1973). *The servant as leader* (Rev. ed.). Cambridge, MA: Center for Applied Studies.

Halpin, A. W., & Winer, B. J. (1957). A factorial study of the leader behavior descriptions. In R. M. Stogdill & A. E. Coons (Eds.), *Leader behavior: Its description and measurement* (pp. 39–51). Columbus, OH: Bureau of Business Research, Ohio State University.

Heilman, M. E., Block, C. J., Martell, R. F., & Simon, M. C. (1989). Has anything changed? Current characterizations of men, women, and managers. *Journal of Applied Psychology, 74*, 935–942.

Herold, D. M., Fedor, D. B., Caldwell, S., & Lui, Y. (2008). The effects of transformational and change leadership on employees' commitment to change: A multilevel study. *Journal of Applied Psychology, 93*, 346–357.

Hersey, P., & Blanchard, K. H. (1969). Life cycle theory of leadership. *Training and Development Journal, 23*, 26–41.

Hersey, P., & Blanchard, K. H. (1988). *Management of organizational behavior* (5th ed.). Englewood Cliffs, NJ: Prentice Hall.

Hollander, E. P., & Offermann, L. R. (1990). Power and leadership in organizations. *American Psychologist, 45*, 179–189.

House, R. J. (1971). A path-goal theory of leader effectiveness. *Administrative Science Quarterly, 16*, 321–339

House, R. J. (1977). A 1976 theory of charismatic leadership. In J. G. Hunt & L. L. Larson (Eds.), *Leadership: The cutting edge* (pp. 189–207). Carbondale: Southern Illinois Press.

House, R. J., & Mitchell, T. R. (1974). Path-goal theory of leadership. *Contemporary Business, 3*, 81–98.

Howell, J. M., & Higgins, C. A. (1990). Leadership behaviors, influence tactics, and career experiences of champions of technological innovation. *Leadership Quarterly, 1*, 249–264.

Indvik, J. (1986). Path-goal theory of leadership: A meta-analysis. *Proceedings of the Academy of Management Meetings, 46*, pp. 189–192.

Judge, T. A., & Piccolo, R. F. (2004). Transformational and transactional leadership: A meta-analytic test of their relative validity. *Journal of Applied Psychology, 89*, 755–768.

Kaiser, R. B. (2010). Introduction to the special issue on developing flexible and adaptable leaders for an age of uncertainty. *Consulting Psychology Journal: Practice and Research, 62*(2), 77–80. doi:10.1037/a0019986

Kaiser, R. B., & Overfield, D. V. (2010). Assessing flexible leadership as a mastery of opposites. *Consulting Psychology Journal: Practice and Research, 62*(2), 105–118. doi:10.1037/a0019987

Kark, R., Shamir, B., & Chen, G. V. (2003). The two faces of transformational leadership: Empowerment and dependency. *Journal of Applied Psychology, 88*, 246–255.

Keller, R. T. (1989). A test of path-goal theory of leadership with need for clarity as a moderator. *Journal of Applied Psychology, 74*, 208–212.

Kets de Vries, M. F. R. (2001). *The leadership mystique: An owner's manual*. London: Financial Times Prentice Hall.

Kets de Vries, M. F. R. (2009). *Reflections on character and leadership*. San Francisco, CA: Jossey-Bass.

Kets de Vries, M. F. R., & Miller, D. (1984). *The neurotic organization: Diagnosing and changing counter productive styles of management*. San Francisco, CA: Jossey-Bass

Kets de Vries, M. F. R., & Perzow, S. (1991). *Handbook of character studies: psychoanalytic explorations*. Madison, CT: International Universities Press.

Kirkpatrick, S. A., & Locke, E. A. (1996). Direct and indirect effects of three core charismatic leadership components on performance and attitudes. *Journal of Applied Psychology, 81*, 36–51.

Kotter, J. P. (1985). *Power and influence: Beyond formal authority*. New York: Free Press.

Machiavelli, N. (1950). *Discourses*. London: Routledge & Kegan Paul. (Original work published 1513.)

Machiavelli, N. (1966). *The Prince*. New York: Bantam. (Original work published 1513.)

Maner, J. K., & Mead, N. L. (2010). The essential tension between leadership and power: When leaders sacrifice group goals for the sake of self-interest. *Journal of Personality and Social Psychology, 99*(3), 482–497. doi:10.1037/a0018559

Morrison, A. M., & Von Glinow, M. A. (1990). Women and minorities in management. *American Psychologist, 45*, 200–208.

Murphy, D. (1994). *A multi-dimensional theory of the glass ceiling* (Unpublished master's thesis). University of Vermont, Burlington.

Murphy, S. E., Blyth, D. E., & Fielder, F. E. (1992). Cognitive resources theory and the utilization of the leader's and group members' technical competence. *Leadership Quarterly, 3,* 237–255.

Nicolaou, N., Shane, S., Cherkas, L., Hunkin, J., & Spector, T. D. (2008). Is the tendency to engage in entrepreneurship genetic? *Management Science, 54*(1), 167–179. doi:10.1287/mnsc.1070.0761

Offerman, L. R., & Gowing, M. K. (1990). Organizations of the future: Changes and challenges. *American Psychologist, 45,* 95–108.

Pattison, K. (2010). *What breed is your CEO? Randy Komisar on leadership and management.* Retrieved from http://www.fastcompany.com/1674779/randy-komisar-kleiner-perkins-caufield-byer-leadership-management-entrepreneurship

Pfeffer, J. (1981). *Power in organizations.* Marshfield, MA: Pitman.

Pfeffer, J. (1992a). *Managing with power: Politics and Influence in Organizations.* Boston, MA: Harvard Business School Press.

Pfeffer, J. (1992b). Understanding power in organizations. *California Management Review, 34,* 29–50.

Piccolo, R. F., & Colquit, J. A. (2006). Transformational leadership and job behaviors: The mediating role of core job characteristics. *Academy of Management Journal, 49,* 327–340.

Podsakoff, P. M., MacKenzie, S. B., Morrman, R. H., & Fetter, R. (1990). Transformational leader behaviors and their effects on followers' trust in leader, satisfaction, and organizational citizenship behaviors. *Leadership Quarterly, 1,* 107–142.

Powell, G. N. (1988). *Women and men in management.* Newbury Park, CA: Sage.

Powell, G. N. (1990). One more time: Do female and male managers differ? *Academy of Management Executive, 4,* 68–75.

Ragnis, B. R., & Sundstrom, E. (1989). Gender and power in organizations: A longitudinal perspective. *Psychological Bulletin, 105,* 51–88.

Senge, P. M. (1990). *The fifth discipline: The art and practice of the learning organization.* New York: Doubleday/Currency.

Shin, S. J., & Zhou, J. (2003). Transformational leadership, conservation, and creativity: Evidence from Korea. *Academy of Management Journal, 46,* 703–714.

Smith, B. J. (1982). *An initial test of a theory of charismatic leadership based on the response of subordinates (Unpublished doctoral dissertation).* University of Toronto.

Stajkovic, A. D., Lee, D., & Nyberg, A. J. (2009). Collective efficacy, group potency, and group performance: Meta-analyses of their relationships, and test of a mediation model. *Journal of Applied Psychology, 94*(3), 814–828. doi:10.1037/a0015659

Sutton, R. (2010). True leaders are also managers. *Harvard Business Review.* Sourced on-line http://blogs.hbr.org/cs/2010/08/true_leaders_are_also_managers.html

Tichy, N. M., & Devanna, M. A. (1986). *The transformational leader.* New York: John Wiley & Sons.

Twenge, J. M., & Campbell, W. K. (2009). *The narcissism epidemic: Living in the age of entitlement.* New York: Free Press.

van Dierendonck, D. (2011). Servant leadership: A review and synthesis. *Journal of Management, 37*(4), pp. 851–862. doi:10.1177/0149206310380462

van Dierendonck, D., & Nuijten, I. (2011). The servant leadership survey: Development and validation of a multidimensional measure. *Journal of Business and Psychology, 26*(3), 249–267. doi:10.1007/s10869-010-9194-1

Vecchio, R. P. (1987). Situational leadership theory: An examination of a prescriptive theory. *Journal of Applied Psychology, 72,* 444–451.

Vecchio, R. P. (1990). Theoretical and empirical examination of cognitive resource theory. *Journal of Applied Psychology, 75,* 141–147.

Vinchur, A. J., & Koppes, L. L. (2011). A historical survey of research and practice in industrial and organizational psychology. In S. Zedeck (Ed.), *APA handbook of industrial and organizational psychology* (Vol. 1, p. 686). Washington, DC: American Psychological Association.

Yukl, G. (1989). Managerial leadership: A review of theory and research. *Journal of Management, 15*(2), 251–289. doi:10.1177/014920638901500207

Yukl, G. (1994). *Leadership in organizations* (3rd ed.). Englewood Cliffs, NJ: Prentice Hall.

Yukl, G. (2010). *Leadership in organizations.* Upper Saddle River, NJ: Prentice Hall.

Yukl, G., & Falbe, C. M. (1991). The importance of different power sources in downward and lateral relations. *Journal of Applied Psychology, 76,* 416–423.

Yukl, G., & Mahsud, R. (2010). Why flexible and adaptive leadership is essential. *Consulting Psychology Journal: Practice and Research, 62*(2), 81–93. doi:10.1037/a0019835

Yukl, G., & Van Fleet, D. (1992). Theory and research on leadership in organizations. In M. D. Dunnette & L. M. Hough (Eds.), *Handbook of industrial and organizational psychology* (pp. 147–197). Palo Alto, CA: Consulting Psychologists' Press.

Zaccaro, S. J. (2007). Trait-based perspectives of leadership. *American Psychologist, 62*(1), 6–16. doi:10.1037/0003-066X.62.1.6

Zaccaro, S., Foti, R. J., & Kenny, D. (1991). Self-monitoring and trait-based variance in leadership: An investigation of leader flexibility across multiple group situations. *Journal of Applied Psychology, 76,* 308–315.

Zaleznik, A. (1992). *Managers and leaders: Are they different?* Boston, MA: Harvard Business School Pub.

Workforce Diversity and Ethics

CHAPTER OVERVIEW

This chapter focuses on identifying barriers that dampen or prevent the enhancement of diversity or getting hired and examines forces that promote the inclusion of women, persons of color, and sexual minorities in organizational decision making. In the discussion, we identify the role of privilege as a major barrier to diversity and inclusion and investigate tactics to minimize or eliminate barriers to full participation.

Historically, when organizations were largely local affairs, they tended to reflect the mores and customs of their region. However, with the rise of multinational corporations and the influence of worldwide telecommunications, many of us are in constant contact with people from around the globe. In addition, as organizations have become open to diverse people, the easy historic certainties of "the old-boys' club" have given way to the forces of globalization.

Corbis/SuperStock

Paul Chesley/National Geographic
Image Collection/Alamy

Jon Arnold Images Ltd/Alamy

The resulting diversity and inclusion have enormous potential, but may for some create fear, tension, and conflict. We review specific civil rights laws and regulations that address barriers to employment and career advancement. Many organizations have taken up the challenge of diversity and inclusion and have constructed their own cultural values well in advance of what is federally mandated. As a result, such organizations routinely appear on lists of best places to work, suggesting that it may actually be possible to do good by doing right.

The chapter concludes with remarks on the importance of ethics and suggestions for ways to foster ethical conduct to enhance diversity and inclusion.

LEARNING OBJECTIVES

When you have finished reading this chapter, you will be prepared to do the following:

- Define diversity, inclusion, and the role of privilege as a major barrier to workforce participation
- Describe the barriers to entrance and inclusion in decision-making processes for women, persons of color, and sexual minorities in the workforce
- Discuss regulatory mechanisms of laws, court cases, and executive orders to promote and strengthen equality of opportunity in hiring, promoting, and other personnel decisions
- Describe sexual harassment in the workplace and distinguish between quid pro quo and hostile environment forms of sexual harassment

- Identify tactics that can reduce sexual harassment in the workplace and summarize two U.S. Supreme Court decisions that resulted in major settlements in favor of women plaintiffs and also strengthened further sexual harassment prevention programs
- Define the four types of organizational justice and describe the connection between organizational justice and ethics in the workplace

WORKFORCE DIVERSITY AND INCLUSION

Almost wherever you go in the world today, you find people place a high premium on work in their lives because it provides for their physical and psychological well-being. Although job opportunities in most organizations are open to all qualified applicants, we know that in many cases not all people are equally or fairly considered for jobs. In addition, even if they are hired, they may not participate fully in decision making. Thomas (2005) defines *diversity* as individual differences (gender, race, and sexuality) that are socially and historically significant, and that have resulted in organizational power and privilege differentials. Accordingly, this chapter focuses on barriers to participation in the workplace that confront women, people of color, and sexual minorities because members of these three groups are becoming an increasingly larger proportion of the workforce each day.

Olly/Fotolia

Treatment of diversity and inclusion is based on three fundamental premises: (1) work is a major focus in the lives of most people and is important for individual and societal well-being; (2) it is ethically and financially wise to actively advance and support a diverse and inclusive workforce in any organization, given the increasingly diverse overall labor force and marketplace; and (3) in a free society that is grounded in equity across categories of race, age, gender, disability, religion, national origin, and other characteristics, every individual has an inalienable right to compete for any job for which he or she is qualified (Blustein, 2008; Cascio & Aguinis, 2011; Jackson & Joshi, 2011).

Contemporary U.S. workplaces are undergoing rapid and dramatic changes reflected in increased globalization, flattened organizational hierarchies, the growing influx of women and people of color, technological innovation, and widespread use of work groups and teams. These changes, when considered individually and especially when combined, have generated an unprecedented need to support and increase worker diversity both in terms of access—"bringing people in the door"—and inclusion—"bringing people to the table" (Fassinger, 2008). In short, diversity and inclusion are the reality and not just a goal to satisfy legal, moral, or ethical imperatives.

Diversity and inclusion management is evolving. The historic focus on getting diverse persons into an organization by means of affirmative action and targeted recruitment is now broadening to include strategies that better integrate minority persons into the core fabric of the organization. In the next section, we focus on how current federal law and emerging practices are employed to make organizations more diverse and inclusive.

BARRIERS TO DIVERSITY AND INCLUSION

A major hidden barrier to occupational entry and active inclusion in organizational decision-making processes by members of marginalized groups is *privilege*. Thomas (2006, p. 120) defines privilege as "the luxury to ignore aspects of one's identity that confer unearned advantages and power." As Thomas notes, this type of privilege is *unearned*. It flows from the high status granted those with the favored skin color, gender and gender expression, age, appearance, and social class. People of privilege may be unaware of the benefits they enjoy as a member of a favored group, and they often consider their advantages as natural and deserved, sometimes viewing members of marginalized groups as lacking these natural advantages and therefore not having "earned" the right to be treated in the same fashion as members of the majority group. Furthermore, if lower-status individuals point out the privileges of the majority, they may be considered "pushy" and "complainers" by majority group members and may be viewed as difficult to work with in a variety of situations in the organization (Fiske, 2010). Thus, majority members may be inclined to adopt the strategy of hiring only new employees who are like themselves rather than welcoming workers who are different from the majority. This is known as the *Attraction-Selection-Attrition (ASA)* cycle of organizational behavior (Schneider, Smith, Taylor, & Fleenor, 1998).

According to the ASA model of organizational membership, the organizational founder establishes the organizational goals and puts in place the policies, practices, and procedures that reflect those goals. Job applicants are attracted to an organization based on the congruence of their personal characteristics and the features of the potential work organization. For example, a person who enjoys working closely with people will be attracted to an organization that promotes working in teams rather than to an organization that values individual effort. Likewise, organizations may have recruitment and hiring processes that make them tend to seek out job applicants whose backgrounds are similar to those of current successful employees (i.e., workers whose experience on the job is primarily in teams) and ignore those applicants who do not match the backgrounds of successful members. Finally, attrition is most likely to arise when the new hire does not feel comfortable or valued and quickly exits the organization.

The outcome of this process is to produce and reinforce similarity and homogeneity (Avery, 2011). Schneider, Smith, Taylor, and Fleenor (1998) examined the personality characteristics of 13,000 managers from more than 100 organizations and found that the organizations were relatively homogenous in terms of the personalities of their managers. At first glance, the ASA interaction model might be considered sound because it promotes and sustains stability in an organization—it would seem to encourage the hiring of new employees who look, think, and act like the majority of people already working in the organization. However, as Schneider (1987) has cautioned, after a few years of homogenous hiring, an organization that fails to take advantage of the diversity of educational backgrounds, experience, and knowledge that is inherent in the evolving labor force is most likely going to fail. In short, diverse organizational membership is a necessary feature for the continued success and stability of the organization over time. This is explained in part by the findings from research that examines organizational justice (Greenberg, 2011). Assuming that most people have a preference for justice and fairness, organizations that seek and nurture it can expect higher overall levels of stability and productivity.

Women in the Workforce

Approximately three-quarters of women between the ages of 25 and 55 are now in the workforce, which is a 70% increase since 1978 (Fassinger, 2005, 2008). Despite this significant increase, there is overwhelming evidence of ongoing occupational segregation, underrepresentation in leadership positions, and inequities in compensation. For example, for every dollar a man is paid for his work, an equally qualified women makes about 0.75 cents—and this discrepancy in pay has persisted for the past 30 years (American Association of University Women, 2007). The picture grows even bleaker as workers advance from entry-level jobs right after college graduation to higher positions in an organization. One year after graduation, full-time female workers earn 80% of what their male counterparts are paid, but after 10 years, college-educated women earn only 69% of the pay earned by men in comparable positions, even when women and men are matched in terms of factors that usually influence earnings (American Association of University Women, 2007).

Some of the wage disparities between men and women arise from women's prevalence in occupations and work roles that carry both limited benefits and flexibility (Sauter & National Institute for Occupational Safety and Health, 2002). For example, women make up less than one-fourth of the workforce in the critical globally competitive and lucrative areas of science, technology, engineering, and mathematics (STEM positions), even though women account for half of the workforce with college degrees. Women of color represent a meager 4% of the STEM workforce. Although industry employs most STEM workers, women are almost totally absent from managerial and leadership positions—as of 2012, there were no female chief executive, operating, or financial officers in any of 42 publicly traded chemical companies (Tullo, 2004). Negative stereotypes about women and leadership, in particular, may help explain some of these patterns (Avery, 2011).

Barriers to Work for Women

A subtle but effective barrier often confronting women is a lukewarm reception in the educational or workplace environment, expressed as discriminatory actions that make women feel unwelcome. Some of these actions include an "old boys' network" that may inform men of advancement opportunities before women in the organization learn about them, as well as double standards for women's behavior and accomplishments that can lead to heightened scrutiny and expectations that women must assume additional responsibilities without the provision of support or compensation for the extra work.

Another major barrier for women in organizations is sexual harassment, or sex-based harassment (SBH), which will also be considered later in this chapter. In a review of the sexual-harassment literature, Berdahl and Raver (2011) summarized research that has found reports of SBH in nearly all industries and settings (although they also point out that this is not strictly a problem that women face from male perpetrators). Lastly, the intersection between work and family life is a major barrier to career advancement because women have been and are still expected to handle household management, child care, and care of other family members (Hammer & Zimmerman, 2011). Thus, an organization's leadership as well as other members of the organization need to take constructive actions to eliminate the kinds of barriers that make it extremely difficult or impossible for women to be active and valued members of the organization.

Persons of Color in the Workforce

Persons of color (e.g., African Americans, Hispanic/Latino Americans, Asian Americans, and Native Americans) now make up about one-third of the U.S. population and are projected to compose just over one-half of the population by 2050 (Fassinger, 2008). Presently, people of color are more likely than white people to experience unemployment and underemployment. African-American women are twice as likely to have temporary jobs than white women. Salaries for whites are higher than for people of color, even when education and experience are equivalent. For example, in 2006, white men earned an average annual salary of $62,446, and the average salary for white women was $45,752, compared to $49,171 for African American men and $41,765 for African-American women, respectively (U.S. Census Bureau, 2007). In the STEM fields, fewer than 100 African Americans or Hispanic/Latino Americans were employed in engineering in 2001, and incredibly, not even 20 of these minority workers each were employed in leadership roles in mathematics or computer science (Tullo, 2004). Asian Americans have generally found more opportunities in engineering and computer science than have other minorities.

Barriers to Work for Persons of Color

The cardinal barrier to occupational entry and subsequent organizational participation faced by people of color in the workplace is racism, both institutional and interpersonal. Racism is manifested by inadequate educational experiences, lack of mentors and role models, and low expectations for achievement (Avery, 2011). Also, people of color in organizations are most likely to experience exclusion from information and support networks as well as stress caused by the isolation of tokenism.

Another source of racism at the individual and institutional levels is implicit or unconscious bias that occurs when commonly held preferential attitudes toward certain groups put the non-preferred group at a disadvantage. These insidious biases are expressed by negative stereotypical statements found in the larger social environment. A sound antidote to negative social messages for people of color is social support, especially when it derives from family and from membership in support groups at work (Aronson, 2002).

Sexual Minorities in the Workplace

Lesbian, gay, bisexual, transgender, queer, and other gender and/or sexual identifications and self-labels make up sexual minorities, many of whom are invisible at work given the hostile environment they may find there. For example, sexual minorities can be fired in 31 states on the basis of sexual orientation and in 39 states on the basis of gender identity/expression.

Same-sex marriage is legal at the time this text is being written in only a few states. In most U.S. states, couples and their children cannot participate in average benefit plans at work (health, dental, and life insurance programs), which usually constitute about 20% of the employee's total compensation package. Approximately 64% of transgender people report annual incomes below the $15,000 poverty level, and about 35% of this group of people are unemployed (American Psychological Association, 2007).

Barriers to Work for Sexual Minorities

Sexual minorities face a major barrier in educational and work organizations with respect to the issue of coming out versus identity management strategies that center on concealment. This obstacle exacts a psychological price that may be associated with lower workplace performance. Antigay prejudice is pervasive in the workplace, and sexual minorities experience lowered job satisfaction, increased absenteeism, decreased organizational commitment, and compromised psychological and physical health. Despite the profound difficulties they currently face in the workplace, the outlook for sexual minorities is improving, as reflected in the results of a recent public opinion poll that indicated 85% of

Americans support equal opportunity for gay people in the workplace (Human Rights Campaign, 2007). In addition, some recent findings suggest that being "out" in the workplace has beneficial aspects reflected by less work-home conflict, greater organizational commitment, and enhanced job satisfaction.

REGULATIONS: LAWS, COURT CASES, AND EXECUTIVE ORDERS

Equality involves opportunity, creating a level playing field for everyone, whereas *equity* focuses on outcomes that are driven by merit-based performances of the individual (Avery, 2011). The underlying assumption of equal opportunity regulations is that everyone is entitled to a fair chance, but outcomes are still determined primarily by individual effort, measured by a bias-free evaluation system. Despite this aspiration, it was not until the 1960s—about 50 years ago—that discrimination in hiring was *not* illegal; until that time, job openings could be posted for "Whites Only." In addition, the concept of "employment at will" was prevalent; this meant that any employer could terminate the employment relationship with any employee at any time—with or without reason.

There has since been movement away from the "employment at will" doctrine toward "just cause" discharge policies that require an employer to show acceptable reasons for discharging an employee. Another important legal construct designed to minimize discrimination in hiring practices is the notion of adverse impact. *Adverse impact* is said to exist when an organization uses practices that unintentionally have negative consequences for employees who belong to a protected group. For example, hiring police officers or firefighters based on height requirements can have an adverse impact on women who apply for the positions, and using cognitive ability tests that are biased toward whites can cause fewer African-American and Hispanic/Latino workers to be hired (De Corte, Lievens, & Sackett, 2007). You will learn more about adverse impact in dealing with recruitment, hiring, and performance evaluation in Chapter 6.

Table 5-1 presents a list of federal laws that apply to employment, with a brief statement of the intent of each law. The Equal Pay Act (EPA) of 1963 provides that an employer cannot pay different wages to one gender (such as lower pay for women) compared to the other gender for equal work at jobs that require equal skill, effort, and responsibility and that are performed under similar working conditions. In 1972, Congress expanded coverage of the Equal Pay Act to employees working in executive, administrative, or professional positions. It is noteworthy that the first legislation that President Barack Obama signed into law was the Lilly Ledbetter Fair Pay Act on January 29, 2009, which provides more flexibility to file cases of pay discrimination based on each gender-unequal paycheck an individual receives. Since the enactment of the EPA, women's salaries have risen from 62% of comparable men's salaries in 1970 to 80% of men's earnings in 2004.

Title VII of the Civil Rights Act of 1964 was introduced by President John F. Kennedy on June 11, 1963; was signed into law by President Lyndon B. Johnson

TABLE 5-1	A Sampling of Federal Laws That Assure and Promote Equality in Hiring and Conditions of Employment in the United States		
Law	**Year**	**Provisions**	
Equal Pay Act	1963	Provides for equal pay regardless of sex for equally skilled persons for work performed under similar conditions	
Lilly Ledbetter Fair Pay Act	2009	Provides increased flexibility for filing pay discrimination lawsuits based on sex	
Civil Rights Act (Title VII)	1964	Makes it illegal to discriminate on the basis of race, sex, religion, color, or national origin in hiring and all other aspects of employment	
Americans with Disabilities Act (ADA)	1990	Declares it unlawful to discriminate against qualified persons with disabilities in hiring, compensation, terms, conditions, and privileges of employment	
Family and Medical Leave Act (FMLA)	1993	Ensures that eligible employees can take up to 12 weeks of unpaid leave for a serious health condition or to care for a sick child or family member	
Genetics Non-Discrimination (Act)	2009	Makes it illegal to discriminate on the basis of genetic background that might indicate a predisposition for certain diseases such as cancer	

on July 2, 1964; and was amended in 1972, making it illegal to discriminate against individuals on the basis of race, color, religion, national origin, or sex. As part of the Civil Rights Act, the Equal Employment Opportunity Commission (EECO) and state Fair Employment Practices Agency (FEPAs) were established to enforce Title VII, and they can file lawsuits on behalf of employees. Individuals can also bring a private lawsuit against an organization that violates Title VII. In 2003, 119,000 cases of employment discrimination were investigated by the EEOC, with 31,200 cases awarded damages totaling $290 billion. Discrimination in the workplace is illegal, unethical—and very expensive.

The Americans with Disabilities Act (ADA) of 1990 was signed into law by President George Herbert Walker Bush in 1990 and became effective on July 26, 1992. Title I of this law prohibits discrimination against qualified persons with disabilities in employment decisions. If a qualified person can perform the essential functions of a job with the aid, if necessary, of reasonable accommodations, that individual must be considered equally with other candidates for the position. The determination of disability is made on a case-by-case basis. Substance abuse and visual impairment are not considered disabilities under this law. Titles II and III of ADA prohibit discrimination involving access to services and programs offered by public and commercial facilities respectively.

The Family and Medical Leave Act (FMLA) was signed into law by President William Jefferson Clinton in August 1993. The law allows an employee to take up to 12 weeks of job-protected unpaid leave to recover from a serious health condition, to care for a sick family member, or to care for a new child. Upon return from a FMLA leave, the employee must be able to return to the same position or an alternate position that provides equal pay, benefits, and responsibilities he or she held previously. A handful of states have expanded the definition of "family" to include civil union partners and parents-in-law. Prior to the FMLA, an employee's request for leave could be denied for any reason, and they could be fired for taking family and medical leave. A number of European countries provide paid family and medical leave, in some cases for longer than the 12 weeks provided by FMLA in the United States.

It is beyond the scope of this chapter to review the extensive body of laws, court cases, and other governmental guidelines regulating aspects of employment from selection to promotion to termination. However, we want to present two recent developments that have the potential for broad and significant impact on equality in the workplace.

In the first case, the impact is negative and involves a U.S. Supreme Court ruling (5 to 4) in June 2009. The case was brought by white firefighters in New Haven, Connecticut, who claimed they were subject to race discrimination when the city threw out a promotional examination on which they did well and African-American firefighters did poorly. This ruling in favor of the white firefighters by the Supreme Court will make it much harder for employers to discard hiring and promotional tests that have been administered, even if they have a negative impact on members of a given racial group (Sataline, Bravin, & Koppel, 2009).

The second case promises to have a positive impact on workplace discrimination. It is the Genetic Non-Discrimination Act, which became effective on November 21, 2009, and which applies to a whole new group of people who have been the subject of discrimination. The law provides for a federal ban on discriminating on the basis of genetic background and forbids employers from asking for genetic tests that can warn of a predisposition for certain diseases such as cancer. Prior to the passage of this law, employers could take genetic background information into account in hiring, firing, or promotions. This law also prohibits discrimination on the basis of genetic background in group and individual health insurance plans.

SEXUAL HARASSMENT IN THE WORKPLACE

Sexual harassment in the workplace is a major problem that impacts not only the victim and the harasser involved in the incident but also co-workers and the entire organization. In 2007, the Equal Employment Opportunity Commission (EEOC) and related state agencies received 12,510 new charges of sexual harassment on the job. Title VII of the Civil Rights Act of 1964 states that "it is unlawful for an employer to discriminate against any individual with respect to her or his compensation, terms, conditions, or privileges of employment because of such individual's race, color, religion, sex, or national origin." Sexual harassment includes behaviors that typically are experienced as offensive in nature in which unwanted sexual advances are made in the context of a relationship of unequal power or authority.

The Civil Rights Act of 1991 established two types of sexual harassment. The first type is *quid pro quo* (this for that) harassment that arises, for example, when promotion or continuation of employment in an organization is contingent on sexual favors. This is probably the most blatant form of sexual harassment in an organization. The second type is *hostile environment* harassment, in which an employee is subjected to remarks, innuendos, and/or physical acts of a sexual nature that are ongoing and so derogatory that they create an offensive work environment.

Sexual harassment relationships arise under a variety of situations, and the harasser can be anyone—a client, co-worker, student, professor, friend, or stranger. The victim can be any gender, as can the harasser, and the harasser does not have to be of the other gender.

Sexual orientation is not a protected class under the provisions of the Civil Rights Act of 1991. For this reason, gay, lesbian, and bisexual (GLB) employees are not protected against workplace discrimination by any federal laws to date. Fortunately, many states provide protection against workplace discrimination for GLB employees. According to the National Gay and Lesbian Task Force (2008), 20 states ban discrimination in the workplace based on sexual orientation, and more than 100 municipalities in 30 states without non-discrimination laws do so as well.

The effects of sexual harassment on the victim range from annoying to life-altering, particularly when the harassment arises from severe and chronic abuses or when there are repercussions for the victim who complains openly about it. These effects range from decreased performance and increased absenteeism to extreme stress on relationships with significant others, involving divorce in some cases, as well as lack of trust in peer and/or work colleagues. At the organizational level, we may find decreased productivity accompanied by increased absenteeism and team conflict, as well as increased health care and sick pay costs arising from the health consequences of harassment (Berdahl & Raver, 2011).

The following tactics can reduce instances of sexual harassment in the workplace:

- Present the organization's comprehensive sexual harassment policy as part of every employee's orientation to the organization and job training.
- Educate employees about what constitutes sexual harassment and consequences of engaging in sexual harassment.
- Train employees to recognize sexual harassment and establish how to report it to the appropriate organizational authorities.

In 1998, the U.S. Supreme Court established affirmative defense guidelines in response to claims of sexual harassment that require an employer to demonstrate an attempt to prevent and correct the inappropriate behaviors and to prove that the victim failed to use the opportunities that the employer provided to correct the situation.

ORGANIZATIONAL JUSTICE AND ETHICS

An important and potent condition for promoting diversity and productivity in the workplace is to pursue organizational justice tirelessly. Justice is a person's perception of fairness. An unjust or discriminatory workplace is very costly to the organization and to its members. For example, individuals that experience injustice at work have a variety of feelings, including anger, rage, shame, and guilt. Individuals often engage in retaliation and can also experience increased anxiety, insomnia, depression, and exhaustion (Greenberg, 2011). Research on organizational justice has identified the following four components or facets of organizational justice:

> *Procedural justice:* the perceived fairness of decision-making procedures that are ethical, consistent, and free from bias
>
> *Distributive justice:* the perceived fairness of decision outcomes involving, for example, pay, recognition, and promotions relative to the outcomes for co-workers
>
> *Interpersonal justice:* the perceived fairness of treatment by others, especially with reference to respect and concern
>
> *Informational justice:* the perceived fairness of information used as the basis for decision making

We all experience change almost constantly in our working lives, and one way to cope with change is anticipating how fairly the change will take place in our organizations—a concept that is referred to as *anticipatory justice*. According to Rodell and Colquitt (2009), anticipatory justice arises from the global perceptions of fairness that employees attribute to their supervisors. When a supervisor is polite, sincere, and respectful when discussing a change, the employee is more likely to embrace rather than resist the change. It is important to keep in mind that these different components or facets of organizational justice can act in harmony with each other to promote a broadly just workplace. Thus, for example, when outcomes of a decision are unfavorable, such as the announcement of cuts to the salaries of every employee, organization members are more likely to accept the decision if fair and transparent procedures are employed. On the other hand, employee reactions to favorable outcomes are little affected by the fairness of the procedure.

Organizational justice is the foundation for ethics and ethical practices, and we don't need to dwell on the widespread corruption found in the United States as well as in other countries around the globe. *Ethics* refers to the standards of conduct that guide our behaviors, and *moral values* refer to people's fundamental beliefs about what is right and wrong or good and bad. Organizations in general can prescribe standards of behavior while refraining from teaching moral values, which are usually viewed as what the person brings to the organization. It is an organization's responsibility to set clear standards of behavior and to educate employees to recognize these standards and follow them. In fact, an enlightened organization will have an ethics program that consists of a code of ethics, ethics training, and ethics audits.

In closing, it is imperative to have a just and ethical organization because the costs of not doing so can be astronomical—not only in terms of money but more importantly in terms of the well-being and the very survival of your organization.

Chapter Summary

This chapter focused on barriers to participation in the workplace that confront women, people of color, and sexual minorities, as members of these groups represent an increasing proportion of the workforce each day. We presented a definition of workforce diversity and the role of privilege in barriers to work for women, persons of color, and sexual minorities. We also presented a brief description of the laws, court cases, and executive orders that have been implemented in the United States to strengthen and promote equality for all persons. We distinguished between quid pro quo and hostile environment forms of sexual harassment and identified several tactics that can reduce sexual harassment in the workplace. Lastly, we defined the four types of organizational justice and indicated that they are the foundation for ethical actions and programs.

Chapter References

American Association of University Women. (2012). *The simple truth about the gender pay gap*. Retrieved from http://www.aauw.org/learn/research/upload/simpletruthaboutpaygap1.pdf/ June 18, 2012

American Psychological Association. (2007). *Report of the APA task force on socioeconomic status.* Washington, DC: Author.

Aronson, J. M. (2002). *Improving academic achievement: Impact of psychological factors on education.* Boston: Academic Press.

Avery, D. R. (2011). Why the playing field remains uneven: Impediments to promotions in organizations. In S. Zedeck (Ed.), *APA handbook of industrial and organizational psychology* (Vol. 3, pp. 577–613). Washington, DC: American Psychological Association.

Berdahl, J. L., & Raver, J. L. (2011). Sexual harassment. In S. Zedeck (Ed.), *APA handbook of industrial and organizational psychology* (Vol. 3, pp. 641–669). Washington, DC: American Psychological Association.

Blustein, D. L. (2008). The role of work in psychological health and well-being: A conceptual, historical, and public policy perspective. *American Psychologist, 63*(4), 228–240.

Cascio, W. F., & Aguinis, H. (2011). *Applied psychology in human resource management.* Boston: Prentice Hall.

De Corte, W., Lievens, F., & Sackett, P. R. (2007). Combining predictors to achieve optimal trade-offs between selection quality and adverse impact. *Journal of Applied Psychology, 92*(5), 1380–1393. doi:10.1037/0021-9010.92.5.1380

Fassinger, R. E. (2005). Theoretical issues in the study of women's career development: Building bridges in a brave new world. In W. B. Walsh & M. L. Savickas (Eds.), *Handbook of vocational psychology* (3rd ed., pp. 85–124). Mahwah, NJ: Erlbaum.

Fassinger, R. E. (2008). Workplace diversity and public policy: Challenges and opportunities for psychology. *American Psychologist, 63*(4), 252–268. doi:10.1037/0003-066X.63.4.252

Fiske, S. T. (2010). *Social beings: A core motives approach to social psychology* (2nd ed.). Hoboken, NJ: John Wiley & Sons.

Greenberg, J. (2011). Organizational justice: The dynamics of fairness in the workplace. In S. Zedeck (Ed.), *APA handbook of industrial and organizational psychology* (Vol. 3, pp. 271–327). Washington, DC: American Psychological Association.

Hammer, L. B., & Zimmerman, K. L. (2011). Quality of work life. In S. Zedeck (Ed.), *APA handbook of industrial and organizational psychology* (Vol. 3, pp. 399–432). Washington, DC: American Psychological Association.

Human Rights Campaign. (2007). *State of the workplace for gay, lesbian, bisexual and transgender Americans.* Washington, DC: Human Rights Campaign Foundation.

Jackson, S. E., & Joshi, A. (2011). Work team diversity. In S. Zedeck (Ed.), *APA handbook of industrial and organizational psychology* (Vol. 1, pp. 651–686). Washington, DC: American Psychological Association.

National Gay and Lesbian Task Force. (2008). *Percentage of U.S. population covered by a nondiscrimination law or broad family recognition law over time.* Retrieved from http://www. thetaskforce.org/downloads/reports/fact_sheets/ CoveredByNondiscrimLaws0507Color.pdf.

Rodell, J. B., & Colquitt, J. A. (2009). Looking ahead in times of uncertainty: The role of anticipatory justice in an organizational change context. *Journal of Applied Psychology, 94*(4), 989–1002.

Sataline, S., Bravin, J., & Koppel, N. (2009). *A Sotomayor ruling gets scrutiny.* Retrieved from http://online.wsj.com/article/NA_WSJ_ PUB:SB124354041637563491.html

Sauter, S. L., & National Institute for Occupational Safety and Health. (2002). *The changing organization of work and the safety and health of working people: Knowledge gaps and research directions.* Cincinnati, OH: Department of Health and Human Services, Centers for Disease Control and Prevention, National Institute for Occupational Safety and Health.

Schneider, B. (1987). The people make the place. *Personnel Psychology, 40*(3), 437–453.

Schneider, B., Smith, D. B., Taylor, S., & Fleenor, J. (1998). Personality and organizations: A test of the homogeneity of personality hypothesis. *Journal of Applied Psychology, 83*(3), 462–470.

Thomas, K. M. (2005). *Diversity dynamics in the workplace.* Belmont, CA: Thomson/Wadsworth.

Tullo, A. H. (2004). Women in industry: Numbers on the board and in top management slip in 2004. *Chemical and Engineering News, 82*, 18–19.

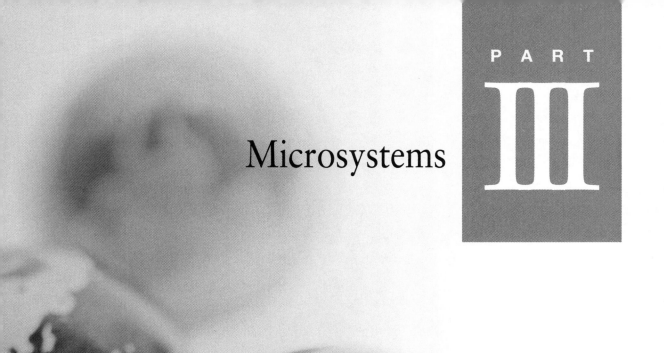

Microsystems

Hiring and Performance Management

The Supe87/Fotolia

CHAPTER OVERVIEW

This chapter examines topics that are especially important for finding work and staying employed in today's highly competitive and globalized marketplace. We approach this as a process. First, it's a matter of building relationships between applicants and organizations seeking to hire new employees. These relationships will be influenced by application materials and various interview procedures.

After a new employee joins an organization, relationships develop between the recently hired member and current members. These relationships may require careful attention, especially when the parties differ across gender, race, or ethnicity. Success may be enhanced, though, with careful socialization, training, and mentoring programs. After new members have received initial training and orientation, their performance will typically be evaluated for the duration of their employment. We will examine the primary performance review techniques, and we will consider some of the most common errors in judgment that can bias performance reviews.

This chapter closes with brief treatments of several other employment topics: dispositional variables that impact work performances; some contemporary issues in performance evaluation, including electronic performance monitoring and cyber loafing; and protected groups and the law.

LEARNING OBJECTIVES

When you have finished reading this chapter, you will be prepared to do the following:

- Explain the role of biographical data and letters of recommendation in the hiring process
- Discuss the differences between structured and unstructured interviews and identify self-presentation tactics that are useful during interviews
- Identify strategies for applying for a job in the context of web-based recruitment and assessment centers
- Identify challenges facing new employees who are entering both a new social culture and a new organizational culture
- Discuss core self-evaluation in the work environment and describe socialization and training programs for new employees
- Describe informal and formal organizational mentoring programs, especially formal programs for new employees who are new to both the country and the organizational culture

Exactostock/SuperStock

- Discuss performance evaluations, how they work, their importance, and sources of error and bias that can contaminate performance evaluations
- Describe the advantages of the 360-degree performance evaluation process, including self-ratings and ratings by others
- Identify and discuss dispositional variables that impact work performance
- Discuss contemporary issues in performance evaluation and describe protected groups and adverse impact

GETTING IN, FINDING YOUR WAY, GETTING AHEAD

By the time students reach college, the vast majority of them have already amassed significant organizational experience. This can include part-time work as well as involvement in extracurricular activities, churches, community groups, and clubs. All of these kinds of organizations are likely to operate according to the principles under discussion in this text. Many college students already have fairly extensive work experience, especially part-time students (The Condition of Education, 2011).

Biographical Information and Letters of Recommendation

Biographical data, or *biodata*, is information, usually collected on an application form, that includes answers to questions about previous jobs, education, specialized training, and personal history. The focus is on a job applicant's past accomplishments and experiences, with the underlying idea that the past behavior is an excellent predictor of future behaviors. For example, an applicant who has worked with the public in a previous position might very well be an excellent employee for the returns department of a discount store or the service department of an automobile dealership.

Letters of recommendation are important, and they represent a commonly used selection tool that provides additional information about an applicant's past performance and qualifications (McCarthy & Goffin, 2001). Such recommendations can confirm or supplement data provided by applicants (Brem, Lampman, & Johnson, 1995), and they can supply intangible information about the applicant's motivation (Tommasi, Williams, & Nordstrom, 1998). It is not unusual for organizations to base hiring and promotion decisions primarily on letters of recommendation. It is worthwhile to keep in mind, however, given potential legal actions initiated by disgruntled applicants, that letters of recommendation usually contain little if any negative observations about a candidate, even if such is warranted. Also, the applicant is usually the person who asks supervisors, colleagues, and/or friends to write a letter of reference, and it is safe to assume that the applicant would only ask those persons who would write a positive letter.

Interview Formats

The job interview is probably the most widely used hiring instrument for all job levels. An employment interview is basically a social interaction between the applicant and the organization's hiring team. In addition to being designed to predict future behavior, interviews also provide the opportunity for the applicant and the organization to look each other over and make judgments based on the interview discussions and the observation of the parties' nonverbal behaviors.

In general, an interview includes questions about job knowledge, abilities, skills, personality, and person-organization fit (Huffcutt, Conway, Roth, & Stone, 2001). The two major types of interviews are the structured and the unstructured interview. The *structured interview* involves the representative of the hiring organization asking the job candidate a series of questions about the unique features and requirements of the job. Every candidate is asked the same questions, presented in the same order. Typically, the candidate's answers describe in specific and behavioral detail how he or she would *respond* to a hypothetical situation. These responses are typically rated so that multiple candidates for a position can be compared. The structured interview with questions formatted to elicit behavior descriptions is usually the preferred type of job interview, especially when the candidates are being considered for a high-level executive position (Huffcutt, Weekley, Wiesner, Degroot, & Jones, 2001).

The *unstructured interview* is composed of broad questions that may vary from one candidate to the next, even for those being considered for the same position. For example, one candidate may be asked to provide details of her experiences and responsibilities in previous jobs, and another candidate may be asked to describe his career goals and interests. The scoring of unstructured interviews is flexible and is at the discretion of the interviewer. Unstructured interviews focus on constructs such as education, work experience, and interests, whereas structured interviews focus more on job knowledge, interpersonal and social skills, and problem solving.

Self-Presentation Tactics

Most interviews begin with a handshake, and this gesture can have a meaningful impact on the rest of the hiring process. Stewart, Dustin, Barrick, and Darnold (2008) investigated the impact of an applicant's handshake on hiring recommendations formed during the interview. The results indicate that individuals from a western culture who follow common prescriptions for shaking hands (namely, a firm handshake and looking the other person in the eye) received higher ratings of employment suitability than those whose handshake was weak or hesitant and did not include eye contact.

Looking more broadly at other features of the job interview process beyond the handshake, Barrick, Shaffer, and DeGrassi (2009) studied the relationship between self-presentation tactics and ratings of interviews and job performance. The investigators focused on three facets of self-presentation:

1. Appearance, which includes hygiene, personal grooming, and appropriate dress
2. Impression management, which refers to the ways people try to make themselves seem right for the job (talking about prior accomplishments) and how they seek to ingratiate themselves with the interviewer (by agreeing with them, paying them compliments, or praising the organization)

3. Nonverbal cues, which include making eye contact, nodding, leaning forward, and making hand gestures, as well as verbal behavior—the more consciously controlled expressions of thoughts and emotions such as verbal fluency and style of delivery (Motowidlo & Burnett, 1995)

Appearance had the strongest correlation to interview ratings, followed by impression management, and then verbal and nonverbal behaviors. In addition, self-presentation tactics had less of an impact on structured interviews than they did on unstructured interviews. Lastly, self-presentation tactics had stronger relationships with interview ratings than with subsequent performance ratings.

RECRUITMENT

Recruitment consists of organizational activities and practices designed to identify and attract potential employees and persuade them to join the organization. It is increasingly clear that in the highly competitive global marketplace, recruitment is a key antecedent to organizational effectiveness (Allen, Mahto, & Otondo, 2007).

Web-Based Recruitment

There is evidence that the source (e.g., newspaper ads, employee referrals) through which organizations make initial contact with potential applicants is very important (Zottoli & Wanous, 2000). Web-based recruitment provides the opportunity to communicate practically unlimited information about an organization and job characteristics, to communicate this information through multiple channels (links, plain text, video clips), and to communicate it to a large number of geographically dispersed job seekers at a relatively low cost (Cober, Brown, Blumental, Doverspike, & Levy, 2000). Allen and colleagues (2007) focused their research on the interaction between an applicant and the recruitment source, especially organization websites. The results indicate that the image of the organization is important even when participants have unlimited opportunity to search for information. These results underscore the importance of shaping and maintaining a clear and positive organizational image.

As more and more job seekers use organization-specific websites in their search for a job, it is important to make sure an organization's online presence attracts high-quality applicants who exhibit a good fit with the position and the organization. Therefore, it is important to determine and implement the richness (text only or text with illustrations and/or videos and sound) and content of the website that will work best to attract qualified applicants, avoid an unwieldy numbers of candidates, increase processing efficiency, minimize the number of applicants that must be rejected, and reduce the cost of identifying suitable job candidates (Dineen & Noe, 2009).

Recently, Walker et al. (2009) investigated job seekers' reactions to organizations, using variables that included or excluded employee testimonials about recruitment websites and quantified the job seekers' reactions to different characteristics of these employment testimonials. Marketing researchers have found that customer testimonials enhance the persuasive power of advertising because consumers prefer to consider the experiences of "ordinary people" when making purchasing decisions (Mittelstaedt, Riesz, & Burns, 2000), and Walker et al. (2009) believed that including employee testimonials might promote more identification with the organization because they would allow job seekers to see the human side of the organization (Cober et al., 2000, p. 487). Walker et al. (2009) found that participants were more attracted to organizations when testimonials were included on recruitment websites and they perceived the information presented as more credible.

Furthermore, testimonials containing video with audio rated higher in attractiveness and information credibility compared to testimonials consisting of only text and photographs. The findings also indicated that African Americans responded more favorably to employee testimonials as the proportion of minorities shown giving testimonials on the recruitment website increased, whereas whites responded more negatively to a recruiting organization that used more minority employee testimonials. Interestingly, the richer medium (video with audio vs. photograph with text) accentuated these group differences.

The findings from the studies by Walker et al. show that the image an organization presents on a recruitment website is important and influences the diversity and quality of applicants who apply for a posted position. An organization's website should include specific information about the job and the organization, but it also must present a positive image of the organization and what it has to offer potential employees (e.g., continuing education opportunities, excellent training and advancement prospects for all employees, or even environmental-friendly alternative energy policies). The recruitment website should include employee testimonials but should take care to show balance by providing testimonials from a diverse group of employees, and the website will benefit from the use of rich medium, including video and audio rather than just presenting static photographs and text.

Weller, Holtom, Matiaske, and Mellewigt (2009) found that individuals recruited through personal recruitment sources (a relative or friend working at the organization) yielded lower turnover than when new employees were recruited through formal sources such as websites or newspaper ads. At the earliest stages of employment in an organization, turnover rates are generally quite low (Morrison & Brantner, 1992), but as employees acquire experience and more information about an organization, turnover rates begin to increase, peaking in the first and second years of employment and then declining thereafter (Hom, Roberson, & Ellis, 2008). Peak turnover rates were delayed from 9 months for employees recruited through formal sources to 17 months for those recruited through personal sources. This research suggests that after an employee is hired, an organization would do well to use socialization tactics, such as facilitating personal contacts with organizational members, to establish a network of relationships with co-workers. Such networks can help newcomers understand organizational culture and can insure that recently hired employees are able to identify knowledgeable people in the organization that can help them resolve specific issues and problems, which may in turn lower turnover rates.

Assessment Centers

Organizations often use assessment centers (ACs) to select individuals to fill management positions and/or to provide direction for career development. AC techniques include exercises that require job candidates to respond to a variety of problems described in memoranda, letters, and/or emails, as well as leaderless group discussions and personality tests that measure a subset of dimensions considered important for a job. There are usually a number of specially trained AC raters who observe the participants and measure candidate abilities, including oral communication, planning and organizing, delegation, written communication, and adaptability (Gatewood, Feild, & Barrick, 2008). An overall assessment rating (OAR) for a candidate combines the performance scores on the all of the AC exercises. Since the 1970s, OAR scores compiled by ACs have shown smaller differences between African-American and white candidates than have standardized paper-and-pencil tests (Huck & Bray, 1976).

SOCIALIZATION, TRAINING, AND MENTORING PROGRAMS

As a consequence of globalization, personnel exchanges across national borders have increased dramatically over the past several decades (Erez, 2011). Many employees have to adjust not only to a new organizational culture but also to the larger culture in which the organization is located. Adapting to a new culture requires that the person understand the norms and customs of a different country, communicate in a language that is not their native language, learn culturally appropriate behaviors, and adapt to unfamiliar living conditions. Fan and Wanous (2008) conducted a field-based longitudinal experiment to test the efficacy of a new type of orientation program focusing on easing entry into a new organization and an unfamiliar culture. Asian students entering a graduate program in the United States were randomly assigned to either a standard three-hour cross-cultural training (CCT) course that addressed the students' immediate needs or to an enhanced course that offered more dynamic and detailed information about how to cope with the demands of graduate education in the United States, including strategies to help them set realistic goals. The findings indicated that participants in the enhanced CCT course had lower pre-entry expectations, felt less stressed, and reported higher levels of academic and interaction adjustment six and nine months after entering the graduate program. Interestingly, many of the positive effects of the enhanced course were not immediately evident but emerged at the six- and nine-month evaluations.

Core Self-Evaluations and Work Environments

A perennial issue in industrial/organizational psychology is the relative contributions of dispositional forces (such as personality and age) relative to situational or environmental forces for shaping performances of organizational members. *Core self-evaluations* (CSEs) are the basic assumptions people make about their worth, competence, and capability. CSEs includes self-esteem, generalized self-efficacy, emotional stability, and locus of control. Longitudinal research has found that persons with above-average core self-evaluations acquire more education, earn more money, and have fewer health problems (Judge & Hurst, 2007).

Kacmar, Collins, Harris, and Judge (2009) examined how core self-evaluations interacted with perceptions of organizational politics and leader effectiveness to influence supervisor ratings of subordinate performance. The results indicate that in less political environments, employees with high core self-evaluations are viewed as more productive by supervisors. Likewise, high leader effectiveness was related to significantly higher performances from individuals with high CSEs, compared to those individuals with low CSEs. These results indicate that the right situation—minimal politics in the work environment coupled with effective leadership—elicits optimal performance and productivity.

Employee Socialization and Training Programs

Newcomer transition is facilitated by formal socialization programs such as orientation, small group work, and mentoring. Small group work is an ideal setting to jump-start newcomer adjustment and socialization, as measured by transition from outsider to insider, role clarity, self-efficacy, and social acceptance (Bauer, Tucker, Bodner, Erdogan, & Truxillo, 2007; Moreland, 1985; Levine & Moreland, 2011). Traditional orientation programs, which tend to be one-sided (employer to employee) and focused on distribution of information about benefits, policies, and work procedures, have little impact on new employees, but engagement in small work groups gives new employees the opportunity to experience the organizational culture while working side by side with more seasoned employees. Small work groups bring together longtime and new employees— some of whom are likely to be diverse and multicultural individuals—in almost daily contact. This contact promotes the sharing of information, establishes networks, communicates organizational values, and serves as an important resource for new employees, encouraging them to become colleagues and form bonds with established employees (Moreland & Levine, 2001). On-the-job training reinforces job commitment, employee satisfaction, performance consistency, and workplace tenure (Bauer et al., 2007; Levine & Moreland, 2011).

Mentoring

Mentoring is an important social and support process that involves a relationship between an experienced mentor and a protégé who is new in a career. Mentoring provides access to information, visibility, and a chance to demonstrate competence. Kram (1985) has suggested that mentoring usually progresses through stages: the initiation stage, beginning the relationship; cultivation, or bonding between the parties; separation, when the protégé strikes out on her own; and finally, redefinition, as the two parties become friends and consider each other as equals.

The gender and the ethnicity of a mentor may be related to the protégé's long-term prospects. Dreher and Cox (1996) looked at salary comparisons derived from 1,108 survey respondents who were graduates of an MBA program and had experienced a mentoring relationship They discovered that the graduates who had a white male mentor had a $22,454 salary advantage over those who did not have a white male mentor in the early stages of their career. Individuals with a white male mentor also had an average salary advantage of $16,840 over those who were mentored by a woman or a person of color. More recently, Wang, Tomlinson, and Noe (2010) studied formal rather than informal organizational mentoring programs in a large energy-management firm in China. Informal mentoring is usually based on mutual attraction between the mentor and the protégé and often has no specific time limit placed on the mentoring experience, whereas formal organizational mentoring programs match mentors and protégés and then support the relationship for a specific time period. The findings indicate that high-quality mentoring relationships arise from promoting both affect- and cognition-based trust between the mentor and protégé. Also, protégés with a higher internal locus of control gained more from the formal organizational mentoring program than did those with a lower internal locus of control.

PERFORMANCE EVALUATION: HOW IT WORKS, HOW IT IS DONE

Almost all organizations use some kind of performance evaluation system to measure employees' contributions to attaining organizational goals. Typically, an evaluation form serves as an agenda for a face-to-face meeting to evaluate work completed during the prior year, highlight areas that could be improved, and begin making a plan for the year to come. The supervisor rates the performance of the employee on tasks that were his or her core responsibilities; a numerical rating system is often used for evaluations, with higher numbers corresponding to greater levels of success. The employee is also typically rated on interpersonal demeanor, cooperation, and imitative behaviors. An example of an evaluation form is shown in Figure 6.1. In this case, the appraisal form is for a medical writer who summarizes research. Notice that the rating scale ranges from 1 for unsatisfactory performance to 5 for exceptional performance, and there is space for the supervisor to write about an employee's goals and accomplishments.

A performance assessment can raise concerns about productivity when the review indicates that an employee's work is high quality but there is insufficient quantity, or the supervisor may discover perceived issues with absences, a history of the employee arriving late and leaving early, or an unacceptable number of mistakes and delays or workplace accidents. When a supervisor's concerns are serious and numerous, then an unfavorable evaluation may instigate a corrective action plan. A corrective action plan typically includes a specific list of concerns with corresponding changes that the supervisor expects the employee to make. The plan usually covers a relatively short time frame (a few weeks to several months), and it may not be tied to the routine performance evaluation. Rather, it may be triggered by a supervisor's concerns. If the employee does not implement the changes in the plan and does not clearly demonstrate improvement, then the employee may face termination.

Employee Evaluation: Medical Writer

Appraisal Date:	Anniversary Date:
Employee:	Title:
Supervisor:	
Period Covered by Appraisal:	

Review of Past Objectives

Objective	Performance	Employee Comments	Supervisor comments
	[ ] Did not meet [ ] Partially met [ ] Met [ ] Exceeded [ ] Not Applicable		

Major accomplishments in the past Appraisal Period

Skills Evaluation

Evaluation criteria

1:	Unsatisfactory Performance
2:	Improvement Desired
3:	Meets Expectations
4:	Exceeds Expectations
5:	Exceptional Performance
n/a:	Not applicable or not observed

MEDICAL WRITER JOB SKILLS	1	2	3	4	5	n/a	Comments
Accuracy of literature interpretation							
Efficiency and reliability in triaging of source literature							
Attention to detail							
Understanding of and responsiveness to supervisory feedback on content work							
Clarity of writing							
Journal review up to date							
Computer skills and autonomy							
Library and literature searching skills							
Cooperativeness with mgt and other staff							

FIGURE 6.1   Sample Employee Evaluation Form

DOES PERFORMANCE EVALUATION HELP?

Performance evaluation is a labor-intensive process, and it takes time away from the tasks at hand because people aren't doing their regular jobs when they are filling out forms and having performance review meetings. So it is important to inquire about the value of the results of a performance assessment for the organization, for mid-level managers, and for the employee. First we will assume that the evaluation process has gone smoothly and has been largely free of systematic error and bias (we will consider error and bias in performance evaluation shortly). Successful performance appraisals can inform decisions about resource allocation by providing detailed information about the contributions of the work of an individual employee as well as a group of employees (Hillstrom & Hillstrom, 2002). A good performance appraisal system also helps organizational leaders make decisions about how the specific duties and responsibilities of various positions can be adjusted to suit each employee's strengths. Finally, when performance appraisal is perceived as fair and equitable, it enhances overall productivity, in part because individuals believe that honest effort is rewarded.

An effective employee evaluation system is useful when an organization is large enough to have mid-level managers between rank-and-file employees and those at highest levels of responsibility and authority. Performance evaluations are valuable in these kinds of situations for several reasons: first, direct supervisors have a solid understanding of their subordinates' duties and responsibilities, so they are the most well-equipped personnel to evaluate the performance of the employees they supervise; second, mid-level managers often supervise several comparable individuals, and they must make decisions about resource allocations among these employees. So the results of performance evaluations can help managers identify situations in which employees can become more productive with the addition of support (for example, by assigning them assistants). In addition, because resources are almost always limited, supervisors can make informed comparisons using the results of performance evaluations and then reward the most productive employees.

Favorable performance evaluations may lead to raises, promotions, and other tangible benefits, but employees stand to gain even more. Formal and structured performance assessment will help employees document their accomplishments and progress. In addition, performance assessment gives employees the opportunity to boost their performance by learning where their supervisor sees problems. Timely feedback can help employees make corrections to their work habits before their shortcomings becomes serious and lead to sanctions, corrective action plans, or termination.

SOURCES OF PERFORMANCE EVALUATION ERROR AND BIAS

When the performance of an employee cannot be fully captured for evaluation through objective measures and is instead a matter of opinion or attitude, then such opinions are vulnerable to a wide range of influences and cognitive limitations, which can cause biased and distorted ratings (Eagly & Chaiken, 1993; Fiske, Gilbert, & Lindzey, 2010). Several of these influences are particularly relevant to the performance evaluation domain and have been the subject of research that is motivated in part by a desire to make such ratings more objective and, ultimately, more useful.

Halo Effect

Managers can reach general conclusions about a subordinate that are not accurate, especially when such conclusions are based on limited information that may or may not be typical and truly representative. So a global rating is given to an employee based solely on the rater's general feeling about the employee; that is, a broad impression that the rater has about an employee influences the evaluation the employee will receive. When the impression formed by the person evaluating an employee is based on aspects of the individual that are irrelevant to his or her job performance, this is referred to as the *halo effect* or *halo error*, and it can be positive or negative. For example, attractive people are likely to be regarded as competent, especially in the social domain. Conversely, a reverse halo effect may occur when a person is regarded in a generally negative way because he is unattractive, or an employee is labeled incompetent because she lacks social poise rather than because she is truly bad at her job (Fiske, 2010).

Leniency, Severity, and Distributional Errors

In addition to overgeneralizing about an individual, managers are also sometimes prone to viewing their subordinates as more alike than they actually are. In some cases, managers commit leniency errors, in which they give underperforming employees positive ratings. Other managers may err in the opposite direction, falling prey to severity errors, in which high-performing employees are given low ratings. The result of either unwarranted leniency or severity is a distributional error: if high-achieving and low-performing employees are given similar ratings, then the performance appraisals will not accurately reflect important individual differences. Especially when performance appraisals are used to justify raises and advancement in an organization, systematic bias can erode confidence in the process—even when a manager is "nice" and shows leniency toward underperforming employees. Leniency in performance evaluation can set the stage for resentment on the part of employees who are doing their jobs well. It also makes it less likely that low-performing employees will improve.

360-DEGREE FEEDBACK AND SELF-RATINGS

Our discussion of performance evaluation has largely been limited to one-way feedback from a supervisor to a subordinate. Historically, this has been the most common approach, and it is still widely used. When preparing to conduct a performance evaluation, most supervisors will seek out information about an employee, for example, by talking to colleagues and customers or by compiling information as it comes in as unsolicited feedback. In this model, though, the supervisor remains the principal conduit for information, which she will analyze and interpret.

   An alternative to this reliance on the supervisor's opinion is known as *360-degree feedback* (Bracken, Timmreck, & Church, 2001). This approach metaphorically puts the employee in the middle of a circle surrounded by all the sources of performance-relevant information. These sources include supervisors, colleagues, subordinates, customers, and any other individuals with direct knowledge of the employee's work. In the most sophisticated systems, there may be distinctive survey forms for people in each category. Finally, 360-degree systems also tend to place more emphasis on the employee's self-perception as well as his perception of relationships with others (Craig & Hannum, 2006).

About a third of all organizations currently use 360-degree feedback approaches for performance evaluation (Bracken et al., 2001). In a review of 360-feedback research, Atwater and colleagues (2007) came to the following conclusions about this method:

- Overall, feedback is more likely to produce change when there is a perception that it is warranted.
- Although positive feedback is generally better received, negative feedback may motivate managers to set performance goals, even though the employee may initially have a negative response to this continuous improvement approach.
- When there is a discrepancy between high self-ratings and relatively low ratings by subordinates, leaders may be more motivated to change than when their own self-ratings are consistent with low marks from other raters.
- Following a 360-degree review, the organization needs to provide opportunities for training and coaching to help employees implement and sustain change.
- Giving members the chance to participate in 360-degree reviews may increase their overall positive perception of the organization, especially when there are follow-up meetings to discuss the process as well as training and development opportunities.

Some researchers and organizational consultants as well as proponents of 360-degree feedback urge caution in using this approach (Bracken & Center for Creative Leadership, 1997; Craig & Hannum, 2006). They conclude that 360-degree feedback is potentially useful and appropriate for helping employees grow and develop, but it should not be used for performance assessment that is tied to decisions about promotion, compensation, or termination.

DISPOSITIONAL VARIABLES AND WORK PERFORMANCE

There are many variables that impact work performance, including situational, environmental, or contextual variables such as outdated equipment. Dispositional variables, which are parameters more directly associated with the individual employee, also impact performance. We will review two of these factors: locus of control and self-esteem.

Locus of Control

An important aspect of individual variation in personality is locus of control. People with an external locus of control tend to explain the outcomes of their behavior by appeals to external forces—they look at things like fate or luck, chance, or the actions of people who are in positions of power and influence. In contrast, individuals with an internal locus of control are more likely to explain success and failure as the result of their own actions and choices (Phares, 1976). It is important to acknowledge that locus of control is not a matter of accuracy but of attribution; it references the ways people interpret behavior, including our own (Fiske, 2010). So as a dispositional variable, it is not a simple matter of "reality" or of being right or wrong but instead is the result of an individual's habitual frame of mind.

In organizational settings, individuals with a strong external locus of control are likely to have relatively poor outcomes, possibly because this attributional style creates a sort of "victim mentality" (Twenge & Campbell, 2008, p. 310). A meta-analysis of various factors related to workplace success found that people with an external locus of control are less likely to get promoted into jobs with more responsibility. They tend to make less money and are much less satisfied with their work (Ng, Eby, Sorensen, & Feldman, 2005).

Self-Esteem

Self-esteem is a dispositional variable that seems as if it would be a positive attribute to find in employees. From an organizational perspective, however, an excess of unwarranted confidence among its youngest and newest members poses a potential problem. Optimism is good; overconfidence is not. In addition, the relationship between self-esteem and performance is unclear at best. In an exhaustive survey of the self-esteem research literature, Baumeister and colleagues (2003) found no evidence that high self-esteem was related to many of the things we want and want to encourage (good grades, good jobs), nor does it protect against things we'd all probably rather avoid (bad relationships, children experimenting with drugs and sex). Despite this evidence, these self-esteem skeptics did find two noteworthy benefits that are apparently associated with good self-esteem. First, people with high self-esteem are happier than their counterparts with low self-esteem, and second, in laboratory studies, even though people with high self-esteem aren't *better* at standardized tasks, they are more persistent after failure.

CONTEMPORARY ISSUES IN PERFORMANCE EVALUATION

Electronic Performance Monitoring

Members of many professions now spend much of their day using computers and computer networks (Madden & Jones, 2008). As a result, their work activity is open to being directly recorded, monitored, and analyzed. This has led to the development of systems for *electronic performance monitoring* (EPM). These are primarily computer-based technologies, although they may also monitor activity on devices such as mobile phones or make use of tools such as The Global Positioning System (GPS) to track employee movements. EPMs are usually quite unobtrusive and may record the employee's every move—electronic, physical, or both (Moorman & Wells, 2003). Although EPM systems are unpopular with some employees, a 2008 meta-analysis by Carroll (2008) found that their use was correlated with better work performance. However, the researchers discovered a negative correlation between the intensity of monitoring and job performance: the most closely watched employees were less productive than those who were monitored via less invasive techniques (Carroll, 2008). In addition, other researchers (Wells, Moorman, & Werner, 2007) have reported that employees regard EPM as fair when it is largely developmental (helping employees improve their own performance) but view it as unfair when they believe it is being implemented as a deterrent to unauthorized computer use, a topic we'll now briefly consider.

Cyberloafing

Some electronic monitoring is intended to ensure compliance with organizational policies, which include guidelines about use of company-owned equipment for conducting personal business. In addition to deterring rare but problematic activity such as viewing child pornography, computer usage guidelines are usually intended to curb distractions to employees at work (sometimes known as cyberloafing or cyberslacking). By 2004, this new way of avoiding work had become pervasive in web-enabled workplaces. In a survey of 3,245 workers in the United Kingdom, 97% of the respondents admitted to cyberloafing—on average, for three hours a day (Amble, 2004).

Research is currently inconclusive about the relationship between cyberloafing and productivity. Estimates of the "cost" to organizations are often dramatic—you may have heard reports that unauthorized use of computers for personal use costs companies billions of dollars per year (Robbins, 2007). However, the same workers who engage in cyberloafing are also more likely to work from home, including checking and answering work email when they are not actually at work (Madden & Jones, 2008). In addition, judicious use of social media (such as Facebook) and interactive online games may actually increase productivity by giving workers a break from their routine, and in the case of social media, may provide a way to strengthen relationships among employees and foster a sense of teamwork (Opperman, 2007).

Some researchers propose that workers may browse the Web as a way to manage their emotions, although sending and responding to personal email can often have the opposite effect (Lim & Chen, 2009). Lim (2002) found that cyberloafing was more common when employees felt that their workplaces were inherently unjust, although it may be that the employees who were doing this most often were rationalizing their own misbehavior. Beugre and Kim (2006) proposed that non-work-related computer usage is most destructive when it clearly violates the local norms for such behavior. This suggests that new members of an organization would be wise to take note of the patterns of computer usage of their colleagues and keep their own cyberloafing at or below the levels established as acceptable. Managers may want to make these norms explicit, with policies that give guidance about the type and amount of non-work computer usage that is considered tolerable (Kidwell, 2010; Needleman, 2010).

Personality and Risk of Burnout

Burnout is a term that is frequently and somewhat informally used to describe a sort of emotional depletion. It is an occupational hazard in many settings, especially for people who work in helping professions. But some researchers have focused on how personality traits may be burnout risk factors. Alarcon, Eschleman, and Bowling (2009) conducted a meta-analysis of burnout research that employed a standard questionnaire, the Maslach Burnout Inventory (or MBI). The MBI taps three dimensions of this syndrome: depersonalization and emotional exhaustion (which increase as an employee reaches burnout) and a sense of personal accomplishment (which decreases when burnout is imminent). The researchers developed some hypotheses about how those dimensions related to differences in several personality measures, including the familiar Big Five model of personality. They also looked at what is known as the Type-A personality, which is characterized by a driven and chronically impatient style of working. In addition, they looked at self-esteem, locus of control, self-efficacy (basically, a sense that you are capable of meeting your goals—a topic we will explore more fully in Chapter 8 on motivation), optimism, and several other factors.

The researchers found evidence that there may be a sort of burnout-prone personality: low on self-esteem and self-efficacy; having an external locus of control; tending both to high levels of negative emotion and low levels of positive emotion as well as general emotional instability; and a lack of optimism and hardiness. The Big Five personality traits play a role as well; the likelihood of burnout is associated with lower levels of extraversion, conscientiousness, and agreeableness. Finally, the role of the Type-A personality in burnout is somewhat more complicated: it does not correlate with the MBI's dimensions of moral exhaustion and depersonalization. Personal accomplishment *was* correlated—a positive trait—although the researchers wondered if it was also tempered by the tendency of Type-As to be irritable and anger-prone.

PERFORMANCE EVALUATION AND THE LAW: PROTECTED GROUPS

As discussed in Chapter 5, various federal laws prohibit workplace-related discrimination against individuals in protected groups, as defined by gender, ethnicity (or race), age, and religious affiliation. Affirmative action (AA) programs are designed to comply with these laws and to encourage diversity in organizations. Levi and Fried (2008) studied the attitudes of whites and African Americans toward AA programs in hiring, promotion, training, and layoffs. The findings indicated that among whites, AA policies for layoffs were perceived most negatively, followed by promotions, and then training and hiring. For African Americans, the most negative reactions were toward the AA policies for layoffs, while there were no differences in their reactions to the three other AA policies. The findings also indicated that African Americans were much more favorable toward the AA policies in general than were whites, across all human resource activities and within each of them independently. Whites viewed both moderate (race used as a tie breaker in employment decisions) and strong (race accorded substantial weight in employment decisions) AA programs quite negatively.

A claim of discrimination may arise when there is a concern over potential bias in the recruitment, selection, and initial training of employees. But after a member of a protected group is employed by an organization, there also can be systematic discrimination in the employee's performance evaluations. Because discriminatory performance evaluation practices are prohibited by federal law, when violations are substantiated in court, a finding of noncompliance can be quite costly. Mayhew reported that actions by the U.S. Equal Employment and Opportunity Commission (the EEOC) cost employers more than $294 million in 2009 alone (Mayhew, 2010).

When we look at how nondiscrimination laws are related to performance evaluation, one important concept to understand is *adverse impact,* which is the result of organizational practices that lead to substantial deficits in the rate at which members of protected classes are hired, promoted, and retained (De Corte, Lievens, & Sackett, 2007). One example involves the use of standardized tests of cognitive ability. There are differences between ethnic groups on intelligence test performance. African-American and Hispanic/Latino test takers typically have lower scores than Asian Americans or whites. When tests of this sort are used to make hiring decisions, then the selection process itself may be discriminatory (Hough & Oswald, 2008). But as described in this chapter, organizational performance may also be strongly related to other personality characteristics. In general, there are no consistent differences among ethnic groups or between genders in scores on the Big Five model's personality traits (Hough, Oswald, & Ployhart, 2001). Foldes and colleagues (Foldes, Duehr, & Ones, 2008) largely reached the same conclusion by conducting a meta-analysis of more than 700 reported differences, but they did identify some areas of concern. In general, they found no systematic adverse impact when comparing African-American and white respondents. However, group differences between African Americans and Asian Americans may be more potentially problematic.

Although there has been more research into the potential for adverse impact during recruitment and selection, this literature can be extended to give useful guidance about performance evaluation. Hough and Oswald (2008) concluded that the best insurance of fair and unbiased performance evaluation may be to avoid focusing on intelligence test performance and instead measure the specific skills and competencies that are most critical for success.

Chapter Summary

This chapter focused on the strategies and specific actions involved in enhancing an individual's chances of getting and keeping a job. We first described the interactions between a job applicant and the organization that determine if an applicant will be hired. Then we examined the role of performance assessment in keeping the job for which the individual was hired. We also described the socialization processes and training used by organizations to facilitate the integration of newly hired employees into the culture and operation of the organization.

The second part of this chapter focused on performance assessment, which requires a systematic, accurate, and fair appraisal system for evaluating people's work. We presented some of the major concepts and trends in performance evaluation. We reported research findings that indicate how systems thinking led to the development of performance evaluation techniques (such as 360-degree feedback) that explicitly seek out multiple perspectives to develop evaluations that are more complete, accurate, and useful.

Although job performance is ultimately a matter of the employee succeeding in his or her duties and responsibilities, we reviewed research on personality differences that indicate an association with individual and overall organizational success. We presented some recent research on the impact of dispositional variables on work performance, we identified some contemporary issues in performance management, and we concluded with a brief treatment of protected groups and adverse impact in hiring, performance evaluation, and promotion.

Chapter References

Alarcon, G., Eschleman, K. J., & Bowling, N. A. (2009). Relationships between personality variables and burnout: A meta-analysis. *Work & Stress, 23*(3), 244–263.

Allen, D. G., Mahto, R. V., & Otondo, R. F. (2007). Web-based recruitment: Effects of information, organizational brand, and attitudes toward a Web site on applicant attraction. *Journal of Applied Psychology, 92*(6), 1696–1708. doi:10.1037/0021-9010.92.6.1696

Amble, B. (2004). Does cyberloafing undermining productivity? *Management-Issues Ltd.* Retrieved from http://www.management-issues. com/2006/8/24/research/does-cyberloafing-undermining-productivity.asp

Atwater, L. E., Brett, J. F., & Charles, A. C. (2007). Multisource feedback: Lessons learned and implications for practice. *Human Resource Management, 46*(2), 285–307.

Barrick, M. R., Shaffer, J. A., & DeGrassi, S. W. (2009). What you see may not be what you get: Relationships among self-presentation tactics and ratings of interview and job performance. *Journal of Applied Psychology, 94*(6), 1394–1411. doi:10.1037/a0016532

Bauer, T. N., Tucker, J. S., Bodner, T., Erdogan, B., & Truxillo, D. M. (2007). Newcomer adjustment during organizational socialization: A meta-analytic review of antecedents, outcomes, and methods. *Journal of Applied Psychology, 92*(3), 707–721.

Baumeister, R. F., Campbell, J. D., Krueger, J. I., & Vohs, K. D. (2003). Does high self-esteem cause better performance, interpersonal success, happiness, or healthier lifestyles? *Psychological Science in the Public Interest, 4*(1), 1–44. doi:10.1111/1529-1006.01431

Beugre, C. D., & Kim, D. (2006). *Cyberloafing: Vice or virtue?* Paper presented at Emerging Trends and Challenges in Information Technology Management, Washington, D.C.

Bracken, D., & Center for Creative Leadership. (1997). *Should 360-degree feedback be used only for developmental purposes?* Greensboro, NC: Center for Creative Leadership.

Bracken, D., Timmreck, C. W., & Church, A. H. (2001). *The handbook of multisource feedback: The comprehensive resource for designing and implementing MSF processes* (1st ed.). San Francisco: Jossey-Bass.

Brem, C., Lampman, C., & Johnson, M. (1995). Preparation of applications for academic positions in psychology. *American Psychologist, 50,* 533–553.

Carroll, W. R. (2008). The electronic workplace: The effects of electronic performance monitoring on performance outcomes: A review and meta-analysis. *Employee Rights and Employment Policy Journal, 12*(1), 29–48.

Cober, R. T., Brown, D. J., Blumental, A. J., Doverspike, D., & Levy, P. (2000). The quest for the qualified job surfer: It's time the public sector catches the wave. *Public Personnel Management, 29*(4), 479–496.

Craig, S. B., & Hannum, K. (2006). Research update: 360-degree performance assessment. *Consulting Psychology Journal: Practice and Research, 58*(2), 117–124. doi:10.1037/1065-9293.58.2.117

De Corte, W., Lievens, F., & Sackett, P. R. (2007). Combining predictors to achieve optimal trade-offs between selection quality and adverse impact. *Journal of Applied Psychology, 92*(5), 1380–1393. doi:10.1037/0021-9010.92.5.1380

Dineen, B. R., & Noe, R. A. (2009). Effects of customization on application decisions and applicant pool characteristics in a web-based recruitment context. *Journal of Applied Psychology, 94*(1), 224–234. doi:10.1037/a0012832

Dreher, G. F., & Cox, T. H., Jr. (1996). Race, gender, and opportunity: A study of compensation attainment and the establishment of mentoring relationships. *Journal of Applied Psychology, 81*(3), 297–308. doi:10.1037/0021-9010.81.3.297

Eagly, A. H., & Chaiken, S. (1993). *The psychology of attitudes*. Fort Worth, TX: Harcourt Brace Jovanovich College Publishers.

Erez, M. (Ed.). (2011). *Cross-cultural and global issues in organizational psychology* (Vol. 3). Washington, DC: American Psychological Association.

Fan, J., & Wanous, J. P. (2008). Organizational and cultural entry: A new type of orientation program for multiple boundary crossings. *Journal of Applied Psychology, 93*(6), 1390–1400. doi:10.1037/a0012828

Fiske, S. T. (2010). *Social beings: A core motives approach to social psychology* (2nd ed.). Hoboken, NJ: John Wiley & Sons.

Fiske, S. T., Gilbert, D. T., & Lindzey, G. (2010). *Handbook of social psychology* (5th ed.). Hoboken, NJ: John Wiley & Sons.

Foldes, H. J., Duehr, E. E., & Ones, D. S. (2008). Group differences in personality: Meta-analyses comparing five U.S. racial groups. *Personnel Psychology, 61*(3), 579–616. doi:10.1111/j.1744-6570.2008.00123.x

Gatewood, R. D., Feild, H. S., & Barrick, M. R. (2008). *Human resource selection* (6th ed.). Mason, OH: Thomson/South-Western.

Hillstrom, K., & Hillstrom, L. C. (2002). *Employee performance appraisals Encyclopedia of Small Business,* (Vol. 1, pp. 398–400). Detroit: Gale.

Hom, P. W., Roberson, L., & Ellis, A. D. (2008). Challenging conventional wisdom about who quits: Revelations from corporate America. *Journal of Applied Psychology, 93*(1), 1–34. doi:10.1037/0021-9010.93.1.1

Hough, L. M., & Oswald, F. L. (2008). Personality testing and industrial-organizational psychology: Reflections, progress, and prospects. *Industrial and Organizational Psychology, 1*(3), 272–290. doi:10.1111/j.1754-9434.2008.00048.x

Hough, L. M., Oswald, F. L., & Ployhart, R. E. (2001). Determinants, detection and amelioration of adverse impact in personnel selection procedures: Issues, evidence and lessons learned. *International Journal of Selection and Assessment, 9*(1/2), 152–194. doi:10.1111/1468-2389.00171

Huck, J. R., & Bray, D. W. (1976). Management assessment center evaluations and subsequent job performance of white and black females. *Personnel Psychology, 29,* 13–30.

Huffcutt, A. I., Conway, J. M., Roth, P. L., & Stone, N. J. (2001). Identification and meta-analytic assessment of psychological constructs measured in employment interviews. *Journal of Applied Psychology, 86*(5), 897–913.

Huffcutt, A. I., Weekley, J. A., Wiesner, W. H., Degroot, T. G., & Jones, C. (2001). Comparison of situational and behavior description interview questions for higher-level positions. *Personnel Psychology, 54*(3), 619–644.

Judge, T. A., & Hurst, C. (2007). Capitalizing on one's advantages: Role of core self-evaluations. *Journal of Applied Psychology, 92*(5), 1212–1227. doi:10.1037/0021-9010.92.5.1212

Kacmar, K. M., Collins, B. J., Harris, K. J., & Judge, T. A. (2009). Core self-evaluations and job performance: The role of the perceived work environment. *Journal of Applied Psychology, 94*(6), 1572–1580. doi:10.1037/a0017498

Kidwell, R. E. (2010). Loafing in the 21st century: Enhanced opportunities—and remedies—for withholding job effort in the new workplace. *Business Horizons, 53*(6), 543–552. doi:10.1016/j.bushor.2010.06.001

Kram, K. E. (1985). *Mentoring at work: Developmental relationships in organizational life*. Glenview, IL: Scott, Foresman.

Levi, A. S., & Fried, Y. (2008). Differences between African Americans and whites in reactions to affirmative action programs in hiring, promotion, training, and layoffs. *Journal of Applied Psychology, 93*(5), 1118–1129. doi:10.1037/0021-9010.93.5.1118

Levine, J. M. & Moreland, R. L. (2011). A history of small group research. In A. Kruglanski & W. Stroebe (Eds.), *Handbook of the history of social psychology* (pp. 233–255). New York: Psychology Press.

Lim, V. K. G. (2002). The IT way of loafing on the job: Cyberloafing, neutralizing and organizational justice. *Journal of Organizational Behavior, 23,* 675–694.

Lim, V. K. G., & Chen, D. J. Q. (2009). Cyberloafing at the workplace: Gain or drain on work? *Behaviour & Information Technology, 31*(4), 343–353. doi:10.1080/01449290903353054

Madden, M., & Jones, S. (2008). *Networked workers*. Washington, DC: Pew Research Center.

Mayhew, R. (2010). *What are the consequences of discrimination on the job?* Retrieved from http://smallbusiness.chron.com/consequences-discrimination-job-1312.html

McCarthy, J. M., & Goffin, R. D. (2001). Improving the validity of letters of recommendation: An investigation of three standardized reference forms. *Military Psychology, 13,* 199–222.

McCormick, E. J., Mecham, R. C., & Jeanneret, P. R. (1992). *Technical manual for the position analysis questionnaire (PAQ)* (3rd ed.). Logan, UT: PAQ Services.

Merton, R. K. (1968). The Matthew Effect in science: The reward and communication systems of science are considered. *Science, 159*(3810), 56–63.

Miner, M. G., Miner, J. B., & Sharf, J. (1980). *Uniform guidelines on employee selection procedures.* Washington, DC: Bureau of National Affairs.

Mittelstaedt, J. D., Riesz, P. C., & Burns, W. J. (2000). Why are endorsements effective? Sorting among theories of product and endorser effects. *Journal of Current Issues and Research in Advertising, 22,* 55–65.

Moreland, R. L. (1985). Social categorization and the assimilation of "new" group members. *Journal of Personality and Social Psychology, 48*(5), 1173–1190.

Moreland, R. L., & Levine, J. M. (2001). Socialization in organizations and work groups. In M. E. Turner, *Groups at work: Theory and research.* Mahwah, NJ: Lawrence Erlbaum Associates, pp. 69–106.

Moorman, R. H., & Wells, D. (2003). Can electronic monitoring be fair? Exploring relationships among mentoring characteristics, perceived fairness and job performance. *The Journal of Leadership and Organizational Studies, 10,* 2–6.

Morrison, R. F., & Brantner, T. M. (1992). What enhances or inhibits learning a new job? A basic career issue. *Journal of Applied Psychology, 77*(6), 926–940. doi:10.1037/0021-9010.77.6.926

Motowidlo, S. J., & Burnett, J. R. (1995). Aural and visual sources of validity in structured employment interviews. *Organizational Behavior and Human Decision Processes, 61*(3), 239–249. doi:10.1006/obhd.1995.1019

Needleman, S. E. (2010). A Facebook-free workplace? Curbing cyberslacking. *Wall Street Journal, Small Business.* Retrieved on May 20, 2010 http://online.wsj.com/article/NA_WSJ_PUB: SB10001424052748703691804575254443707831052. html#dummy

Ng, T. W. H., Eby, L. T., Sorensen, K. L., & Feldman, D. C. (2005). Predictors of objective and subjective career success: A meta-analysis.

Personnel Psychology, 58(2), 367–408. doi:10.1111/j.1744-6570.2005.00515.x

Opperman, S. (2007). *"Surfin' USA"—Accessing the Net at work and other time-wasting activities—are they a cost or benefit to your agency?* Retrieved from http://www.fedsmith.com/article/1298/surfin-usa-accessing-net-at-work-other.html

Phares, E. (1976). *Locus of control in personality.* Morristown, NJ: General Learning Press.

Robbins, S. P. (2007). *The truth about managing people* (2nd ed.). Upper Saddle River, NJ: FT Press.

Stewart, G. L., Dustin, S. L., Barrick, M. R., & Darnold, T. C. (2008). Exploring the handshake in employment interviews. *Journal of Applied Psychology, 93*(5), 1139–1146. doi:10.1037/0021-9010.93.5.1139

Tommasi, G. W., Williams, K. B., & Nordstrom, C. R. (1998). Letters of recommendation: What information captures HR professionals' attention? *Journal of Business and Psychology, 13,* 5–18.

Twenge, J. M., & Campbell, S. M. (2008). Generational differences in psychological traits and their impact on the workplace. *Journal of Managerial Psychology, 23*(8), 862–877. doi:10.1108/02683940810904367

Walker, H. J., Feild, H. S., Giles, W. F., Armenakis, A. A., & Bernerth, J. B. (2009). Displaying employee testimonials on recruitment web sites: Effects of communication media, employee race, and job seeker race on organizational attraction and information credibility. *Journal of Applied Psychology, 94*(5), 1354–1364. doi:10.1037/a0014964

Wang, S., Tomlinson, E. C., & Noe, R. A. (2010). The role of mentor trust and protégé internal locus of control in formal mentoring relationships. *Journal of Applied Psychology, 95*(2), 358–367. doi:10.1037/a0017663

Weller, I., Holtom, B. C., Matiaske, W., & Mellewigt, T. (2009). Level and time effects of recruitment sources on early voluntary turnover. *Journal of Applied Psychology, 94*(5), 1146–1162. doi:10.1037/a0015924

Wells, D. L., Moorman, R. H., & Werner, J. M. (2007). The impact of the perceived purpose of electronic performance monitoring on an array of attitudinal variables. *Human Resource Development Quarterly, 18,* 121–138.

Zottoli, M. A., & Wanous, J. P. (2000). Recruitment source research: Current status and future directions. *Human Resource Management Review, 10*(4), 35. doi:10.1016/S1053-4822(00)00032-2

Group Dynamics and Teams

CHAPTER OVERVIEW

In this past decade, we have experienced an escalation in downsizing, restructuring, mergers, and acquisitions as organizations seek to survive in an increasingly complex and unyielding world economy. Everyone has witnessed the toll these transitions take on the lucky people who remain employed, and the stress it induces on the employees "let go," as each invents ways to accept a gain or loss of status. Possessing the savvy to preserve existing bonds and the know-how for building new alliances is paramount. Failure to make adjustment at group levels risks system dysfunction.

Sergej Khackimullin/Fotolia

Groups are a fundamental feature of our daily lives. It is important to understand how groups work to accomplish goals as individuals, as co-workers, and as members of society. Although groups have been a central concern of social psychology from the start (Lawson, Graham, & Baker, 2007), most researchers have worked in highly specialized subdisciplines. We review recent efforts at linking theory across many areas of group process research, followed by an examination of popular and practical models describing the stages of group development.

A discussion about groups and teams includes reasons for joining groups, group roles and norms, and provision of group stability and predictability. We offer an explanation of how group activity reflects systems phenomena and consider how group membership changes people. We look at the unique capacity of teams to maximize goal attainment as well as some antidotes for the many challenges that contemporary teams encounter.

LEARNING OBJECTIVES

When you have finished reading this chapter, you will be prepared to do the following:

- Explain the similarities and differences between groups and teams
- Discuss the reasons for joining groups or work teams
- Define the concept of a team and discuss the different types of teams, including virtual teams and empowered or autonomous teams
- Identify systems characteristics as they apply to group dynamics and teamwork

Tetra Images/SuperStock

• Specify strategies to build and maintain quality teamwork
• Describe teamwork challenges and ways to address these challenges

GROUPS

A *group* is defined as a collective of two or more interdependent and interacting persons, sharing common purpose(s), whose members possess a unique relationship, as distinguished from non-members. Group members share unique actions and experiences that give rise to boundaries that may be physical, psychological, social, or some combination of these elements that serve to define the group.

Groups and Teams: Similarities and Differences

Groups and teams are similar in that both involve social interaction, every member has influence on every other member, and members share a common purpose. They differ in that performance in a group depends primarily on the work of individual members, whereas in teams performance requires both individual and collective contributions to complete a project.

Reasons for Joining

The daily lives of most people across the globe revolve around occupational activities. Work not only provides for people's subsistence but also helps to define who they are and how they behave. Family, work, and community membership shape personal identity, self-evaluation, social connectedness, and the ever-clarifying perception of self versus others (Tajfel & Turner, 1979, 1986). Even though an organizational member may have little choice in joining a group at work, each individual brings unique needs for security or power. Haslam and Ellemers (2005) propose that everyone has a desire to belong and to share unique relationships and meaningful experiences with other members of an organization. In addition to providing a paycheck, a well-functioning organization facilitates fulfillment of varying personal needs by strengthening relations and fostering employee work commitment (Gómez, Seyle, Huici, & Swann, 2009; Haslam & Ellemers, 2005; Hogg & Terry, 2001).

Predictable patterns of group behaviors and close relationships give a sense of "who we are," and "how we are to behave in relation to others" (Moreland, 1987). When a group identity is formed, it is satisfied and enhanced through frequent and positive affective or emotional experiences (Brewer, 2003; Brewer & Miller, 1996; Turner & Reynolds, 2008). Healthy employee relationships, frequent interactions, and shared positive emotional experiences need not be ignored in the name of economic considerations, as research data link meaningful work relations to enhanced employee satisfaction, productivity, and outcome consistency (Harris, 1979; Lickel et al., 2000).

Types of Groups

Basically, there are two types of groups: formal and informal. A *formal group* is one created by the organization that is intended to focus the resources of members on important organizational goals. The traditional organizational structure is function focused and relies on *command groups* in which members are subordinate to a specific manager or supervisor and report directly to that supervisor. For example, a command group might be formed by a vice president, unit director, or department head, for the purpose of identifying specific strategies to enhance organizational marketing, production, or new product development.

Usually, but not exclusively, command groups are formed by directors or heads of *line units,* or persons directly involved in delivering the product or service of the organization. *Staff units*, which can also construct command groups, are units or positions that are not part of the direct product or service-delivery command chain, although they provide support to line units or personnel. For example, a large manufacturing organization will include line units for marketing, production, and sales. Most organizations will also have staff units or positions to handle human resources, payroll, housekeeping, and other administrative support.

The other kind of formal group is team structured and process focused and relies on *task groups* to perform specific projects. Unlike command groups, members of task groups can be selected from different units or positions in the organization (line or staff), providing that they have some knowledge, experience, or special interest relative to the task before the group. Task groups can operate as a standing or permanent committee, or an organization may form an *ad hoc committee* or a *task force*, both of which describe a temporary group formed to solve a specific problem, such as setting parking policies or establishing guidelines for access and use of organizational electronic information systems and instruments. Task groups are charged with a set of goals or objectives, empowered by means of delegated authority and resources (money, time, and so on) and held accountable in some fashion. For example, suppose an organization wants to diversify their workforce, clients, or customer base. Leadership might create a task group that includes representatives from line units or positions (such as production) as well as administrative staff members (such as human resources) to work together to find a solution.

The second major type of group that is frequently found in organizations is the *informal group*. Informal groups arise without any direction from the organization and reflect clearly the fundamental need of humans to belong to groups (Baumeister & Leary, 1995; Hogg & Terry, 2001). There are two types of informal groups: interest groups and friendship groups.

Interest groups bring together like-minded employees of an organization who have a common goal or issue. Members may form a group to tackle modification of employee benefits, to enhance organizational concern for environmental pollution and action around recycling projects and programs, or to support and arrange an organizational party, picnic, or some kind of celebration. Unlike formal groups, membership in informal groups is almost always voluntary and largely independent of organizational line or staff positions. Usually, but not always, interest groups will construct their own mission or goal, gather their own resources, and establish their own accountability, rather than have these group features mandated by the organization.

The other type of informal group is the *friendship group*. These kinds of groups usually extend outside of the organization to bring people together around a common interest or activity, such as an athletic team or event, or some type of entertainment, community action project, or financial investment club. Usually, friendship groups are less structured than either formal groups or informal interest groups.

Both types of informal groups are found in almost every organization around the world and are intended to promote interaction between people as well as to achieve specific objectives or goals. Both types of groups are important to organizations and members alike, and when managers and leaders recognize and understand the role of informal groups, they are better equipped to better manage and know the organization and its people.

Stages of Group Development

The classic work of Tuckman (1965) and Tuckman and Jensen (1977), supported by contemporary literature (Cannon-Bowers & Bowers, 2011; Kozlowski, Gully, Nason, & Smith, 1999), describes groups as moving through five stages: forming, storming, norming, performing, and adjourning.

In the first stage, *forming*, members seek information about the purpose(s) of the group, begin to learn how the group will work—the "rules of the road"— and become acquainted with other team members. During this phase of group development, it is important to reduce uncertainty and indicate the costs of being involved with the group.

In the second stage, *storming*, group members are frequently in conflict about defining the group's goals and compete with each other for leadership roles. During *norming*, the third stage, informal and formal rules or guidelines about cohesiveness and teamwork begin to emerge. Members are more upbeat and positive about the group, their membership, and the work in the group. The group begins to get work completed, members begin to shape project reports, and a clear performance record begins to emerge. The norming stage is completed when members solidly agree about what to do and how to do it, and they earnestly engage in work projects.

Performing, the fourth stage, is characteristic of a fully functional group. Intragroup interactions and relationships are harmonious, and everyone attends to getting the group work done. Finally, in the *adjourning* stage, the group prepares to dissolve. Members focus on completing the job and getting group activities in order, rather than focusing on high task performance. Some group members may be pleased that the group is breaking up, but others may be concerned about the loss of camaraderie, friendship, and time structuring of their organizational life.

In reality, group development advances in a more circular or nonlinear path, rather than in this clear linear progression. The more emotionally charged or conflict-ridden the group experience, the more likely group stages will be interrupted, particularly movement from storming to norming (Wheelan, 2004). Groups that provide time for venting concerns and seeking resolution to problem issues enhance group bonding and employee satisfaction (Wheelan, 2004). Over time the group builds knowledge, skills, and capabilities to enhance self-regulation, continuous improvement, and collective adaptability (Cannon-Bowers & Bowers, 2011; Kozlowski & Ilgen, 2006).

Gersick's Punctuated Equilibrium

Gersick (1988) proposed a two-phase punctuated equilibrium model to explain group development. In Phase I group members construct guidelines that establish how the group will accomplish its task, attempt to make sense of the task in light of collective experiences, and diagnose the issues before making decisions about how to solve the problem. According to Gersick (1988, 1991), there is a shift from Phase I (framing the problem) to a new framework for performance that occurs at the halfway point of the group's collaborative work. In Phase II, (transition) the group focus turns to task completion and engages in the tasks essential for project completion, during which time the group may or may not contact stakeholders to challenge group biases (Cannon-Bowers & Bowers, 2011; Myers & Anderson, 2008).

Group Roles and Norms

The structure of groups tends to reflect the pattern of relationships between the members, driven in large part by roles and norms. A *role* is a set of expected behaviors attached to a position in an organized set of social relationships (Merton, 1967; Sluss, van Dick, & Thompson, 2011; Stryker & Burke, 2000). Roles give meaning to actions (Ashforth & Johnson, 2001; Ashforth & Mael, 1996) and serve as a framework for organizing, storing, interpreting, and making sense of individual, group, or team work (Stets & Burke, 2000). Some typical group roles include timekeeper, information seeker, recorder, facilitator, and devil's advocate (Chen & Lawson, 1996). Interactions are often role driven, so it can be surprising and even unsettling when a member acts out of role or transgresses group norms. To enhance group cohesiveness, it is beneficial to have group members rotate through different roles from one group meeting to the next so that group members are not seen as performing only one role each.

Norms are informal rules that are shared by group or team members. They prescribe appropriate and inappropriate behavior within the group. Most groups develop norms that relate to performance and associated processes, such as how long to work and how best to accomplish work, and how to get work done relative to the practices of other group members (Goodman & Leyden, 1991). Most groups and teams have appearance norms that include appropriate dress, appearance of loyalty to the team, and guidance on when or how to look busy as well as when it is okay to just "hang out." Also, most groups develop norms that revolve around issues of informal social arrangements (who interacts with whom inside and outside the workplace) and allocation norms (who gets what— extra payments, special equipment, the smallest space or biggest office, and so on).

Norms usually emerge from explicit discussions by group members. They may be absorbed from the larger organizational culture, or they may result from initial or primary reactions to meaningful group situations or events. A sound knowledge and appreciation of roles and norms will help you appreciate the forces that contribute to group structure and can also enhance the stability and predictability of the behaviors and experiences of a group or team.

GROUP DYNAMICS

As social systems, groups strive for stability by engaging in open/closed exchange to accommodate membership interdependence (von Bertalanffy, 1969). The forming, storming, and norming stages of group development transform "I" systems into a "We" system. After a group has formed, it sustains homeostasis by being receptive to positive feedback and disinclined to accept negative feedback (Tajfel & Turner, 1979). Collective action generates *nonsummativity*, when the sum of the group's work is greater than the total of what would be produced by the people in the group on their own, independent of the contributions of each other.

Group Identity As Influence on Behavior

Social identity theory examines how individuals move from "I" to "We" as they come to understand where they belong (their in-group) and where they do not (out-group). Once formed group members seek distinction from other groups by viewing their group in the best of lights to feel good about who they are and what they do (Brewer, 2003; Brewer & Miller, 1996; Haslam & Ellemers, 2005; Tajfel & Turner, 1979).

High or low identity salience describes the extent to which the individual identifies with the in-group. A member's identification with group norms and behaviors may be strong (high salience) or it may be relatively weak (low salience) (Tajfel & Turner, 1979; Turner & Reynolds, 2008). The permeability of group boundaries varies greatly from one group to another. Some groups have very permeable boundaries, and joining or leaving these groups is relatively easy—a political party is a good example of a group with permeable boundaries. Other groups have impermeable boundaries and are difficult to leave—family affiliation often entails a group with impermeable boundaries (Campbell, 1958; Lickel et al., 2000).

Benefits to Group Entitativity

Entitativity is the perception of a group as an entity and who are bonded together as a coherent unit (Campbell, 1958). The strength of this bond varies from group to group—some collections of individuals are perceived to be more entitative than other collections (Ashforth & Johnson, 2001; Ashforth & Mael, 1996; Brewer & Miller, 1996; Campbell, 1958). The better individual values and goals align with the group's values and goals, the higher the entitativity. Entitativity is also enhanced by frequent membership interactions, and discussions about values and goal setting (Castano, Yzerbyt & Bourguignon, 2003). Groups with well-established rules, guidelines, and norms, internal homogeneity, clear internal structure, and common outcomes tend to have higher entitativity than groups without these features (Hogg, Sherman, Dierselhuis, Maitner, & Moffitt, 2006).

Member identification is strongest when participants are highly uncertain (of themselves) and the group is highly entitative (Hogg et al., 2006). For example, very young children (in the formative stage of identity) are attracted to superheroes, because they long to be empowered and admired by others.

When a group has high entitativity, then its members are more likely to identity with it and to be influenced by its other members. Conversely, when entitativity is low in a group, its members are less likely to identify with the group or to be influenced by others in the group (Brewer, 2003; Castano et al., 2003; Dovidio, Glick, & Rudman, 2005; Lickel et al., 2000; Oldmeadow, Platow, & Foddy, 2005). High entitativity is an important indicator of continuous membership loyalty and cooperation (Castano et al., 2003; Lickel et al., 2000).

In-Group Bias

As discussed above, once formed a group tends to manipulate its image by casting itself and its collective enterprises in the best light. This can lead to a biased assessment of in-group versus out-group actions. Members are more likely to see all in-group behaviors as positive (Bartel, Blader, & Wrzesniewski, 2007; Haslam & Ellemers, 2005; Turner & Reynolds, 2008), and although such self-assuring behavior ("We are all okay") has a stabilizing effect within a group, it risks negative stereotypes of those outside it. In-group favoritism of this sort can also put undue pressure for conformity on membership—at the peril of individual identity if it happens to conflict with the group identity (Bartel et al., 2007).

The tendency to pressure membership into conformity can be especially troublesome if the group's favored practices are consistent with societal prejudices outside the workplace (Dovidio et al., 2005). In addition, real or perceived conflict tends to intensify in-group bias, which often leads to category accentuation or the exaggeration of differences between disputing groups that minimize common aspects of the groups and undervalue ways in which they are similar. This kind of polarized thinking easily leads to causal attribution, which is placing the blame for conflict outside oneself or domain (Heider, 1958). One way to prevent polarization of team members is by promoting frequent interactions between groups. See Chapter 11 on conflict management for further discussion of bias and causal attribution.

TEAMWORK

A *team* is a group of individuals who see themselves and who are seen by others as a social entity that is embedded in a larger community or a specific organization, and who perform tasks that affect others, such as customers or co-workers. Members of a team interact dynamically, interdependently, and adaptively to meet shared goals; a team's collective product fulfills a shared common purpose (Ilgen, 1999; Salas & Fiore, 2004; Salas et al., 1992). Teams are often organized around work processes—speeding up cycle times or customer orders, launching a new product, or devising new compensation plans—rather than specific functions such as marketing, production, or sales (Wellins, Byham, & Dixon, 1994). Team members often receive specialized training and may also develop a variety of skills arising from cross-functional training. As a result, instead of doing the same thing over and over, team members can do many different things and can stand in for other members, allowing more individual flexibility while still getting the team's work done. Because teams are largely self-governed, they can roam freely within organizational hierarchies and structures, and in some instances teams may elect their own leadership. Teams are often involved in organization-wide decisions rather than leaving decision making to managers who are often removed from the team's product or service. The idea behind team decision making is "if you do it, you decide it."

Current research and organizational practices reflect confidence in teams to produce superior work (Cannon-Bowers & Bowers, 2011). High-functioning teams make good decisions, are adept at adjusting to change, support membership stress management, and are effective at resolving problems (Bartel et al., 2007). Teamwork affords the workplace many advantages to the traditional function-focused organizational structure. Team success depends on members having sufficient freedom and autonomy to contribute to individual goal attainment while collectively coordinating efforts to retain focus on overarching goals and also accommodating change within and outside the collaborative.

Types of Teams

There are many classification schemes for team types that are based on a team's primary mission, purpose, or charge (Cannon-Bowers & Bowers, 2011). For example, work teams focus on accomplishing the tasks of the organization, which might cause them to be labeled production teams or a customer service teams. Another dimension that determines the type of team is its life cycle. For example, some teams are created for a finite or fixed period of time—for example, an organization might establish a space and facilities team to deal with facility challenges during a period of concentrated and extensive construction. Other teams are created for unlimited periods of time, such as an organizational justice or workplace climate teams. In contrast, task forces (such as *quality circles*) are created for the primary purpose of solving specific problems; these are temporary groups that have a specified mandate and that are disbanded when the task is completed.

Teamwork, which is often independently governed and self-generated, depends on healthy relations and cooperation. To achieve cooperation among its membership, a team must be comfortable with the production process and its members must be satisfied with the team's services or products (see Figure 7.1).

Winning Team Formula

The winning formula for quality teamwork involves (1) well-defined goals, (2) relevant knowledge, (3) individual self-efficacy, (4) collective efficacy, (5) the ability to resolve conflict, and (6) management support in the form of social and financial capital (Leach, Wall, Rogelberg, & Jackson, 2005; Stevens & Campion, 1999). Quality teamwork benefits most by articulated goals, the knowledge needed for task completion, belief in one's self, and belief in the team's capacity for accomplishing a given task (Salas & Fiore, 2004; Tasa, Taggar, & Seijts, 2007). For these reasons, each member of the team needs to possess knowledge of the team's goal, understand the specifications of its tasks, and have the necessary skills to complete assignments. This requires ongoing information sharing and timely feedback, because a team's accomplishments depend on two-way communication. Frequent dialogue among members of a team ensures that vital information known to individual members is shared with the other team members. Tasa and colleagues (2007) refer to this process as the provision of "relevant knowledge," or the knowledge needed for quality task completion.

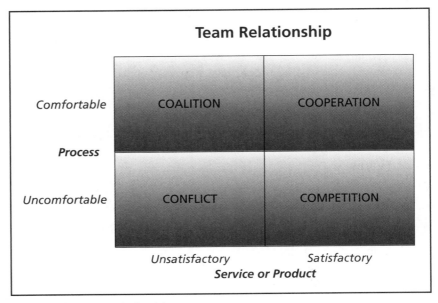

FIGURE 7.1 Team Relationship.

Interpersonal knowledge, skills, and abilities in key areas, namely conflict resolution, collaborative problem-solving, and communication, are essential for consistent quality teamwork. Expertise in these knowledge, skills, and abilities (KSAs) also enhances efficiency and lowers team member stress levels (Leach et al., 2005; Stevens & Campion, 1999).

Consistent team productivity depends on operational systems that insure full access to feedback from within and outside the team. This means that all members must have access to information that is relevant and current. Members must observe other team members using this shared knowledge, and each member must observe the others applying the knowledge to confirm comprehension of shared knowledge (Tasa et al., 2007).

Team Cognition

Team cognition is a shared mental representation of a team's work, which includes the process that developed the collective knowledge and its domain (or outcome) of that knowledge. Sometimes referred to as a *team mental model*, team cognition results from interaction among members who convey their individual perspectives to the team, or who collectively participate in education intended to develop each member's knowledge and enhance the team's effectiveness (Mohammed, Ferzandi, & Hamilton, 2010). Salas and Fiore (2004) and Kozlowski and Ilgen (2006) explain that common understanding and congruence—compatibility or agreement at individual and collective levels—is essential to develop a useful shared mental model. Accuracy of a shared mental model is assessed by the amount of overlap among team members' thoughts and mental representations. To work effectively, team members must know the structure of the problems that underlie their tasks along with the roles and skills of the members of the team as they pertain to the problem, and there also must be a shared awareness that each member of the team possesses this knowledge about the problems and the tools they have to solve them. Shared problem understanding is an important first step in teamwork, because a problem defined is a problem half-solved. The team's negotiation of the problem facilitates the clarity and utility of their shared mental model as well as its strategies for solving the challenges they face (Kozlowski & Ilgen, 2006; Levine, Resnick, & Higgins, 1993; Salas & Fiore, 2004).

Team learning can be likened to building a castle with blocks—as the stacked blocks become walls and the walls are constructed next to one another, the image of the castle-in-the-making becomes clear to the castle builders, which in turn facilitates building the remainder of the castle. Team cognition is organized thought that gives meaning to stimuli and mental models regarding some aspect of the team's work, such as the interpersonal teamwork processes or team's task strategy. The extent to which the team's mental model is shared influences the improvement of the team's performance. The full experience of feelings, behaviors, and cognitions shared among team members is called team member schema similarity or TMSS (Rentsch, Waehr, Salas, & Fiore, 2004). Team cognition, the common understanding among employees, unites teams in shared fundamental assumptions, interpretations, and beliefs. Team cognition or shared learning can be measured by the degree to which each of these three components is congruent with the others (Salas & Fiore, 2004).

As stated earlier, ongoing organizational support is essential for effective teamwork, whether measured by the group's outputs, the consequences the group has for its members, or the enhancement of the team's capacities to perform effectively in the future. It is also important for team members to be aware of the potential for pitfalls faced by teams whose members become so interdependent that their shared cognitive representation of the world is distorted by in-group bias tendencies, and as a result, lacks objectivity about their work and the world around them.

Self-Efficacy and Collective Efficacy

Self-efficacy is a person's judgment of his or her capacity to organize and execute a designated course of action. It focuses on what a person believes is possible, given the skills and talent required for a specific task. Self-efficacy influences how a person manages resources, plans and strategizes work, exerts effort for group endeavors, and responds to failure, as well as affecting how vulnerable the person is to discouragement (Bandura, 1982, 2006a, 2006b). Self-efficacy is reinforced by (1) personal success or mastery, (2) observing a trainer model the target behaviors, and/or (3) specific and realistic praise and feedback about performance (Tasa et al., 2007).

Collective efficacy describes confidence in ones' group or team, believing that it has the capacity to perform a task or reach a goal. As a group product, collective efficacy is born of interactive experience, developing partly through exchanges of information and observed behaviors while interacting and communicating. This accumulated group confidence is influenced by the aggregate amount of cooperative behaviors in a team. Early success may give the team the greatest boost of self-confirmation (Tasa et al., 2007). Collective efficacy also becomes new input to subsequent group work and outcomes, and it can increase the team's ability to accomplish even greater successes. Team support by management strengthens collective efficacy (Choi & Chang, 2009). When performance feedback is directed to the team as a whole, the contextual role of collective efficacy as it relates to individual behavior is strongest (Marks, Mathieu, & Zaccaro, 2001; Tasa et al., 2007).

It is important to distinguish between group potency and collective efficacy. Group potency is a group's enduring ability to perform a wide range of tasks across different activities, whereas collective efficacy is linked to specific tasks. The two concepts are related—the stronger the group potency, the greater the collective efficacy, and vice versa. Group potency and collective efficacy are both positively related to group performance, but collective efficacy more predictably indicates relationship strength (Stajkovic, Lee, & Nyberg, 2009).

Challenges to Quality Teamwork

Workplace-based teams need to know they have the support of management to resolve conflict and generate innovative practices for overcoming obstacles encountered along the way. This support must include adequate social and financial resources to secure quality team support (Porter, 2005; Purvis, Sambamurthy, &

Zmud, 2001; Rogers, 2003; Russell & Hoag, 2004; Tasa et al., 2007). In addition, team performance is enhanced by (1) routinely revisiting goals to ensure continuity of focus and commitment, (2) providing a learning orientation that sees ability as malleable and renewable, and (3) offering support for development and perpetuation of collective efficacy and innovation (Rogers, 2003). Finally, teams need be porous enough to allow resources and information in while remaining resistant to uncertainty about who is on the team and whether these members are accountable for its collective outcomes (Faraj & Yan, 2009). But even when all of these supports are in place, there are several predictable barriers to progress. Following is a list of some of the common challenges you may encounter when working with teams. Each challenge is accompanied by suggestions for addressing them in ways that will help you restore balance and productivity to your teamwork.

1. **Your team hits a rough patch caused in large part by a recent round of layoffs, and morale suffers as a result.** Work and self-image are so closely linked that threats to job security—whether triggered by layoffs or negative performance evaluations—easily translate into attacks on individual employee self-image. When this happens, employee morale sags, work commitment is lowered, and performance suffers (Bartel et al., 2007; Hogg & Terry, 2001).

    Potential Remedies

    • Take measures to enhance the salience of work and collective identity. Strong team identity energizes membership, builds loyalty to the team and the organization (Lickel et al., 2000) and optimizes group performance (Bandura, 2006b).
    • Build proactive support systems to keep employees in step with ever-changing workplace realities, because the more intense the situational turmoil, the greater the need for the self-organization or learning (Hogg & Terry, 2001; Schein, 2004).
    • View change as an opportunity for self-renewal. In the past employees learned a given trade and stayed with it for life, often in the same organization (Juran, 1992), but today's employees must deal with steady change, because knowledge and technical skills are quickly outmoded and workers must frequently update their skills to fit new conditions and evolving technologies.
    • Since interpersonal and task conflict negatively affect performance and satisfaction with the group experience, it is important for management to be reasonably sensitive to employee's emotional needs as well as to professional development (Rogers, 2003; Stevens & Campion, 1999).

2. **You discover that interorganizational collaboration increases the resource pool for addressing complex needs, but it also places novel demands on every participant.** Collaborative initiatives require careful planning and tough up-front decision making, particularly if goals are ambitious and delegated roles are not well defined. By its very nature, interorganizational collaboration unites a hodgepodge of professional people who vary widely in expertise because they bring a variety of knowledge, experience, and educational backgrounds to the team. Finding a common voice to facilitate

building consensus can be a daunting task, particularly when professionals limit communications to include only those people who share a common knowledge base—a well-documented phenomenon. This tendency to withhold information from people who do not possess similar knowledge and skills makes it highly likely that vital information will be withheld from team members who will potentially gain the most from it, and productivity will suffer as a consequence of this lack of collaborative communication (Mesmer-Magnus & DeChurch, 2009).

Potential Remedies

- Developing a shared vision and mission is a necessary first step for transcending multiteam systems into a united front. Next steps include collective goal setting, new task assignment, in-depth role clarity, and equitable evaluation systems (Marks, DeChurch, Mathieu, Panzer, & Alonso, 2005).
- Workshops fostering effective communication practices, enhanced problem solving, and quality change management can improve collective work experience. Side-by-side learning strengthens relations and builds collective efficacy between the work factions (Moreland & Levine, 2000).
- Utilize structured discussions around key topics to increase the common knowledge base by generating in-depth processing of vital information (Salas et al., 1992; Salas & Fiore, 2004).
- Model and reward a cooperative team climate while promoting accountability through systematic measurement of collective outcomes. Remember to celebrate small accomplishments as well as major triumphs.

3. **Your organization encourages the formation of virtual teams, but you find that this kind of team poses special challenges to maximizing productivity.** Virtual teams are united by their mission, but they are separated by physical distance. This means that team members must use electronic communication—email, Skype, videoconferencing, telephone calls, and so forth—for day-to-day information-sharing and program adjustment. If team members fail to bridge the distances among them, the gaps in time, space, or culture that can occur render them vulnerable to interpersonal stress and system dysfunction. Signs of dysfunction are manifested as low task commitment, role ambiguity, social loafing, and lack of follow-through on assigned tasks (Maruping & Agarwal, 2004).

Potential Remedies

- Distance teamwork is more efficient and productive when members have a greater sense of self-efficacy or collective efficacy. To ensure a higher efficacy level, try to arrange for face-to-face interaction when initially setting up the collaborative effort to sustain the distance management that will follow (Leung & Peterson, 2011).
- When regular communication between team members has been established, it must be supported electronically using portable instruments

such as laptops, cell phones, and Internet access to electronic literature or data sharing. Access to distance technology affords teams many
conveniences, particularly for coordinating schedules with other obli-
gations and interests, but it can strain relations and—interestingly—
communications. Make sure you address signs of strain among team
members as soon as they are apparent.
- Management of virtual teams needs to focus on three key interpersonal processes: (1) conflict management, (2) motivation and
  confidence building, and (3) management of emotions (Maruping &
  Agarwal, 2004).

4. **Your organization encourages fierce competitiveness, and you are
   concerned that teamwork is suffering in this competition-entrenched
   culture.** It is widely believed that teams do better work than individual
   employees in many situations. Teams are perceived as more flexible, more
   creative, and more productive. To achieve this creativity and productivity,
   however, teams operate in a context populated with fiercely individualistic,
   competitive, and "win-lose" habits. In such an environment, the focus is
   often on protecting individual turf and distrusting outside forces (Kohn,
   1992, 1999; Salas & Fiore, 2004, p. 84). To counter such tendencies, remember that teamwork requires reaching outside ourselves to strengthen relations with others, to try on ideas generated by team members, to find
   consensus, and above all, to cooperate (Levine, Choi, & Moreland, 2003). If
   the competitive mind-set is too entrenched in an organization, it may damage employee relations and stifle production. A recent study demonstrated
   that while low to moderate interorganizational competition increases group
   identity and members' identification with the group, a highly competitive
   work environment tends to interfere with group identity and is associated
   with feelings of alienation (Spataro & Chatman, 2007).

   ### Potential Remedies

   - Reward the successful outcome of the team rather than individual
     employee success.
   - Set the bar high to tap intrinsic motivation (Gellatly & Meyer, 1992).
   - Foster a learning culture and promote continuous learning—encourage
     team members to learn from their mistakes and from the mistakes of fel-
     low members of their team and other teams (Schein, 2004).
   - Model cooperation and consensus building in your leadership.
   - Strengthen team identity to tap the inherent desire of members for
     connectedness and affiliation.

Chapter Summary

Teams utilize two key elements to attain the
cooperation necessary for quality outcomes: (1) a
shared goal or an understanding of what makes
teamwork interdependent and (2) an appreciation for the role each team member assumes to
coordinate work with the other team members

and maximize group synergy. We explained in this chapter that optimal cooperation is attained when integrity is intact or that which makes the unit unique is in balance. Individual integrity requires intragroup receptivity to feedback exchange, and the higher the group entitativity or confidence, the better the communication needed to keep individuals and the group in balance. Therefore, we advise teams to maintain high entitativity as a priority for quality teamwork, which is sustained through strong relations, full team engagement, and management support.

Chapter References

Ashforth, B. E., & Johnson, S. A. (2001). Which hat to wear? The relative salience of multiple identities in organizational contexts. In M. A. Hogg & D. J. Terry (Eds.), *Social identity processes in organizational contexts* (pp. 31–48). Philadelphia: Psychology Press.

Ashforth, B. E., & Mael, F. A. (1996). Organizational identity and strategy as a context for the individual. In J. A. C. Baum & J. E. Dutton (Eds.), *Advances in strategic management* (Vol. 13, pp. 19–64). Greenwich, CT: JAI Press.

Bandura, A. (1982). Self-efficacy mechanism in human agency. *American Psychologist, 37*(2), 122–147. doi:10.1037/0003-066X.37.2.122

Bandura, A. (2006a). Going global with social cognitive theory: From prospect to paydirt. In S. I. Donaldson, D. E. Berger, & K. Pezdek (Eds.), *The rise of applied psychology: New frontiers and rewarding careers* (pp. 53–70). Mahwah, NJ: Lawrence Erlbaum.

Bandura, A. (2006b). Toward a psychology of human agency. *Perspectives on Psychological Science, 1*(2), 164–180. doi:10.1111/j.1745-6916.2006.00011.x

Bartel, C., Blader, S. L., & Wrzesniewski, A. (2007). *Identity and the modern organization*. Mahwah, NJ: Lawrence Erlbaum.

Baumeister, R. F., & Leary, M. R. (1995). The need to belong: Desire for interpersonal attachments as a fundamental human motivation. *Psychological Bulletin, 117*(3), 497–529. doi:10.1037/0033-2909.117.3.497

Brewer, M. B. (2003). *Intergroup relations* (2nd ed.). Maidenhead, UK: Open University Press.

Brewer, M. B., & Miller, N. (1996). *Intergroup relations*. Buckingham, UK: Open University Press.

Campbell, D. T. (1958). Common fate, similarity, and other indices of the status of aggregates of persons as social entities. *Behavioral Science, 3*(3), 14–25.

Cannon-Bowers, J. A., & Bowers, C. (Eds.). (2011). *Team development and functioning* (Vol. 1). Washington, DC: American Psychological Association.

Castano, E., Yzerbyt, V., & Bourguignon, D. (2003). We are one and I like it: The impact of ingroup entitativity on ingroup identification. *European Journal of Social Psychology, 33*(6), 735–754. doi:10.1002/ejsp.175

Chen, Z., & Lawson, R. B. (1996). Groupthink: Deciding with the leader and the devil. *Psychological Record, 46*(4), 581.

Choi, J. N., & Chang, J. Y. (2009). Innovation implementation in the public sector: An integration of institutional and collective dynamics. *Journal of Applied Psychology, 94*(1), 245–253.

Dovidio, J. F., Glick, P., & Rudman, L. A. (2005). *On the nature of prejudice: Fifty years after Allport*. Malden, MA: Blackwell.

Faraj, S., & Yan, A. (2009). Boundary work in knowledge teams. *Journal of Applied Psychology, 94*(3), 604–617. doi:10.1037/a0014367

Gellatly, I. R. & Meyer, J. P. (1992). The effects of goal difficulty on physiological arousal on physiological arousal, cognition, and task performance, *Journal of Applied Psychology, 77*, 694–704.

Gersick, C. (1988). Time and transition in work teams: Toward a new model of group development. *Academy of Management Journal, 31*, 9–14.

Gersick, C. (1991). Revolutionary change theories: A multilevel exploration of the punctuated equilibrium paradigm. *Academy of Management Review, 16*(1), 10–36.

Gómez, A., Seyle, C., Huici, C. & Swann, W. B., Jr., (2009). Can self-verification strivings fully transcend the self-other barrier? Seeking verification of ingroup identities. *Journal of Personality and Social Psychology, 97,* 1021–1044.

Goodman, P. S., & Leyden, D. P. (1991). Familiarity and group productivity. *Journal of Applied Psychology, 76*(4), 578–586. doi:10.1037/0021-9010.76.4.578

Harris, M. (1979). *Cultural materialism: The struggle for a science of culture* (1st ed.). New York: Random House.

Haslam, S. A., & Ellemers, N. (2005). Social identity in industrial and organizational psychology: Concepts, controversies and contributions. In G. P. Hodgkinson (Ed.), *International review of industrial and organizational psychology* (Vol. 20, pp. 39–118). Chichester, England: Wiley.

Heider, F. (1958). *The psychology of interpersonal relations.* New York: John Wiley.

Hogg, M. A., Sherman, D. K., Dierselhuis, J., Maitner, A. T., & Moffitt, G. (2006). Uncertainty, entitativity, and group identification. *Journal of Experimental Social Psychology, 43*(1), 135–142.

Hogg, M. A., & Terry, D. J. (2001). *Social identity processes in organizational contexts.* Philadelphia: Psychology Press.

Ilgen, D. R. (1999). Teams embedded in organizations: Some implications. *American Psychologist, 54*(2), 129–139.

Juran, J. M. (1992). *Juran on quality by design: The new steps for planning quality into goods and services.* New York: Free.

Kohn, A. (1992). *No contest: The case against competition* (Rev. ed.). Boston: Houghton Mifflin.

Kohn, A. (1999). *Punished by rewards: The trouble with gold stars, incentive plans, A's, praise, and other bribes.* Boston: Houghton Mifflin.

Kozlowski, S. W. J., Gully, S. M., Nason, E. R., & Smith, E. M. (1999). Developing adaptive teams: A theory of compilation and performance across levels and time. In D. R. Ilgen & E. D. Pulakos (Eds.), *The changing nature of performance: Implications for staffing, motivation, and development* (pp. 240–292). San Francisco: Jossey-Bass.

Kozlowski, S. W. J., & Ilgen, D. R. (2006). Enhancing the effectiveness of work groups and teams. *Psychological Science in the Public Interest, 7*(3), 77–124.

Lawson, R. B., Graham, J. E., & Baker, K. M. (2007). *A history of psychology: Globalization, ideas, and applications.* Upper Saddle River, NJ: Pearson Prentice Hall.

Leach, D. J., Wall, T. D., Rogelberg, S. G., & Jackson, P. R. (2005). Team autonomy, performance, and member job strain: Uncovering the Teamwork KSA Link. *Applied Psychology, 54*(1), 1–24. doi:10.1111/j.1464-0597.2005.00193.x

Leung, K., & Peterson, M. F. (2011). Managing a globally distributed workforce: Social and interpersonal issues. In S. Zedeck (Ed.), *APA handbook of industrial and organizational psychology* (Vol. 3, pp. 771–805). Washington, DC: American Psychological Association.

Levine, J. M., Choi, H. S., & Moreland, R. L. (2003). Newcomer innovation in work teams. In P. Paulus & B. Nijstad (Eds.), *Group creativity: Innovation through collaboration* (pp. 202–224). New York: Oxford University Press.

Levine, J. M., Resnick, L. B., & Higgins, E. T. (1993). Social foundations of cognition. *Annual Review of Psychology, 44,* 585 -612.

Lickel, B., Hamilton, D. L., Wieczorkowska, G., Lewis, A., Sherman, S. J., & Uhles, A. N. (2000). Varieties of groups and the perception of group entitativity. *Journal of Personality and Social Psychology, 78*(2), 223–246. doi:10.1037/0022-3514.78.2.223

Marks, M. A., DeChurch, L. A., Mathieu, J. E., Panzer, F. J., & Alonso, A. (2005). Teamwork in multiteam systems. *Journal of Applied Psychology, 90*(5), 964–971. doi:10.1037/0021-9010.90.5.964

Marks, M. A., Mathieu, J. E., & Zaccaro, S. J. (2001). A temporally based framework and taxonomy of team processes. *The Academy of Management Review, 26*(3), 356–376.

Maruping, L. M., & Agarwal, R. (2004). Managing team interpersonal processes through technology: A task-technology fit perspective. *Journal of Applied Psychology, 89*(6), 975–990. doi:10.1037/0021-9010.89.6.975

Merton, R. K. (1967). *Social theory and social structure* (Rev. ed.). New York: Free Press.

Mesmer-Magnus, J. R., & DeChurch, L. A. (2009). Information sharing and team performance: A meta-analysis. *Journal of Applied Psychology, 94*(2), 535–546. doi:10.1037/a0013773

Mohammed, S., Ferzandi, L., & Hamilton, K. (2010). Metaphor no more: A 15-year review of the team mental model construct. *Journal of Management, 36*(4), 876–910.

Moreland, R. L. (1987). The formation of small groups. In C. Hendrick (Ed.), *Group processes* (Vol. 8, pp. 80–110). Newbury Park, CA: Sage.

Moreland, R. L., & Levine, J. M. (2000). Socialization in organizations and work groups. In M. Turner (Ed.), *Groups at work: Theory and research* (pp. 69–112). Mahwah, NJ: Erlbaum.

Myers, S., & Anderson, C. (2008). *The fundamentals of small group communication*. Los Angeles: Sage.

Oldmeadow, J., Platow, M. J., & Foddy, M. (2005). Task-groups as self-categories: A social identity perspective on status generalization. *Current Research in Social Psychology, 10*(18), 268–282.

Porter, C. O. L. H. (2005). Goal orientation: Effects on backing up behavior, performance, efficacy, and commitment in teams. *Journal of Applied Psychology, 90*(4), 811–818. doi:10.1037/0021-9010.90.4.811

Purvis, R. L., Sambamurthy, V., & Zmud, R. W. (2001). The assimilation of knowledge platforms in organizations: An empirical investigation. *Organization Science, 12*(2), 117–135. doi:10.1287/orsc.12.2.117.10115

Rentsch, J. R., Woehr, D. J., Salas, E., & Fiore, S. M. (2004). Quantifying congruence in cognition: Social relations modeling and team member schema similarity. In Salas, E., & Fiore, S. M. *Team cognition: Understanding the factors that drive process and performance* (pp. 11-31). Washington DC: American Psychological Association.

Rogers, E. M. (2003). *Diffusion of innovations* (5th ed.). New York: Free Press.

Russell, D. M., & Hoag, A. M. (2004). People and information technology in the supply chain: Social and organizational influences on adoption. *International Journal of Physical Distribution & Logistics Management, 34*(2), 102–122. doi:10.1108/09600030410526914

Salas, E., Dickens, C., Converse, P. D., & Tannenbaum, S. I. (1992). Toward an understanding of team performance and training. In R. Swezey & E. Salas (Eds.), *Teams: Their training and performance* (pp. 3-29). Washington, DC: American Psychological Association.

Salas, E., & Fiore, S. M. (2004). *Team cognition: Understanding the factors that drive process and performance*. Washington, DC: American Psychological Association.

Schein, E. H. (2004). *Organizational culture and leadership* (4th ed.). San Francisco: Jossey-Bass.

Sluss, D. M., van Dick, R., & Thompson, B. S. (Eds.). (2011). *Role theory in organizations: A relational perspective* (Vol. 1). Washington, DC: American Psychological Association.

Spataro, S. E., & Chatman, J. A. (2007). Identity in the competitive market: The effects of inter-organizational competition on identity-based organizational commitment. In C. Bartel, S. Blader, & A. Wrzesniewski (Eds.), *Identity and the modern organization* (pp. 177–200). Mahwah, NJ: Lawrence Erlbaum.

Stajkovic, A. D., Lee, D., & Nyberg, A. J. (2009). Collective efficacy, group potency, and group performance: Meta-analyses of their relationships, and test of a mediation model. *Journal of Applied Psychology, 94*(3), 814–828. doi:10.1037/a0015659

Stets, J. E., & Burke, P. J. (2000). Identity theory and social identity theory. *Social Psychology Quarterly, 63*(3), 224–237.

Stevens, M. J., & Campion, M. A. (1999). Staffing work teams: Development and validation of a selection test for teamwork settings. *Journal of Management, 25*(2), 207–228.

Stryker, S., & Burke, P. J. (2000). The past, present, and future of an identity theory. *Social Psychology Quarterly Special Issue: The State of Sociological Social Psychology, 63*(4), 284–297.

Tajfel, H., & Turner, J. C. (1979). An integrative theory of intergroup conflict. In W. G. Austin & S. Worchel (Eds.), *Social psychology of intergroup relations* (pp. 33-47). Monterey, CA: Brooks/Cole.

Tajfel, H., & Turner, J. C. (1986). The social identity theory of inter-group behavior. In S. Worchel and L. W. Austin (Eds.), *Psychology of intergroup relations* (pp. 7-24). Chicago: Nelson-Hall.

Tasa, K., Taggar, S., & Seijts, G. H. (2007). The development of collective efficacy in teams: A multilevel and longitudinal perspective. *Journal of Applied Psychology, 92*(1), 17–27. doi:10.1037/0021-9010.92.1.17

Tuckman, B. W. (1965). Developmental sequence in small groups. *Psychological Bulletin, 63*(6), 384–399. doi:10.1037/h0022100

Tuckman, B. W., & Jensen, M. A. (1977). Stages of small-group development revisited. *Group and Organization Studies, 2*(4), 419–426.

Turner, J. C., & Reynolds, K. J. (2008). The social identity perspective in intergroup relations: Theories, themes, and controversies. In

R. Brown & S. L. Gaertner (Eds.), *Blackwell handbook of social psychology: Intergroup processes.* Oxford, UK: Blackwell.

von Bertalanffy, L. (1969). *General system theory: Foundations, development, applications.* New York: George Braziller.

Wellins, R. S., Byham, W. C., & Dixon, G. R. (1994). *Inside teams: How 20 world-class organizations are winning through teamwork.* San Francisco: Jossey-Bass.

Wheelan, S. A. (2004). *Group processes: A developmental perspective* (2nd ed.). Boston: Allyn & Bacon.

Motivation and Productivity at Work

CHAPTER OVERVIEW

What motivates people to reach their goals? This question has inspired an interesting body of research. In this chapter, we review the research by summarizing some of the early theories that laid a foundation for current thinking about motivation. In organizational contexts, we find it useful to think about motivation in individuals and in groups. We present a list of practical motivational tools that are inexpensive, are relatively easy to implement, and can be combined to form customized interventions to enhance productivity.

    Self-regulation is presented as a robust psychological process for building confidence and increasing motivation that is easy to use and gets things done. The chapter

Amy Strycula/Alamy

concludes with a brief survey of research on self-defeating behaviors that can threaten to derail constructive participation in the workforce.

LEARNING OBJECTIVES

When you have finished reading this chapter, you will be prepared to do the following:

- Define motivation and identify the forces that influence motivational levels, making it possible for people to directly influence their own levels of motivation
- Define and explain some traditional and contemporary theories of workplace motivation
- Discuss the potent and valuable motivational tactics of self-fulfilling prophecies and learned industriousness
- Identify several ways to enhance workplace motivation
- Explain the relationship between mood and productivity
- Discuss research on self-defeating behaviors, such as social loafing and procrastination, that derail constructive participation in the workforce

INTRODUCTION TO MOTIVATION

It is fair to say that most people enjoy challenging work, although everyone periodically encounter barriers that reduce or eliminate the initiation and the sustained pursuit of workplace goals. Most of the time, these barriers are a

Kurhan/Fotolia

combination of internal and external forces. An important feature of motivation is its ability to be self-directed; that is, you can influence your own levels of motivation as well as responding to external forces. The information you need to assess your motivation involves the degree of encouragement you are receiving from *your* environment—how much autonomy, competence, and relatedness you have to other people in specific workplace settings. When you have this kind of information, you can then select an appropriate level of motivation for particular situations at work.

There are hundreds of definitions of *motivation*, and almost all of them focus on the initiation, direction, and maintenance of behaviors toward a goal or set of goals (Diefendorff & Chandler, 2011; Steers & Porter, 1991). Recent research into motivational processes demonstrates the importance of self-regulation for understanding how factors inside and outside the person enhance or deter motivated behaviors and cognitive processes essential for goal achievement (Boekaerts, Maes, & Karoly, 2005; Diefendorff & Chandler, 2011; Shell & Husman, 2008; Vancouver, More, & Yoder, 2008). We define motivation as forces within (dispositional or endogenous) or outside (situational or exogenous) of a person that are adjusted by self-regulation to initiate, direct, and sustain actions toward a goal or set of goals. Figure 8.1 presents the general pattern of motivational components that everyone experiences. These include factors from within the person, which are the endogenous forces of motivation such as needs or expectations, as well as factors outside the person, the exogenous forces of motivation such as a tense, conflict-ridden workplace. These forces give rise to actions, thoughts, and feelings—or combinations of these three outcomes—in pursuit of a goal. These outcomes in turn impact the motivational forces that initiated the cycle in the first place.

An important feature of this conceptualization of motivation is that both internal and environmental forces contribute to our level of motivaiton. There

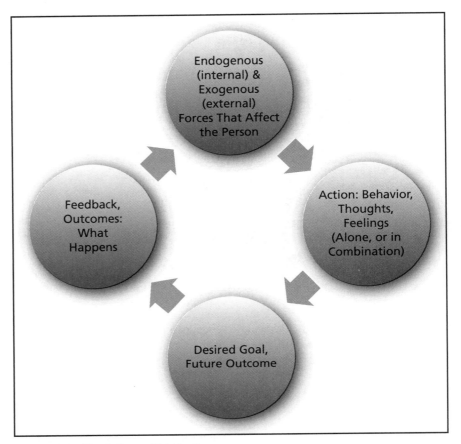

FIGURE 8.1   The Pattern of Motivation.

are also forces that undermine motivation, including demotivating organizational environments, which can dampen individual performance. Such environments can produce what's known as *learned helplessness,* a sort of action paralysis
(Bacharach, Bamberger, & Doveh, 2008; Schaubroeck, Jones, & Xie, 2001). When
this happens, even high levels of motivation are thwarted by the organizational
systems that reinforce the strategy of doing little if any work. Later in this chapter, we will discuss steps you can take to prevent and correct these problems.

THEORIES OF MOTIVATION

Motivation at work is a complex phenomenon, and you can no longer assume
that people will work harder when given higher pay, greater responsibilities,
or higher positions in the organizational hierarchy—the happy worker may not
always be a good worker (Gendolla & Krüsken, 2002). In addition, some employees in the United States may not be motivated by the same things that effectively
motivate workers in Asia or Europe (Erez, 2011). As a consequence, researchers have proposed a number of theories to explain workplace motivation and

TABLE 8-1	Maslow's Hierarchy of Needs	
Levels of Needs	**General Rewards**	**Organizational Rewards**
Physiological	Food, water, sex, rest	Pay and fringe benefits
Safety	Safety, security, stability, protection	Safe working conditions, job security
Social	Love, affection, belongingness	Cohesive work group, friendly supervision, membership
Self-esteem	Self-esteem, self-respect, prestige, status	Social recognition, job title, feedback from customers
Self-actualization	Growth, advancement, creativity	A challenging job, opportunities for creativity, achievement in work, advancement in the organization

Source: Maslow, 1943; 1954.

to predict worker productivity. These theories vary in emphasis: some place greater weight on the value of individuals defining higher-order goals (Covey, 2004); others specify procedures for organizing and attending to the details of day-to-day effort (Allen, 2001).

Maslow's Need Hierarchy

Abraham Maslow, a clinically oriented psychologist, proposed that our human needs could be divided into five levels and arranged in order of importance (Maslow, 1943, 1954). He believed that people do not address the higher level needs (self-esteem and self-actualization) until their basic lower level needs are first satisfied (see Table 8-1, which lists the hierarchy of needs Maslow identified).

Maslow's theory is intuitively appealing, although it has not received much direct testing and may not stand up to rigorous scrutiny (Kohn, 1999). It is based largely on abstract theorizing and clinical practice, mostly with female clients (Koltko-Rivera, 2006). Probably the most durable aspect of Maslow's original formulation that relates to employee motivation is that various employees in an organization may operate at different levels of the needs hierarchy, and therefore managers must be aware of the diversity of needs and have access to appropriate resources to address the different needs.

Equity Theory

An equity theory of motivation was first proposed by Adams (1963; Trevor & Wazeter, 2006). It focuses primarily on the ratio or comparison of inputs (or *I*, what the member brings and puts into the job—specific skills, talents, or extra work effort) and outputs (*O*, what the member gets out of an organization—things like pay, advancement opportunities, and non-pay benefits). Equity exists when individuals believe that they are getting as much out of an organization as they are putting in. However, this perceived equity is always based on a point of reference—a comparable colleague (for self-comparison) or a comparable organization (for measuring one's workplace). Just as an organizational member compares himself with other members of the organization, so too does he make choices involving alternative courses of action based on expected or future outcomes (Pinder, 1984; Trevor & Wazeter, 2006).

Self-Determination Theory

In the early 1970s, Deci found that if people were paid to do what they enjoyed, they tended to lose interest faster than when the activities were not rewarded (Deci, 1971, 1972, 1975). Deci and Ryan (1985) proposed that when employees feel controlled by external forces, their subjective experience is diminished and degraded: they feel they are being bribed. These researchers went on to develop a theory proposing that intrinsic motivation (a subjective sense of reward or pleasure) is an expression of a deeper need for self-determination (choice) and competence (personal efficacy). Deci and Ryan believe that intrinsic motivation arises primarily from choice, and to a lesser extent from controllability (Deci & Ryan, 2008). In addition, it appears that choice is an important moderator of what is sometimes called *flow*, which is the affective, feeling, or experiential side, compared with the behavioral or performance side of motivation. We will discuss flow later in this chapter.

Self-determination theory (SDT) proposes that people want to have control over their actions, and anything that compromises that sense of control will lead to reduced motivation. For example, if you volunteer to take care of a work colleague's pet while she is out of town for a few days on a business trip because you enjoy animals, then your actions have been freely chosen and reflect intrinsic motivation. But if this friend asks you to look after his pet while he is away on a trip a few months later, and he offers to pay you $200, you may feel that the task you previously enjoyed now feels more like an obligation than a freely chosen activity. The money or extrinsic motivator has restricted your autonomy or freedom of choice.

According to self-determination theory, humans are inherently proactive and seek out growth opportunities and integrated functioning that require sustained effort (Deci & Ryan, 2002; Deci & Vansteenkiste, 2004). SDT is built on three universal innate needs—autonomy, competence, and relatedness. *Autonomy* is the universal desire to be the causal agent of what happens in one's own life, *competence* is the ability to control outcomes and experience mastery, and *relatedness* refers to interacting, being connected with, and caring for others.

In critiquing Deci and Ryan's work, Meyer and Maltin (2010) stress the importance of distinguishing between liking an activity for its own sake and liking it because it makes one feel competent. They believe that if intrinsic motivation is eliminated by such factors as incentives and rewards, competition, imposed goals, deadlines, pressure, and so on, then it probably does not have much application to real organizational life (Meyer & Maltin, 2010).

Csikszentmihalyi and Csikszentmihalyi (1988) and colleagues (Nakamura & Csikszentmihalyi, 2002; Seligman & Csikszentmihalyi, 2000) observed people experiencing autotelic or flow experience across a diverse range of difficult and enjoyable activities. Flow arises when the challenge level of a task matches an individual's skill level. Mismatched levels of challenge and skill induce anxiety if the challenge level of a task exceeds an individual's skill level but can lead to boredom if an individual's skill level is much higher than the task challenge. If both the challenge and the skill level are low, an individual may react with apathy or indifference to the assigned task (Csikszentmihalyi & LeFevre, 1989). Thus, managers need to pay close attention to finding good matches between an employee's skill set and the challenges of different tasks to promote high and enjoyable productivity.

Goal Setting

In general, a *goal* is a desired state or object that a person seeks to attain at some point in the future. According to Locke and Latham, goals are immediate regulators of task performance (Latham & Locke, 1979, 2007; Locke & Latham, 2002). In other words, goals greatly influence task performance. Across a variety of organizations and managerial levels, Locke and Latham found that goal setting yields median performance improvements in both quantity and quality of 16%, with a range of 2% to 57.5% above the pre–goal setting performance level. Two consistent findings in the many hundreds of field-based and laboratory studies of goal setting are as follows:

- Increasing goal difficulty is translated almost directly into higher performance levels. Assuming that they are accepted, challenging goals yield greater effort and persistence, with satisfaction arising from higher levels of performance.
- Goals that are specific and difficult yield higher levels of performance than vague, non-quantitative goals such as "do your best" or being given no assigned goal. In general, people welcome challenging, realistic, and specific goals compared to easy, impossible, or unspecified goals.

Table 8-2 presents a brief outline of the components and steps of goal setting, some of the reasons for the effectiveness of establishing goals, and some of the potential pitfalls.

Not only does goal setting directly influence an individual's goal-related performance, but group goals also improve group performances (Diefendorff & Chandler, 2011). For example, in a laboratory-based study, Weingart (1992) found that increasing group goal difficulty increased effort, which also led to increased performance. Success with more complex tasks increased performance because they elicited more high-quality planning and more effort. In a field-based study of work teams, Pritchard , Jones, Roth, Stuebing, and Ekeberg (1988) found that group-level goal-performance feedback, goal setting, and incentives increased productivity from 50% to 76%, compared to an eight-month baseline observation period. More recently, Colbert and Witt (2009) found that goal-focused leaders were especially effective with workers who scored high on conscientiousness, particularly when leaders presented goals that were consistent with the organization overall philosophy, mission, and vision.

Goal setting also works with individuals (Locke & Latham, 2002; Schleicher, Hansen, & Fox, 2011). For simple tasks, the technique tends to encourage

TABLE 8-2   Goal Setting

The components of goal setting

Decide on a specific and challenging goal.

Determine a standard for measuring goal-related performance.

Provide for specific and systematic goal-related performance feedback.

Introduce incentives and rewards for goal accomplishment.

Recalibrate or reset goals based on feedback.

Steps to setting goals

Specify the goal.

Specify how performance will be measured using the following:

Temporal units, e.g., time to goal

Physical units, e.g., number of items to be made

Resource outcomes, e.g., cost cutting measures

Behavioral observation scales, e.g., timely response to customer request

Specify the target to be achieved.

Specify the time to target.

Prioritize goals.

Determine coordination requirements (important for interdependent tasks).

Trust and believe in yourself and others.

Reasons that goal setting is effective

Specific goals direct action or behavior more than a general goal such as "do your best."

Specific goals yield clear expectations.

More challenging goals yield higher performance.

Within limits, people prefer challenging goals.

Ways that goal setting enhances persistence

Goal setting directs attention and action.

Goals mobilizes energy and effort.

Goals help employees develop appropriate task strategies.

Potential pitfalls of goal setting and moderator effects

Excessive risk taking

Stress

Failure

Ignore non-goal areas

Short-range thinking

Dishonesty and cheating

increased effort. Complex individual goals call for and elicit more sophisticated approaches, such as gathering more information and considering alternative strategies (Gilliland & Landis, 1992). When persons are assigned difficult goals, they produce more, experience a stronger sense of self-efficacy (confidence), and even show increased heart rate (Gellatly & Meyer, 1992).

MOTIVATIONAL TOOLS

Perhaps you or other people in your organization find that at times you have a relentless list of tasks or projects, as well as voice mail, email, text messages, letters, memoranda, and reports that keep streaming in and stacking up on your computer screen and your desk, causing you to feel overloaded and overwhelmed. Some of the following motivational tools may be able to assist you and your colleagues in managing your burdensome workload and may even enhance your productivity.

Self-Fulfilling Prophecies

Robert K. Merton (1948) introduced the concept of *self-fulfilling prophecy*, which can be summarized as "what you expect is what you get," whether the expectation is imposed upon or elected by the individual or group. Self-fulfilling prophecies have been studied in a variety of contexts of interpersonal relationships, including educational (Babad, Inbar, & Rosenthal, 1982; Rosenthal, 1973, 2002) and military work setting (Eden & Shani, 1982). There are several types of self-fulfilling prophesies, which we will examine briefly in turn.

In the *Pygmalion effect*, enhanced performance arises when one person (for example, a manager) expects higher performance of another person (a subordinate). In short, if you expect a lot from others at work, that is usually what you will get. Thus, the Pygmalion effect is like goal setting, although perhaps it operates more on a suggestive level, rather than as directly mandated or imposed goals. The Pygmalion effect derives its name from a play by George Bernard Shaw in which a professor bets that he can teach a poor flower girl to speak and act like an upper-class lady. He is successful because the girl rises to meet the expectations of her mentor.

Eden has shown that Pygmalion effects arise within groups as well as with individuals (Eden, 1990; Eden & Ravid, 1982). In a meta-analysis of 17 studies, McNatt (2000) found that Pygmalion effects are stronger for men in military settings or when initial expectations are low. However, in a more recent study, Natanovich and Eden (2008) were able to experimentally elicit the effect regardless of the gender of the supervisor or the employee. Eden and colleagues (Davidson & Eden, 2000) have shown that the opposite may be true as well: in the *Golem effect*, low expectations lead to low levels of performance (Babad et al., 1982). Thus, it is beneficial to expect more rather than less of others as well as oneself as we will next see with the Galatea effect.

The *Galatea effect* is another form of the self-fulfilling prophecy. In this case, an individual raises her own self-expectations for specific performances rather than relying on another person, such as a manager (Eden & Kinnar, 1991) or teacher (Jussim, 1986), to set expectations. The name of this type of self-fulfilling prophesy comes from an updated telling of the original myth of Pygmalion, about a sculptor who creates a statue that comes to life. Galatea, the living statue, believed herself to be as good as any living human, and so she was. When others expect more of you (Pygmalion) or you expect more of yourself (Galatea), your performance improves without any increases in salary or other external resources.

Learned Industriousness

To understand why people's tendencies toward hard work vary so much, Eisenberger (1992) developed a model of learned industriousness. It proposes that people become industrious as a result of the secondary reinforcing properties of working hard, achieving a challenging goal, and enjoying the experience. Thus, in an organizational setting, flow and learned industriousness can be enhanced if members are afforded autonomy whenever possible. A test of Eisenberger's learned industrious model (Converse & DeShon, 2009) found that a consistently challenging and demanding organizational context may encourage adaptation and self-regulation. In this sort of environment, people are likely to learn and apply strategies to maintain a level of productivity that is equal to organizational expectations.

ENHANCING MOTIVATION

Although employees expect to be paid fairly for their work, there are other things besides a higher salary that may be able to enhance their motivation and outcomes. These other methods might include pursuing authentic relationships with colleagues by working on a team or challenging oneself to take on a solo project for the pleasure of taking on unique and engrossing independent work. To increase appreciation for a seemingly meaningless task, one employee may challenge herself to understand how completion of this task fits into the larger whole; another may consult his supervisor to help understand the relevance of his task to the organization's larger purpose (McKnight & Kashdan, 2009).

Climb the Ladder to Success

Koo and Fishbach (2008, 2010) recommend viewing goal attainment as a sequence or ladder, since progress toward greater accomplishments is much more likely when current pursuits are seen as preparatory—a means to an end. This self-induced state of detachment from immediate rewards is utilized by elite experts in sports, performance arts, and scientific research. Across performance domains, the best of the best uniformly frame their skill-improvement activity or training as their primary motivation and the actual *doing* or performing as a secondary outcome that serves as an opportunity to test the effectiveness of the practice routine (Ericsson & Charness, 1994; Ericsson & Williams, 2007).

Self-Regulation

Baumeister and colleagues (Baumeister & Newman, 1994; Vohs & Heatherton, 2000) recommend thinking about increasing capacity for self-regulation in the workplace by comparing it to building physical strength and endurance—the greater the training, the stronger the outcome (Muraven & Baumeister, 2000). Self-control, in this formulation, is a habit that is reinforced or developed through practice. And like physical fitness, self-control requires incremental change to avoid exhausting or depleting an individual's reserve. In fact, incorporating physical exercise and regular breaks into a regular workday routine is believed to complement demanding tasks and bolster productivity (Diefendorff & Chandler, 2011). Self-control is reinforced and sustained by the regular practice of self-affirmation or the personal acknowledgment of a job well done (Schmeichel & Vohs, 2009).

Mood at Work

It's not just about what you do at work (behavior) or what you know about your work (cognitions)—how you *feel* while working (emotional state) also drives productivity (Carver & Scheier, 1990). Diefendorff and Chandler (2011) reviewed the relationships between emotion (affect), thought (cognition), and behavior (habit) to discover that not surprisingly, a negative mood tends to reduce motivation to work and diminish productivity, whereas a good mood is likely to enhance productivity. In addition, when employees make progress on goal attainment, that progress spurs further action, which eventually leads to ultimate goal attainment, and success usually produces a pleasurable state of mind or mood (Gagne, Ryan, & Deci, 2005).

MOTIVATION DYSFUNCTION

Although researchers are still only speculating about the true motivation driving dysfunctional behaviors such as social loafing or procrastination, the outcome is predictably unsatisfying—inactivity and lack of task follow-through not only compromise work relationships; they also destroy collective efficacy.

Social Loafing

The traditional definition of *social loafing* is the tendency for group members to withhold effort when they think that their individual contributions to a group project cannot be easily discerned (Latané, Williams, & Harkins, 1979). A systems theorist might view social loafing as a form of systems breakdown—the attempt to correct overfunctioning in one the part of the system (caused by an overzealous employee, for example) by underfunctioning in another (as when an employee disengages from goal attainment). Tan and Tan (2008) found that social loafing is less likely to occur when there is visibility and clarity around task assignments (who is to perform which task), task coordination (advance notice about deadlines, clear information about who reports to whom, etc.), and completion (a concept of the ideal product or service). When given support for autonomy, team members often contribute *more* than originally required to complete the work. Greater task visibility yielded greater employee engagement, facilitated group cohesiveness, and significantly increased employee task engagement (Tan & Tan, 2008).

Procrastination

We saved this topic for last—not to procrastinate, but to emphasize that high levels of motivation are possible in an organization, that motivation can be controlled by individual employees, and that it can have a ripple effect on colleagues and units. Employee procrastination, the failure to meet deadlines, threatens organizational stability based on underfunctioning at the employee level, rather than at higher team levels. Procrastination is manifested psychologically at three levels: self-doubt at the emotional level triggers self-efficacy issues at the cognitive level that give rise to task aversion and persistent lack of follow-through at the behavioral level. Procrastination is a perfect example of transactional redundancy (repeating the same behaviors but expecting different results) because habitual task aversion perpetuates an individual's failure to measure up to intended aspirations, thus blocking any sense of accomplishment, and lowering self-efficacy, which initiated the procrastination in the first place (Neenan, 2008), creating a circular and self-perpetuating pattern of procrastination. Kim, Chiu, and Zou (2010) observed that procrastinators possess either too high or too low an opinion of their own abilities.

Students are especially prone to procrastination behaviors (Klassen et al., 2009; Lubbers, Van Der Werf, Kuyper, & Hendriks, 2010), and 15% to 20% of adults perpetuate this conflict-avoidance practice (Steel, 2007). Because of the self-perpetuating nature of procrastination behaviors—continuing to generate negative feedback about lack of follow-through, sinking into low self-esteem and self-doubt—they require intervention to end the downward spiraling motion. Interestingly, people who seek out information about themselves and their performance are less likely to engage in procrastination (Berzonsky & Ferrari, 1996).

Chapter Summary

In this chapter, we first reviewed some of the important models for motivation, including Maslow's hierarchy of human needs, equity, self-determination theory, and goal setting. We then turned our attention to the centrality of goal setting for understanding the relationship between motivation and productivity. We considered various ways that people live up to their own expectations and the expectations of others by means of several different types of self-fulfilling prophecies, referred to as the Pygmalion effect, the Golem effect, and the Galatea effect. We examined the highly subjective but compelling experience of flow, where activity is so engrossing and engaging that time literally seems to fly.

Lastly, we discussed two self-defeating behaviors, social loafing and procrastination, and offered advice for preventing the dynamics that render a workforce vulnerable to these forms of system dysfunction.

Chapter References

Adams, J. S. (1963). Wage inequities, productivity and work quality. *Industrial Relations, 3*, 9–16.

Allen, D. (2001). *Getting things done: The art of stress-free productivity*. New York: Penguin.

Babad, E. Y., Inbar, J., & Rosenthal, R. (1982). Pygmalion, Galatea, and the Golem: Investigations of biased and unbiased teachers. *Journal of Educational Psychology, 74*(4), 459–474. doi:10.1037/0022-0663.74.4.459

Bacharach, S. B., Bamberger, P. A., & Doveh, E. (2008). Firefighters, critical incidents, and drinking to cope: The adequacy of unit-level performance resources as a source of vulnerability and protection. *Journal of Applied Psychology, 93*(1), 155–169.

Baumeister, R. F., & Newman, L. S. (1994). Self-regulation of cognitive inference and decision processes. *Personality and Social Psychology Bulletin, 20*(1), 3–19.

Berzonsky, M. D., & Ferrari, J. R. (1996). Identity orientation and decisional strategies. *Personality and Individual Differences, 20*(5), 597–606.

Boekaerts, M., Maes, S., & Karoly, P. (2005). Self-regulation across domains of applied psychology: Is there an emerging consensus? *Applied Psychology: An International Review, 54*(2), 149–154.

Carver, C. S., & Scheier, M. F. (1990). Origins and functions of positive and negative affect: A control-process view. *Psychological Review, 97*(1), 19–35.

Colbert, A. E., & Witt, L. A. (2009). The role of goal-focused leadership in enabling the expression of conscientiousness. *Journal of Applied Psychology, 94*(3), 790–796. doi:10.1037/a0014187

Converse, P. D., & DeShon, R. P. (2009). A tale of two tasks: Reversing the self-regulatory resource depletion effect. *Journal of Applied Psychology, 94*(5), 1318–1324. doi:10.1037/a0014604

Csikszentmihalyi, M., & Csikszentmihalyi, I. S. (1988). *Optimal experience: Psychological studies of flow in consciousness.* New York: Cambridge University Press.

Csikszentmihalyi, M., & LeFevre, J. (1989). Optimal experience in work and leisure. *Journal of Personality and Social Psychology, 56*(5), 815–822. doi:10.1037/0022-3514.56.5.815

Davidson, O. B., & Eden, D. (2000). Remedial self-fulfilling prophecy: Two field experiments to prevent Golem effects among disadvantaged women. *Journal of Applied Psychology, 85*(3), 386–398. doi:10.1037/0021-9010.85.3.386

Deci, E. L. (1971). Effects of externally mediated rewards on intrinsic motivation. *Journal of Personality and Social Psychology, 18*(1), 105–115. doi:10.1037/h0030644

Deci, E. L. (1972). Intrinsic motivation, extrinsic reinforcement, and inequity. *Journal of Personality and Social Psychology, 22*(1), 113–120. doi:10.1037/h0032355

Deci, E. L. (1975). *Intrinsic motivation.* New York: Plenum.

Deci, E. L., & Ryan, R. M. (1985). *Intrinsic motivation and self-determination in human behavior.* New York: Plenum.

Deci, E., & Ryan, R. (Eds.). (2002). *Handbook of self-determination research.* Rochester, NY: University of Rochester Press.

Deci, E. L., & Ryan, R. M. (2008). Facilitating optimal motivation and psychological well-being across life's domains. *Canadian Psychology/Psychologie canadienne, 49*(1), 14–23.

Deci, E. L., & Vansteenkiste, M. (2004). Self-determination theory and basic need satisfaction: Understanding human development in positive psychology. *Ricerche di Psicologia, 27,* 17–34.

Diefendorff, J. M., & Chandler, M. M. (2011). Motivating employees. In S. Zedeck (Ed.), *APA handbook of industrial and organizational psychology* (Vol. 3, pp. 65–135). Washington, DC: American Psychological Association.

Eden, D. (1990). *Pygmalion in management: Productivity as a self-fulfilling prophecy.* Lexington, MA: Lexington Books.

Eden, D., & Kinnar, J. (1991). Modeling Galatea: Boosting self-efficacy to increase volunteering. *Journal of Applied Psychology, 76*(6), 770–780. doi:10.1037/0021-9010.76.6.770

Eden, D., & Ravid, G. (1982). Pygmalion versus self-expectancy: Effects of instructor- and self-expectancy on trainee performance. *Organizational Behavior and Human Performance, 30*(3), 351–364. doi:10.1016/0030-5073(82)90225-2

Eden, D., & Shani, A. B. (1982). Pygmalion goes to boot camp: Expectancy, leadership, and trainee performance. *Journal of Applied Psychology, 67*(2), 194–199. doi:10.1037/0021-9010.67.2.194

Erez, M. (Ed.). (2011). *Cross-cultural and global issues in organizational psychology* (Vol. 3). Washington, DC: American Psychological Association.

Ericsson, K. A., & Charness, N. (1994). Expert performance: Its structure and acquisition. *American Psychologist, 49*(8), 725–747. doi:10.1037/0003-066X.49.8.725

Ericsson, K. A., & Williams, A. M. (2007). Capturing naturally occurring superior performance in the laboratory: Translational research on expert performance. *Journal of Experimental Psychology: Applied, 13*(3), 115–123. doi:10.1037/1076-898X.13.3.115

Eisenberger, R. (1992). Learned industriousness. *Psychological Review, 99,* 248–267.

Gagne, M., Ryan, A. M., & Deci, E. L. (2005). Self-determination theory and work motivation. *Journal of Organizational Behavior, 26*(4), 331–362. doi:10.1002/job.322

Gellatly, I. R., & Meyer, J. P. (1992). The effects of goal difficulty on physiological arousal, cognition, and task performance. *Journal of Applied Psychology, 77*(5), 694–704. doi:10.1037/0021-9010.77.5.694

Gendolla, G. H. E., & Krüsken, J. (2002). The joint effect of informational mood impact and performance-contingent consequences on effort-related cardiovascular response. *Journal of Personality and Social Psychology, 83*(2), 271–283. doi:10.1037/0022-3514.83.2.271

Gilliland, S. W., & Landis, R. S. (1992). Quality and quantity goals in a complex decision task: Strategies and outcomes. *Journal of Applied Psychology, 77*(5), 672–681. doi:10.1037/0021-9010.77.5.672

Jussim, L. (1986). Self-fulfilling prophecies: A theoretical and integrative review. *Psychological Review, 93*(4), 429–445. doi:10.1037/0033-295X.93.4.429

Kim, Y.-H., Chiu, C.-Y., & Zou, Z. (2010). Know thyself: Misperceptions of actual performance undermine achievement motivation, future performance, and subjective well-being. *Journal of Personality and Social Psychology, 99*(3), 395–409.

Klassen, R. M., Ang, R. P., Chong, W. H., Krawchuk, L. L., Huan, V. S., Wong, I. Y. F., et al. (2009). Academic procrastination in two settings: Motivation correlates, behavioral patterns, and negative impact of procrastination in Canada and Singapore. *Applied Psychology, 59*(3), 361–379. doi:10.1111/j.1464-0597.2009.00394.x

Kohn, A. (1999). *Punished by rewards: The trouble with gold stars, incentive plans, A's, praise, and other bribes.* Boston: Houghton Mifflin.

Koltko-Rivera, M. E. (2006). Rediscovering the later version of Maslow's hierarchy of needs: Self-transcendence and opportunities for theory, research, and unification. *Review of General Psychology, 10*(4), 302–317. doi:10.1037/1089-2680.10.4.302

Koo, M., & Fishbach, A. (2008). Dynamics of self-regulation: How (un)accomplished goal actions affect motivation. *Journal of Personality and Social Psychology, 94*(2), 183–195. doi:10.1037/0022-3514.94.2.183

Koo, M., & Fishbach, A. (2010). Climbing the goal ladder: How upcoming actions increase level of aspiration. *Journal of Personality and Social Psychology, 99*(1), 1–13. doi:10.1037/a0019443

Latané, B., Williams, K., & Harkins, S. (1979). Many hands make light the work: The causes and consequences of social loafing. *Journal of Personality and Social Psychology, 37*(6), 822–832. doi:10.1037/0022-3514.37.6.822

Latham, G. P., & Locke, E. A. (1979). Goal setting: A motivational technique that works. *Organizational Dynamics, 8*(2), 68–80.

Latham, G. P., & Locke, E. A. (2007). New developments in and directions for goal-setting research. *European Psychologist, 12*(4), 290–300. doi:10.1027/1016-9040.12.4.290

Locke, E. A., & Latham, G. P. (2002). Building a practically useful theory of goal setting and task motivation: A 35-year odyssey. *American Psychologist, 57*(9), 705–717. doi:10.1037/0003-066X.57.9.705

Lubbers, M. J., Van Der Werf, M. P. C., Kuyper, H., & Hendriks, A. A. J. (2010). Does homework behavior mediate the relation between personality and academic performance? *Learning and Individual Differences, 20*(3), 203–208. doi:10.1016/j.lindif.2010.01.005

Maslow, A. H. (1943). A theory of human motivation. *Psychological Review, 50*(4), 370–396. doi:10.1037/h0054346

Maslow, A. H. (1954). *Motivation and personality* (1st ed.). New York: Harper.

McKnight, P. E., & Kashdan, T. B. (2009). Purpose in life as a system that creates and sustains health and well-being: An integrative, testable theory. *Review of General Psychology, 13*(3), 242–251. doi:10.1037/a0017152

McNatt, D. B. (2000). Ancient Pygmalion joins contemporary management: A meta-analysis of the result. *Journal of Applied Psychology, 85*(2), 314–322. doi:10.1037/0021-9010.85.2.314

Merton, R. K. (1948). The self-fulfilling prophecy. *The Antioch Review, 8*(2), 193–210. doi:10.2307/4609267

Meyer, J. P., & Maltin, E. R. (2010). Employee commitment and well-being: A critical review, theoretical framework and research agenda. *Journal of Vocational Behavior, 77*(2), 323–337. doi:10.1016/j.jvb.2010.04.007

Muraven, M., & Baumeister, R. F. (2000). Self-regulation and depletion of limited resources: Does self-control resemble a muscle? *Psychological Bulletin, 126*(2), 247–259.

Nakamura, J., & Csikszentmihalyi, M. (2002). The concept of flow. In C. R. Snyder & S. J. Lopez (Eds.), *Handbook of positive psychology* (pp. 89–105). New York: Oxford University Press.

Natanovich, G., & Eden, D. (2008). Pygmalion effects among outreach supervisors and tutors: Extending sex generalizability. *Journal of Applied Psychology, 93*(6), 1382–1389. doi:10.1037/a0012566

Neenan, M. (2008). Tackling procrastination: An REBT perspective for coaches. *Journal of Rational-Emotive & Cognitive Behavior Therapy, 26*(1), 53–62.

Pinder, C. C. (1984). *Work motivation: Theory, issues, and applications.* Glenview, IL: Scott, Foresman.

Pritchard, R. D., Jones, S. D., Roth, P. L., Stuebing, K. K., & Ekeberg, S. E. (1988). Effects of group feedback, goal setting, and incentives on organizational productivity. *Journal of Applied Psychology, 73*(2), 337–358. doi:10.1037/0021-9010.73.2.337

Rosenthal, R. (1973). *On the social psychology of the self-fulfilling prophecy: Further evidence for Pygmalion effects and their mediating mechanisms.* New York: M S S Modular Publications.

Rosenthal, R. (2002). Covert communication in classrooms, clinics, courtrooms, and cubicles. *American Psychologist, 57*(11), 839–849. doi:10.1037/0003-066X.57.11.839

Schaubroeck, J., Jones, J. R., & Xie, J. L. (2001). Individual differences in utilizing control to cope with job demands: Effects on susceptibility to infectious disease. *Journal of Applied Psychology, 86*(2), 265–278.

Schleicher, D. J., Hansen, S. D., & Fox, K. E. (Eds.). (2011). *Job attitudes and work values* (Vol. 3). Washington, DC: American Psychological Association.

Schmeichel, B. J., & Vohs, K. (2009). Self-affirmation and self-control: Affirming core values counteracts ego depletion. *Journal of Personality and Social Psychology, 96*(4), 770–782. doi:10.1037/a0014635

Seligman, M. E. P., & Csikszentmihalyi, M. (2000). Positive psychology: An introduction. *American Psychologist, 55*(1), 5–14.

Shell, D. F., & Husman, J. (2008). Control, motivation, affect, and strategic self-regulation in the college classroom: A multidimensional phenomenon. *Journal of Educational Psychology, 100*(2), 443–459.

Steel, P. (2007). The nature of procrastination: A meta-analytic and theoretical review of quintessential self-regulatory failure. *Psychological Bulletin, 133*(1), 65–94. doi:10.1037/0033-2909.133.1.65

Steers, R. M., & Porter, L. W. (1991). *Motivation and work behavior* (5th ed.). New York: McGraw-Hill.

Tan, H. H., & Tan, M. L. (2008). Organizational citizenship behavior and social loafing: The role of personality, motives, and contextual factors. *The Journal of Psychology, 142*(1), 89–108.

Trevor, C. O., & Wazeter, D. L. (2006). A contingent view of reactions to objective pay conditions: Interdependence among pay structure characteristics and pay relative to internal and external referents. *Journal of Applied Psychology, 91*(6), 1260–1275.

Vancouver, J. B., More, K. M., & Yoder, R. J. (2008). Self-efficacy and resource allocation: Support for a nonmonotonic, discontinuous model. *Journal of Applied Psychology, 93*(1), 35–47. doi:10.1037/0021-9010.93.1.35

Vohs, K. D., & Heatherton, T. F. (2000). Self-regulatory failure: A resource-depletion approach. *Psychological Science, 11*(3), 249–254. doi:10.1111/1467-9280.00250

Weingart, Ł. R. (1992). Impact of group goals, task component complexity, effort, and planning on group performance. *Journal of Applied Psychology, 77*(5), 682–693. doi:10.1037/0021-9010.77.5.682

Organizational Decision Making

CHAPTER OVERVIEW

Organizations are constantly making choices, so it is useful to understand the process and the outcomes of decision making. Decision making is defined as the process of choosing among alternatives, implementing the decision, and using outcome data to refine or reshape the initial choice. In this chapter, we present the components of decision making, distinguish between programmed and non-programmed decisions,

Wavebreak Media Ltd/Alamy

and examine individual and organizational decision making. In discussing organizational decision making as primarily a social process, we explore the rational, bounded rational, participative, political, and garbage can models of decision making. We then describe some unique nuisances of collective decision making as influenced by politics, namely groupthink and the Abilene paradox, both of which are common problems in organizational decision making. We also present specific strategies to prevent or minimize the forces that can yield defective and harmful organizational decisions.

We also introduce strategies for getting the good ideas or alternatives that are critical for effective decision making; these strategies include electronic brainstorming (EBS), nominal group techniques (NGT), and the stepladder technique (ST), each of which can be readily implemented in an organizational setting.

LEARNING OBJECTIVES

When you have finished reading this chapter, you will be prepared to do the following:

- Define decision making and its process and implementation components
- Discuss five models of organizational decision making and the advantages and limitations of each model
- Define groupthink and explain the Abilene paradox and offer strategies to deal with each
- Discuss electronic brainstorming, nominal group technique, and the stepladder technique as strategies to generate the good ideas that are essential for effective decision making

Yuri Arcurs/Shutterstock

• Discuss ethical and unethical decision making as well as strategies to promote ethical decision making at work

INTRODUCTION TO DECISION MAKING

Life is a series of choices: save or spend, work or play, stay or go, keep at it or give up. Life can also be thought of as a series of outcomes, related (in part at least) to the choices you make. Along with unpredictable and unexpected factors, how well you do is strongly associated with where you put your focus and your effort. Since everyone makes decisions, you are already familiar with them, you know how it feels to make a decision, and you recognize the effects they tend to produce. We do not, however, all make decisions in the same way. Variations in personality are associated with a corresponding variety of decision-making styles. What's more, choices today (and the outcomes associated with them) influence the choices we're likely to make tomorrow.

Remember the definition of decision making introduced in the chapter overview: it is the process of choosing among alternatives, implementing a decision, and using subsequent outcome data or the results of the decision to shape any further decisions associated with the earlier decision. Organizational decision making often arises within turbulent, cacophonous, and rapidly changing environments, and therefore it is important to have a working knowledge of the components of decision making to operate efficiently in such environments.

Process and Outcome Components

Table 9-1 presents the process and outcome components of decision making, either or both of which can be used to measure the effectiveness of the decision

TABLE 9-1	The Components of Decision Making

Process Component

Identification of the opportunity or problem
Determination of the importance of the opportunity or problem
Search for and evaluation of alternatives
Selection of alternative(s)

Outcome Component

Implementation of decision
Feedback and evaluation of decision outcome(s)

making. The process component includes identifying the problem, making a judgment on the importance of the problem for the individual or group (if the problem is not important, the process is terminated at this stage), searching for alternatives to evaluate if the problem is judged important, and selecting an alternative to prevent or respond to the problem. The outcome component includes implementing or initiating the actions of the selected alternative and evaluating the results by some type of performance measure.

In general, most organizational members are much more willing to make decisions than to implement them because implementation can be time consuming, extensive, and labor intensive.

Types of Decisions

In general, decisions can be classified as either *programmed* or *non-programmed* (Simon, 1977). Programmed decisions usually involve highly repetitive and routine problems in which the procedures for decision making are well established, applied frequently, and triggered by structured or clearly defined problems that require immediate action. In programmed decision making, the focus is on the implementation of the decision with the decision steps clearly indicated and highly standardized. Non-programmed decisions are rare, infrequently encountered, and are unique opportunities or problems that cannot be accommodated by routine standard operating procedures. This type of decision is usually made by upper-level managers or self-directed work teams.

MODELS OF ORGANIZATIONAL DECISION MAKING

In most instances, decision making involves perceived rather than objective measures of risk. We turn now to five models of organizational decision making that seek to minimize risk using different strategies and mechanisms (Browne, 1993; Harrison, 1987).

Rationality Model

The rational model of organizational decision making is based on the assumptions that decision makers are entirely rational and seek to optimize or select the best or most effective alternative for a given problem (Browne, 1993). The rational model represents the ideal approach to decision making and assumes further that decision makers (1) have complete information about the opportunity or problem, (2) have complete information about all alternatives and the consequences of selecting one alternative relative to any other, and (3) make decisions based solely on expectations about future outcomes, rather than basing them on power or political considerations.

Bounded Rationality Model

The bounded rationality model has been put forth as a more accurate description of how decisions are actually made in a variety of organizations (Cyert & March, 1963; March & Simon, 1958; Simon, 1955, 1976). A fundamental assumption of this model is that decision makers behave rationally within the constraints of their cognitive capabilities to attend to and define the problem and gain information about alternatives. In other words, decision makers aspire to make optimal choices but are hampered by the following two boundaries or barriers to rationality:

- All possible information about the problem and alternatives cannot be known within a given period of time.
- A decision may be based on criteria other than rational and logical evaluation of information, such as consideration of the preferences of members and coalitions within the organization.

As a consequence of the cognitive constraints of not being able to gather and process all of the possible information about a problem and all alternatives, decision makers seek to *satisfice* rather than *optimize* by selecting the alternative that appears good enough to solve the present problem.

Participation Model

The participation model of decision making increases the pool of information and insights held by membership to better inform organizational decisions, builds confidence in the decision-making process, and heightens satisfaction with decision outcomes (Galinsky, Magee, Gruenfeld, Whitson, & Liljenquist, 2008; Galinsky, Magee, Inesi, & Gruenfeld, 2006; Mannix & Neale, 2005). According to Vroom and Jago (1988), decision making is the critical leadership activity with groups. They identified four decision-making styles of leadership including making decisions alone characteristic of Autocratic leaders as contrasted with the remaining three styles of participative leadership, namely requesting information from the group and then making the decision, consulting one to one with relevant parties to the decision, and using group decision-making based on consensus.

Political Model

The political model proposes that decisions result from bargaining by individuals or coalitions rather than from the operation of routine organizational information gathering processes. Accordingly, decision making using the political model is a matter of seeking a solution that is acceptable to all parties and following a strategy of incrementalism in search of what is possible rather than what is optimal or satisficing (Lindblom, 1959; Wildavsky, 1975). The political model seeks *consensus*. An incremental approach to decision making—inching along a step at a time—limits the definition of the problem, the information search processes, the number of alternatives, and the number of participants (to only those who have a stake in the outcome *and* the power to block or implement the decision).

Garbage Can Model

Cohen, March, and Olson (1972) believe that collective decision making is based on successive and limited comparisons of alternatives. The garbage can model is the practice of utilizing disorderly streams of decision makers, problems, solutions, and choice opportunities for making choices loosely coupled or linked only by their arrival and departure times within the organization. The garbage can model is considered applicable primarily to public service and non-hierarchical organizations, and it focuses mainly on reactive rather than proactive decision making (Bass, 1983; Perrow, 1977).

Central to each of the five models described is the fact that organizational decision making is primarily a group or social process. Accordingly, we turn now to consider empirical studies of group decision making.

COLLECTIVE DECISION MAKING

Most decisions in organizations are made by groups rather than individuals because it is assumed that group decision making better sustains a competitive position essential for organizational work (Heil, 1991; Sundstrom, Demeuse, & Futrell, 1990). However, the growing reliance on group decision making is not risk free because this process can be influenced markedly by an "agreement norm" that may restrict or suppress disagreements that may be necessary for making effective decisions (Gero, 1985; Harvey, 1974). Levine and Moreland (1990) reported that generic group norms (such as norms to prevent or minimize conflict and to regulate contact between group members and outsiders) emerge in almost every group. Groupthink and the Abilene paradox are two examples of problematic, dysfunctional group decision making, and each is the product of too much cooperation born of untested assumptions.

Groupthink

Groupthink is defined by Irving Janis as "a mode of thinking that people who are deeply involved in a cohesive in-group exercise, when the members' strivings for unanimity override their motivation to realistically appraise alternative courses of action" (Janis, 1972, p. 9). Symptoms of groupthink include illusory invulnerability, belief in the inherent morality of the group (unmanaged in-group bias), self-censorship or ignoring contradictory thoughts or self-doubts about the emerging decision, and self-appointed "mind guards" to shield the group from adverse decision-related information.

Groupthink is overzealous attention to compatibility—protecting one's turf and keeping colleagues happy—that risks inattention to forces outside the group or organization. That is, individuals who engage in groupthink may ignore dissenting opinions and the concerns of their families or colleagues in the business community (Faraj & Yan, 2009; Schein, 2010). From a systems perspective, groupthink is an example of *entropic* tendencies— a refusal to adapt to external forces. If prolonged, entropic tendencies (also known as inertia) can lead to self-elimination or system demise (Flood, 1999).

Some ways to discourage groupthink include using a devil's advocate approach in which one member of the group deliberately challenges features of the decision-making process to insure that divergent thought goes into group decision making. Rotating the role of devil's advocate to different members of the team across different agenda items in a meeting—or across different meetings—promotes diversity of perspectives. Another preventive strategy is to give group members a second chance to debate the pros and cons of a decision that was made during a meeting or through a chain of email messages.

Abilene Paradox

The Abilene paradox refers to a situation in which an organization makes a decision that is the opposite of what the members actually want to do, thus setting them on a journey that takes them from their desired goals (Harvey, 1974). The paradox arises from failure to manage agreement (for example, when all or almost all of the decision makers agree publicly on one alternative during the decision meeting but state privately, usually after the meeting has ended, that they actually preferred some other alternative). The name comes from an anecdote used to explain the paradox originally, in which a family agrees to take a long, hot, dusty drive to Abilene because each of the family members think the others want to go, but they find out after the trip—which is just as miserable as they expected—that none of them really wanted to go, but they thought the others did.

The inability to manage agreement rather than disagreement is the defining feature of the Abilene paradox (Harvey, 1974). That no one goes to Abilene alone indicates that decision makers collude with each other to agree rather than risk being an outcast or separated from the group. The role of devil's advocate in group decision making (group-sanctioned presentations of alternative decisions and problems with each decision) is appropriate for preventing decisions that reflect the Abilene paradox. Other possibilities to help a group avoid agreeing to a bad decision include taking a straw vote, calling a brief recess, or circulating around the meeting room or in the hallways to solicit individual members' opinions about the decision before it becomes final. Any of these tactics provides a break and an opportunity for individuals to think about the decision and hear what other people think about it. Then, when the meeting reconvenes, if you sense there is private disagreement with the straw vote or the opinions you heard in the hallway, take the risk of raising the potential for disagreement with the proposed decision and perhaps appoint someone to play the role of the devil's advocate as the discussion continues.

GOOD IDEAS: HOW TO GET THEM

The generation of good ideas is a critical component of decision making, Since the influential work of Osborn (1957), it had been assumed that group idea generation or *brainstorming* generates more and better ideas than individuals working alone (Dennis & Valacich, 1993; Gallupe, Bastianutti, & Cooper, 1991). The claim is that when members of a group engage in brainstorming, hearing the ideas of other members triggers the generation of ideas that members may not have thought of if they had been working alone. This, of course, would be good news, especially given the emphasis on self-managed teams in organizations, and would further reinforce the value of employing teamwork in the workplace. However, much of the available evidence indicates that individuals working separately (in what is known as nominal groups) generate many more ideas and more creative ideas than do brainstorming groups (Diehl & Stroebe, 1987). In an experimental test of brainstorming training, Putnam and Paulus (2009) gave participants rules for effective brainstorming plus additional techniques to increase the number of ideas generated and then had them list their ideas while working alone (in nominal groups). All participants then discussed and chose the five best ideas from the individually generated ideas. Consistent with other research, individuals assigned to groups in which the participants first worked alone came up with more—and better—ideas compared with those who brainstormed in groups. The additional instructions on how to increase the number of ideas worked, but the ideas were no more original than in the other conditions.

Brazel, Carpenter, and Jenkins (2010) were interested in improving the generation of ideas among accountants performing financial audits who are expected to brainstorm as part of the standard audit process. They noted that although the experimental evidence of brainstorming is inconclusive, most of this research has been conducted with college students as participants. Accordingly, to study brainstorming with other types of participants, the researchers recruited accountants and had them fill out surveys about recent audits. They found a correlation between the quality of the audit and the accountant participants' rating of the quality of the brainstorming. Higher ratings were awarded brainstorming sessions when all of the accountants involved in the audit were present, when there was an agenda and checklist for the meeting, and when the audit team seemed open to the ideas being generated. Hunton and Gold (2010) also recruited more than 2,600 accountants who participated in the audits of 150 clients. Audit teams were randomly assigned to use three different techniques to generate ideas: nominal group, round robin, or open discussion (essentially an unstructured approach). After independently generating ideas, each audit team member took turns reading her or his list. Finally, the members had a chance to talk about anything that came to mind as they listened to other members list their ideas. The nominal group technique and the round robin brainstorming were equally better than open discussion brainstorming.

Nominal Group Technique

There are many strategies that have been developed to enhance creative problem solving that involve conventional verbal interacting groups. The nominal group technique (NGT) uncouples idea generation from idea evaluation while incorporating both these activities into the group decision-making process (Bartunek & Murningham, 1984; Delbecq, Van de Ven, & Gustafson, 1986; Fox, 1987). The NGT technique is a robust mechanism for generating creative ideas that can provide solution(s) to existing problems as well as generating ideas for innovative and new organizational products and services. There are four steps to the NGT, as follows:

1. **Generation of ideas.** Group members are presented with a question such as, "What should be our three major goals, products, or services for the upcoming fiscal year?" They write down their ideas in response to the question.
2. **Recording the ideas.** Each member, in turn, reads her or his ideas, and a designated person writes down each idea so that all members can view the list of ideas. During the recording stage, there is no discussion or evaluation of the presented ideas. This process is repeated until all members have had the opportunity to share their ideas, which remain posted for group members to see. The posted public ideas are now ideas in the name of the group and do not belong to any particular group member.
3. **Clarification of ideas.** Each posted idea is discussed so that members can better understand the rationale of all the ideas. The primary aim is to clarify the ideas rather than to debate the merits of one idea versus another.
4. **Voting on ideas.** Each member privately votes on the top three, five, or whatever number is decided to rank the ideas; these rankings are summarized and the top ideas emerge in the name of the group. If there are no clear-cut preferences in the first round of voting, the process is repeated until the top ideas emerge from the group. The results of the final vote represent the group's decision(s).

The NGT is an easy and effective group decision-making procedure and can be used with groups of 8 to 25 people. It is most suited to the exploration of new ideas and possible courses of action (where do we want our organization to be in three years, for example) rather than for making specific budgetary or personnel decisions.

Stepladder Technique

The stepladder technique introduced by Rogelberg, Barnes-Farrell, and Lowe (1992) is designed to enhance group decision making by regulating the entry of group members into the core decision-making group. For example, with a four-member decision group, two members (the initial core group) work together on the problem for a certain length of time, after which the third member enters the group and presents her suggestions. Then the fourth member joins the three-member group, and presents his suggestions. Staggering the entry of members into the decision-making group addresses some of the problems of members' dominance, conformity, and social loafing that usually arise in conventional groups (fully constituted groups in which all members interact and work on the same problem at the same time). Rogelberg et al. (1992) found that stepladder groups produced significantly higher quality decisions than did conventional group generated decisions.

Rogelberg, O'Connor, and Sederburg. (2002) found that the stepladder technique was as effective in a teleconference format as when conducted face to face. However, in a more recent report of five experiments, Winquist and Franz (2008) could not reproduce the results of other researchers. Even when following the exact same procedure as the technique's formulators, there were no differences between the stepladder group and the control group. It is likely that more studies will be pursued to understand the discrepancies in the results from the recent research.

Electronic Brainstorming

Electronic brainstorming is a computerized version of the brainstorming technique that involves participants sharing ideas by posting them to an electronic meeting system or network. There are three reasons why face-to-face brainstorming groups may not be as productive as nominal groups (Gallupe et al., 1992). First, social loafing is often a problem in groups that interact verbally; members often don't work as hard as when they work alone. Second, production blocking occurs in groups because only one person can speak at a time, and some members may be more verbal than others. Third, group members may feel apprehensive about how other group members will react to their verbally expressed ideas.

DeRosa, Smith, and Hantula (2007) conducted a meta-analysis of research looking at electronic brainstorming. They found that electronic brainstorming groups reported higher ratings of satisfaction than comparable groups who worked face-to-face. Unlike face-to-face methods, large electronic groups outperformed nominal groups, but electronic groups with eight or fewer members were no more effective than nominal groups.

ETHICAL AND UNETHICAL DECISIONS AT WORK

Behavioral ethics has become a legitimate and necessary field of social science inquiry. Investigations in this area have focused on identifying the individual or dispositional variables (level of self-esteem, locus of control) and the organizational or situational variables (ethical culture, codes of conduct) that may be antecedents to unethical decision making (Treviño, & Youngblood, 1990). Recently, Kish-Gephart, Harrison, and Treviño (2010) examined ethical behavior and decision making in organizations. Using meta-analytical techniques, the researchers set out to summarize the influence of individual characteristics (cognitive moral development, locus of control, Machiavellianism, moral philosophy, and demographics), moral intensity, and environmental characteristics. These investigators found that unethical choices were more common in organizational members with the following characteristics: a willingness to obey unethical directives from superiors; a tendency to avoid punishment (low in cognitive moral development); high in Machiavellian attitudes; external locus of control, a belief that ethical choices are driven by circumstances (so they subscribe to a relativistic moral philosophy). Individuals with the profile described are willing to manipulate others to advance their own personal gain, are not team players, and could do extensive damage to the reputation and image of an organization. Demographics such as age, gender, and education level had a weak relationship or had no effect on the likelihood to engage in unethical decision making. To reduce moral disengagement and unethical decision making, organizations can seek out members predisposed to an internal locus of control, who exhibit empathy and a moral identity and score low in cynicism. Such individuals see others as trustworthy and attempt to bring out the best in them (Detert, Treviño, & Sweiter, 2008). In addition, organizations can educate current employees to look for the ethical dimensions of their work and provide examples of high moral identity, low cynicism, and high empathy. It may be especially important for these values and behaviors to be modeled by managers as well as by formal and informal leaders to minimize moral disengagement and subsequent unethical decision making.

Results of the meta-analysis also indicated that organizations in which there is an environment that encourages "everyone for oneself" thinking are more likely to also support unethical choices. But promoting a culture encouraging attention to the well-being of multiple stakeholders yields more ethical behaviors and decision making. Lastly, codes of conduct by themselves have no detectable influence on ethical choices; however, if these codes are firmly enforced, then they can have a powerful impact.

DECISION-MAKING TOOLS

Communication Channels

Open dialogue between leadership, management, and employee groups is crucial for insuring the integrity of interdependent work; the rule of thumb is "the greater the interdependence, the more sophisticated the choice of communication." Regular communication is a boost to building relations, monitoring in-group bias (to broaden the workplace image beyond the individual group or team), and assisting in timely adjustment to change inside and outside the workplace. Structured communication channels (written and oral communications) assist individual and group learning to help members keep up with a collective identity that is continuously evolving, which unites the membership and defines its unique contribution to society (Bartel, Blader, & Wrzesniewski, 2007; Hogg & Terry, 2001).

Receptivity to information, as exchanged among leadership, management, and employees from within and outside of the organization, is reflective of the quality of the relationship shared between messenger and receiver. The openness of leadership and management to messages from anywhere within the organization can be as important for comprehension as is clarity or the type of the information being shared. Faraj and Yan (2009), building on the work of earlier organizational scholars, refer to receptivity to information from within the organization and external to the system as *boundary work* (Lewin, Lippit, & White, 1939; Likert, 1961, 1967; Schein, 2004). Boundary work is expressed in three forms: boundary spanning (BS) to insure access to vital information about resources related to system survival; boundary buffering (BB) to shield the inner system from outside distraction or harmful forces; and boundary reinforcement (BR) to retain internal integrity, stability, and resilience (Faraj & Yan, 2009). BR ensures satisfactory delivery of basic social, cognitive, and financial resources essential for quality work, and BB keeps out unnecessary details while enhancing receptivity to essential communications, decision making, and negotiations for present and future goals and needs. The primary focus of boundary work is to retain organizational uniqueness, resilience, interdependence, and efficiency while respecting employee rights to exercise autonomy or freedom to make independent decisions without approval of an immediate supervisor or manager (Faraj & Yan, 2009).

Feedback Loop Systems

An active and inclusive feedback loop facilitates organization-wide communications as well as providing an important tool for addressing challenges, guiding systems development, and rallying support for oppressed organizational members (Belschak & Den Hartog, 2008; Bilewicz, 2009).

Choice of media must reflect message type, sensitivity of subject matter, and/or the need for confidentiality. Open communication via formal and informal sources renders the system accessible to all, as well as providing a way to exchange messages that require anonymity and/or sensitive information that may embarrass or offend targeted parties.

Too little attentiveness to choosing appropriate media for communication is a source of immeasurable grief and suffering. A good rule of thumb is to place yourself in the position of the person receiving the communication, asking yourself, "How would I prefer to hear this news?" When you reflect on the best type of communication to use, it is important to remember that negative feedback is weighted at twice the impact of positive feedback (Belschak & Den Hartog, 2008).

Chapter Summary

Decision making in organizations is a social process that consists of process and outcome components. Organizational decisions are programmed (routine) or non-programmed (unique and infrequent); the former requires increasingly refined decision processes, whereas the latter requires strategies that contribute to the generation of new and creative alternatives.

We described five models of organizational decision making in which decisions arise from primarily social or group processes: the rational model, the bounded rationality model, the participation model, the political model, and the garbage can model. We also introduced groupthink and the Abilene paradox, both of which are examples of dysfunctional group decision making. Specific strategies were identified to prevent or minimize these widespread and frequently occurring organizational anomalies.

A review of electronic brainstorming, nominal group, and stepladder techniques provided sound techniques to generate good ideas. We examined moral disengagement, its antecedents, and their relationship to unethical decision making and identified strategies to reduce unethical decision making at work. We also presented findings that identify dispositional and situational forces that impact ethical decision making, which in turn can provide principles to construct intervention programs at work to enhance ethical decision making.

Lastly, we provided several decision-making tools, including communication channels and feedback loop systems, that can help an organization strengthen relations among its members, facilitate the integrity of interdependent work, and enhance collective decision making.

Chapter References

Bartel, C., Blader, S. L., & Wrzesniewski, A. (2007). *Identity and the modern organization*. Mahwah, NJ: Lawrence Erlbaum.

Bartunek, J. M., & Murningham, J. K. (1984). The Nominal Group Technique: Expanding the basic procedure and underlying assumptions. *Group & Organization Studies, 9*(3), 417–432. doi:10.1177/105960118400900307

Bass, B. M. (1983). *Organizational decision making*. Homewood, IL: Irwin.

Belschak, F. D., & Den Hartog, D. N. (2009). Consequences of positive and negative feedback: The impact on emotions and extra-role behaviors. *Applied Psychology, 58*(2), 274–303. doi:10.1111/j.1464-0597.2008.00336.x

Bilewicz, M. (2009). Perspective taking and intergroup helping intentions: The moderating role of power relations. *Journal of Applied Social Psychology, 39* (12), 2779–2786.

Brazel, J. F., Carpenter, T. D., & Jenkins, J. G. (2010). Auditors' use of brainstorming in the consideration of fraud: Reports from the field. *The Accounting Review, 85*(4), 1273–1301. doi:10.2308/accr.2010.85.4.1273

Browne, M. (1993). *Organizational decision making and information*. Norwood, NJ: Abex.

Cohen, M. D., March, J. G., & Olsen, J. P. (1972). A garbage can model of organizational choice. *Administrative Science Quarterly, 17,* 1–25.

Cyert, R. M., & March, J. G. (1963). *Behavioral theory of the firm*. Engelwood Cliffs, NJ: Prentice Hall.

Delbecq, A. L., Van de Ven, A. H., & Gustafson, D. H. (1986). *Group techniques for program planning: A guide to nominal group and Delphi processes*. Middleton, WI: Green Briar Press.

Dennis, A. R., & Valacich, J. S. (1993). Computer brainstorms: More heads are better than one. *Journal of Applied Psychology, 78,* 532–537.

Detert, J. R., Treviño, L. K., & Sweitzer, V. L. (2008). Moral disengagement in ethical decision making: A study of antecedents and outcomes. *Journal of Applied Psychology, 93*(2), 374–391. doi:10.1037/0021-9010.93.2.374

DeRosa, D. M., Smith, C. L., & Hantula, D. A. (2007). The medium matters: Mining the long-promised merit of group interaction in creative idea generation tasks in a meta-analysis of the electronic group brainstorming literature. *Computers in Human Behavior, 23*(3), 1549–1581. doi:10.1016/j.chb.2005.07.003

Diehl, M., & Stroebe, W. (1987). Productivity loss in brainstorming groups: Toward the solution of a riddle. *Journal of Personality and Social Psychology, 53*(3), 497–509. doi:10.1037/0022-3514.53.3.497

Faraj, S., & Yan, A. (2009). Boundary work in knowledge teams. *Journal of Applied Psychology, 94*(3), 604–617. doi:10.1037/a0014367

Flood, R. L. (1999). *Rethinking the fifth discipline: Learning within the unknowable*. London: Rouledge.

Fox, W. M. (1987). *Effective group problem solving: How to broaden participation, improve decision making, and increase commitment to action*. San Francisco: Jossey-Bass.

Galinsky, A. D., Magee, J. C., Gruenfeld, D. H., Whitson, J. A., & Liljenquist, K. A. (2008). Power reduces the press of the situation: Implications for creativity, conformity, and dissonance. *Journal of Personality and Social Psychology, 95*(6), 1450–1466. doi:10.1037/a0012633

Galinsky, A. D., Magee, J. C., Inesi, M. E., & Gruenfeld, D. H. (2006). Power and perspectives not taken. *Psychological Science, 17*(12), 1068–1074. doi:10.1111/j.1467-9280.2006.01824.x

Gallupe, R. B., Bastianutti, L. M., & Cooper, W. H. (1991). Unblocking brainstorms. *Journal of Applied Psychology, 76*(1), 137–142. doi:10.1037/0021-9010.76.1.137

Gallupe, R. B., Dennis, A. R., Cooper, W. H., Valacich, J. S., Bastianutti, L. M., & Nunamaker, J. F. (1992). Electronic brainstorming and group size. *The Academy of Management Journal, 35*(2), 350–369. doi:10.2307/256377

Gero, A. (1985). Conflict avoidance in consensual decision processes. *Small Group Research, 16*(4), 487–499. doi:10.1177/104649648501600405

Harrison, E. F. (1987). *The managerial decision-making process* (3rd ed.). Boston: Houghton Mifflin.

Harvey, J. B. (1974). The Abilene paradox: The management of agreement. *Organizational Dynamics, 3*, 63–80.

Heil, W. B. (1991). *Reviewing participation in decision making: Toward a multi-dimensonal model.* Paper presented at the 99th annual convention of the American Psychological Association, San Francisco.

Hogg, M. A., & Terry, D. J. (2001). *Social identity processes in organizational contexts.* Philadelphia: Psychology Press.

Hunton, J. E., & Gold, A. (2010). A field experiment comparing the outcomes of three fraud brainstorming procedures: Nominal group, round robin, and open discussion. *The Accounting Review, 85*(3), 911–935. doi:10.2308/accr.2010.85.3.911

Janis, I. L. (1972). *Victims of groupthink.* Boston: Houghton Mifflin.

Kish-Gephart, J. J., Harrison, D. A., & Treviño, L. K. (2010). Bad apples, bad cases, and bad barrels: Meta-analytic evidence about sources of unethical decisions at work. *Journal of Applied Psychology, 95*(1), 1–31. doi:10.1037/a0017103

Levine, J. M., & Moreland, R. L. (1990). Progress in small group research. *Annual Review of Psychology, 41*, 585–634.

Lewin, K., Lippit, R., & White, R. K. (1939). Patterns of aggressive behavior in experimentally created social climates. *Journal of Social Psychology, 10*, 271–301.

Likert, R. (1961). *The human organization: Its management and value.* New York: Free Press.

Likert, R. (1967). *The human organism.* New York: McGraw-Hill.

Lindblom, C. E. (1959). The science of muddling through. *Public Administration Review, 19*, 79–88.

Mannix, E., & Neale, M. A. (2005). What differences make a difference? The promise and reality of diverse teams in organizations. *Psychological Science in the Public Interest, 6*(2), 31–55. doi:10.1111/j.1529-1006.2005.00022.x

March, J. G., & Simon, H. A. (1958). *Organizations.* New York: John Wiley.

Osborn, A. F. (1957). *Applied imagination* (Rev. ed.). New York: Scribner's.

Perrow, C. (1977). Review of ambiguity and choice in organizations. *Contemporary Sociology, 6*, 295–298.

Putman, V. L., & Paulus, P. B. (2009). Brainstorming, brainstorming rules and decision making. *The Journal of Creative Behavior, 43*(1), 23–39.

Rogelberg, S. G., Barnes-Farrell, J. L., & Lowe, C. A. (1992). The stepladder technique: An alternative group structure facilitating effective group decision making. *Journal of Applied Psychology, 77*(5), 730–737. doi:10.1037/0021-9010.77.5.730

Rogelberg, S. G., O'Connor, M. S., & Sederburg, M. (2002). Using the stepladder technique to facilitate the performance of audioconferencing. *Journal of Applied Psychology, 87*(5), 994–1000. doi:10.1037/0021-9010.87.5.994

Schein, E. H. (2010). *Organizational culture and leadership* (4th ed.). San Francisco: Jossey-Bass.

Simon, H. A. (1955). A behavioral model of rational choice. *Quarterly Journal of Economics, 69*(1), 99–118. doi:10.2307/1884852

Simon, H. A. (1976). *Administrative behavior* (3rd ed.). New York: Free Press.

Simon, H. A. (1977). *The new science of management.* Englewood Cliffs, NJ: Prentice Hall.

Sundstrom, E., Demeuse, K. P., & Furtell, D. (1990). Work teams: Applications and effectiveness. *American Psychologist, 45*, 120–133.

Treviño, L. K., & Youngblood, S. A. (1990). Bad apples in bad barrels: A causal analysis of ethical decision-making behavior. *Journal of Applied Psychology, 75*(4), 378–385. doi:10.1037/0021-9010.75.4.378

Winquist, J. R., & Franz, T. M. (2008). Does the stepladder technique improve group decision making? A series of failed replications. *Group Dynamics: Theory, Research, and Practice, 12*(4), 255–267. doi:10.1037/1089-2699.12.4.255

Vroom, V. H., & Jago, A. G. (1988). *The new leadership: managing participation in organizations.* Englewood Cliffs, NJ: Prentice Hall.

Wildavsky, A. (1975). *Budgeting: A comparative theory of budgetary process.* Boston: Little, Brown.

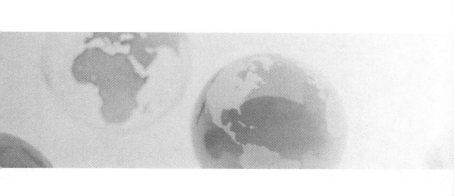

CHAPTER 10

Workplace Negotiation

CHAPTER OVERVIEW

Negotiation is something everyone does every day—from choosing who has first dibs on the coffeemaker in the morning to deciding who walks the dog at night, negotiated decisions get a person through a busy day. The basic dynamics of negotiation, whether it involves two people or a multitude, are always the

Kurha/Shutterstock

same, which is to influence access to desired resources, with each success building momentum for success at the next encounter.

This chapter introduces organizational negotiation, which is a formal systematic process that combines distributive (fixed-pie) negotiation and integrative (enlarge the pie) negotiation to maximize resource utilization and produce satisfactory outcomes. You will learn about the importance of having a BATNA or best alternative to a negotiated agreement, and you will be encouraged to reflect on the influence that gender, context, disposition, power relations, and multicultural variance have on negotiation outcomes.

LEARNING OBJECTIVES

When you have finished reading this chapter, you will be prepared to do the following:

- Explain how distributive negotiation and integrative negotiation are similar and how they are different, and know the advantages and disadvantages of each negotiation type

- Understand the limitations of position-based negotiation compared to interest-based negotiation

- Define BATNA and critique bargaining strategies in relation to principled negotiations

- Understand how integrative negotiation facilitates team building, prevents conflict, and stimulates constructive organizational development

- Explain how inclusive practices facilitate cooperation, enhance negotiated outcomes, and ensure greater employee satisfaction

- List key tool sets and skills that facilitate and guide effective negotiation

Vladgrin/Fotolia

INTRODUCTION TO NEGOTIATION

Negotiation is the way in which individuals and organizations manage interdependence through an interactive give and take process aimed at achieving a desired outcome (Gelfand, Fulmer, & Severance 2011; Mayer, 2000). Success in today's global market demands agility, flexibility, innovation, and strategic advantage (Eisenhardt & Martin, 2000; Eisenhardt, Schoonhoven, & Lyman, 2001). In this section, you will learn a formula for effective negotiation grounded in theory and coupled with tool sets and skills that strengthen relations and build trust to ease power allocation, thereby accomplishing goals, enriching lives, and warding off future conflict. You also discover how successful negotiation rests on overcoming challenges born of entrenchment in a competitive mindset, expanding political inequality, diminished tolerance, and withering trust (Putnam, 2000). Because negotiation centers around issues that hold the greatest potential for conflict, the better prepared people are to manage conflict, the smoother the process and the more successful the negotiated outcome.

Distributive Negotiation: Focus on Now

Distributive negotiation is a fixed-pie or zero-sum orientation to "here and now" resource allocation, which tends to be rights-based and guided by precedent. Distributive negotiation is inclined to be low trust, competitive, and win/lose. To maximize personal gain, parties are reluctant to share information about needs and interests, because they assume that being forthcoming renders them vulnerable to manipulation by their adversaries. This is a low-level construal, which is characterized by voluminous conversation regarding concrete, specific, and incidental details about how best to distribute existing resources. The focus in distributive negotiation is on the short term, and each party attempts to prevail in many small battles, hoping to build momentum to reach ultimate goals.

During any negotiation, the level of trust is a good predictor of potential impasse, and the lower the trust level, the more likely negotiation will come to a standstill. This is especially true during distributive negotiation (Naquin & Kurtzberg, 2009) because only single-loop learning occurs at this low construal level. Fixed-pie perceptions at beginning of the negotiation significantly and negatively affects individual and joint gains (Gelfand et al., 2011), and an increase in distributive behaviors decreases the likelihood of reaching integrative outcomes (Gelfand et al., 2011; Moran & Ritov, 2002). In some situations, however, the minimal processing required for distributive negotiation makes it the best choice, particularly for one-time-only interactions and situations requiring quick resolution (such as an emergency). In general, this deliberative process produces relatively minor changes, is low risk, and requires unimaginative negotiation (Giacomantonio et al., 2010; Liberman, Trope, McCrea, & Sherman, 2007; Liberman, Trope, & Stephan, 2007).

Integrative Negotiation: Focus on Now and Later

Integrative negotiation focuses on "enlarging the pie" to maximize joint benefit from resource distribution. This cooperative focus on meeting the needs of all negotiating parties tends to strengthen relations between the parties as well as heighten satisfaction with negotiated outcomes, producing less conflict following the agreement (Deutsch, Coleman, & Marcus, 2006; Mayer, 2000).

Unlike distributive negotiation, which has the connotation of leading to "win-lose" outcomes, successful integrative negotiation delivers "win-win" agreements. And whereas distributive negotiation is rights-based (e.g., meets criteria to qualify), integrative negotiation seeks overlapping interests of the parties that comprise the entity. As distinct from the here-and-now nature of distributive negotiation, integrative negotiation is now-and-later oriented, which broadens support for future and evolving interdependent needs and interests. Respect for the perspectives of all parties builds trust and increases satisfaction with the negotiation process, leading the parties in the negotiation to believe, "You have my back and I have yours" (Bilewicz, 2009; Galinsky, Maddux, Gilin, & White, 2008; Katz & Kahn, 1978).

Integrative negotiation offers a systems approach to decision making, which implies that to meet the needs of the one subsystem is to meet the needs of the other. In other words, "Meeting your needs is meeting my needs because we are in this together." Inclusive round-table decision making at a high construal level must include discussion of intangible long-term goals—a discussion that answers "why" questions—as well as discussion of the tangible "how- to" issues that surround short-term goals and action plans. A high-level construal nature (characterized by complex abstraction and important details) promotes problem-solving behavior and facilitates "win/win" agreements when integrative potential resides in underlying interests (Giacomantonio et al., 2010).

The ultimate goals of integrative negotiation are to maximize time and resources by satisfying individual and shared interests and to grow social capital for optimal productivity. Ambiguities and unknowns of future-oriented decisions are cushioned by psychological distancing, which involves the postponement of detailed discussion (e.g., specifics about who will do what, when, and how). Deferring these questions frees the parties from the cognitive burden of trying to think about the present and future all at once. Psychological distance is characterized by the use of few and abstract words, with the conscious understanding that the specifics will be addressed later, when the group knows more about each other and the realities unique to that future date of implementation are known (Liberman, Trope, McCrea, & Sherman, 2007; Liberman, Trope, & Stephan, 2007; Stephan, Liberman, & Trope, 2010; Trope & Liberman, 2003).

The leap of faith necessary to sustain the integrative process requires high-level trust and high entitativity (a strong group bond), while the psychological distance helps the negotiating parties tolerate the ambiguities inherent to integrative negotiation. The earlier parties become aware that their counterpart's interests are not diametrically opposed to their own, the higher the quality of the negotiated agreement. Cooperative dialogue of this nature is "money in the bank" because it also builds confidence in the success of future relations (Gelfand et al., 2011). Negotiation essentially occurs at two levels, the here-and-now, concrete- distribution level—"today we distribute resources appropriate to current realities and status quo"—and the later-date, abstract-integrative level—"when we are on firmer ground we will manage shared long-term gains." This higher level latter negotiation welcomes double-loop learning (Argyris & Schön, 1978), and the inherently ambiguous nature of future-oriented decision making is better managed in a cooperative environment (Deutsch et al., 2006; Mayer, 2009).

Quality Negotiation: Combining Integrative and Distributive Negotiation

A skilled negotiator overcomes concerns about opportunism by modeling transparent inclusion, accountability, and cooperation (Bohte & Meier, 2000). She keeps conflicting motives in check by making adjustments to the use of integrative and distributive strategies to match the social—as opposed to individual—motives (Weingart, Brett, Olekalns, & Smith, 2007). To maintain an organizational climate that is conducive to success, the negotiator works to inspire confidence in her ability to move nimbly from issues (e.g., specific distribution of resource) to interests (i.e., underlying need) and back again from interests to issues (Giacomantonio et al., 2010; Sullivan, O'Connor, & Burris, 2006), while remaining flexible and informal (Katz & Kahn, 1978). The greater a negotiator's confidence or self-efficacy, the more nimble she is at switching from distributive to integrative negotiation and back again (Giacomantonio et al., 2010). Collective efficacy grows with successful negotiation (Naquin & Kurtzberg, 2009).

Integrative negotiation, also known as interest-based negotiation, looks to the future while negotiating in the present, thereby simultaneously managing all elements essential for optimal gain. The cognitive ability to negotiate with both the present and the future in mind is instrumental in attaining joint outcomes in which integrative potential exists (Barry & Friedman, 1998). A discussion of interests between the negotiating parties guides a constructive conversation that moves from the general to specific issues involving real-world tangibles (e.g., resources and services) to produce effective negotiation (Giacomantonio et al., 2010). Negotiators achieve consensus through integration of individual wants for satisfying interdependent needs. Those who engage in integrative negotiation must win the trust of participants by turning insight into action while modeling confidence, cooperation, and good humor. People with high self-esteem, ample self-efficacy, and low uncertainty identity are a comfortable fit for this interest-based, present-and future-oriented, fast-dance negotiation process because risk taking is a core element for success in integrative negotiating (Sullivan et al., 2006).

Position-Based Bargaining to Interest-Based Negotiation

Interests are always at the heart of negotiation. Everyone around the table represents the interests of his or her constituency. The exchange process of every negotiation type involves a discussion of financial compensation, acceptance of working conditions, and so on. What separates interest-based or integrative negotiation from position-based negotiation is the amount of attention—or inattention—given to the underlying shared interests of all parties.

People who exhibit a high need for cognitive closure or NFC (Kruglanski & Webster, 1996) have a tendency to freeze at their initial position, to ignore contradictory information, to use heuristics, and to stereotype opponent behaviors (De Dreu & Carnevale, 2003), all of which impede their ability to benefit from contributions of fellow negotiators (Bar-Joseph & Kruglanski, 2003). NFC is sometimes a stable individual influence (reflective of personality or habits), but it can also present as a situationally induced effect, produced by fatigue and/or time pressure (Webster, Richter, & Kruglanski, 1996).

The best way to protect everyone from NFC is to take a break or postpone negotiation proceedings on a contentious issue to give the parties time and space to reflect on the realities of the negotiation—a temporary impasse has been observed to lower NFC (Gelfand et al., 2011; Harinck & De Dreu, 2004).

It is important to carefully pace the information-gathering process in negotiations, to allow time for building alliances, attaining satisfaction with the negotiation process all around, and assuring joint gain outcomes. High performance negotiators do their homework before coming to the table; they are fully present once there through attentive listening, remaining observant of the cues of others, and asking questions. When unsure of how to process information being shared, the reflective negotiator suspends judgment until cognizant of all the facts at hand.

BATNA: Its Appeal and Its Traps

Negotiation is the least expensive form of conflict resolution because it gives negotiating parties the greatest control over the negotiated outcome, and it holds the potential to strengthen relations and set precedence for future collective decision making. But it is always advisable to have a backup plan when negotiating—a concept popularly referred to as a BATNA, for a Best Alternative To a Negotiated Agreement (Fischer & Ury, 1981). You use your "best alternative" to guide your actions if the negotiation process fails to produce the intended results. Having a BATNA ready can boost your confidence when things at the table become challenging; when workplace negotiations stall or come to an impasse, the BATNA often serves as a type of third-party assistance, providing an option that can range from minimally invasive (mediation or non-binding arbitration) to a major power play (binding arbitration or litigation).

Sometimes BATNA falls in the category of *nuisance power,* such as when a union threatens an employee walkout. Interestingly, implied power, a threat to disrupt work and the production schedule (that is, a strike), affords more advantage to workers than applied power, actually walking out, because when the strike actually happens, all the parties in the negotiations—union reps and striking employees as well as management—will have to deal with disgruntled, customers, family members, and co-workers (Mayer, 2000).

KEY ELEMENTS OF QUALITY NEGOTIATION

Lasting agreement is enhanced by meaningful dialogue among negotiating parties. Allowing people to air their differences strengthens relations, builds trust in the negotiation process, and fosters innovative problem solving (Josvold, Wong, & Wan, 2010). Cooperative conflict management strengthens belief in distributive justice, which is the concern for a fair distribution of tangible outcomes—both rewards and burdens—that will be shared among group members as a result of the negotiations, as well as in interactional justice, which indicates how affirmed people feel as they make just decisions (Bies, 2001). Meaningful discussion requires overcoming challenges typical to today's workplace and involves constructive management of emotions to aid rather than compromise quality negotiation, making room for diverse perspectives to win consensus, keeping negotiations friendly to avoid cutthroat practices that can tear at the social fiber, and resisting the urge to stereotype others or fall victim to stereotypical behavior.

To Be Understood, One Must First Seek to Understand

Healthy relations between parties are essential for successful negotiation because the lack of familiarity quickly breeds distrust and fear of opportunism (Bohte & Meier, 2000). Legitimizing diverse perspectives and tapping the wisdom of each participant wins cooperation and satisfaction with the negotiation process and outcome (Bilewicz, 2009; Galinsky et al., 2008; Galinsky, Magee, Inesi, & Gruenfeld, 2006). Argyris (1999) and Senge (1994) recommend climbing a *ladder of inference,* which involves having participants "try on" the thoughts, values, and practices of opposing perspectives to understand the assumptions of others and broaden one's own perspective.

Attentive communication is essential for social system interdependence and stability (Katz & Kahn, 1978), whether between microbial life-forms, too small to be visible to the naked eye (Bassler, 2002; Miller & Bassler, 2001), or between megasized social systems such as multinational organizations.

The kind of communication you choose to use should be based on what type best fits the criteria for mood (formal or informal), security, privacy, speed of delivery, quantity, number of recipients, and effectiveness in facilitating information exchange. The best choice for information media cannot necessarily be found objectively. Empirical data supports electronic programs for attaining the greatest amount of negotiated agreement, but negotiating through "paper advice" elicits the most positive perceptions of the negotiation process, and live mediation is preferred to the e-mediation process (Druckman, Druckman, & Arai, 2004; Gelfand et al., 2011). Attentive one-on-one contact is generally considered to be the most enlightening problem-solving medium (Druckman et al., 2004; Gelfand et al., 2011).

Studies shows that face-to-face contact is consistently heralded for facilitating collaboration and problem solving (LeRoux, Brandenburger, & Pandey, 2010), and research indicates that engagement in active listening and assertive speaking facilitates discussion of diverse perspectives, leading to the resolution of even long-held disputes (Mayer, 2009). A fundamental goal of communication in the negotiating process is to get beneath the superficial conditions that divide the parties and reach the commonality that unites them by seeking the intended message of the speaker. To do this involves listening with all the senses, asking open-ended questions, identifying feelings being expressed, and summarizing back to the speaker the main ideas the listener heard the speaker share. Quality listening requires patience on the part of the curious listener who seeks to discover the intended message of the speaker by listening with all his senses. It is important to ask open-ended questions, to periodically summarize what you hear being communicated, and to request clarification for any misunderstanding in your role as attentive listener.

Assertive voice is designed to respect the perspectives of all parties, and therefore it circumvents the use of inflammatory language. You use it to share a troubling situation as you personally experience it, thus avoiding casting blame for the source of a problem. Assertive voice communicates "I" statements about major frustrations you encounter without drawing conclusions about the source of the problem.

Resist Thinking of Negotiation As a Win/Lose Game

Competition produces one win at a time, whereas cooperation is a collective experience that gives rise to the possibility of multiple wins at any time. Competition theory promotes the enhancement of power differences and reduced awareness of similarities in values and needs; its focus on opposing interests encourages individuals to find an advantageous position for personal gain (Deutsch et al., 2006). In the workplace, low to moderate competition improves performance, but highly competitive practices risk the possibility of alienation and resistance. Constant exposure to the success of one team to the detriment of another fuels suspicion, hostile attitudes, polarization, and damaged relations (Bartel, Blader, & Wrzesniewski, 2007; Deutsch et al., 2006; Spataro & Chatman, 2007). Perhaps the greatest damage caused by constant exposure to a highly competitive environment is a narrowing of focus that hampers creative thinking and innovative problem solving (Kohn, 1992, 1999).

Deutsch reviews three types of motivation that fall within the competitive-cooperative framework; they are cooperative, competitive, and individualistic motivation (Deutsch, 1949, 1973, 1994). Cooperative motivation is a positive interest in the welfare of others as well as your own, competitive motivation is an interest in doing better than others and as well you can for yourself, and individualistic motivation is an interest in doing well for yourself without any concern for the welfare of the other (Deutsch, 1949, 1973). It is healthier to promote competition at the personal level ("Bring out the best in each and every one of you") or sportingly between teams, as opposed to using a kind of heavy-handed employee-against-employee tug-of-war, because an overreliance on competition leads to coercive, threatening, and deceptive practices (Deutsch et al., 2006).

The dual concern model introduced by Pruitt (1983) and expanded on by Pruitt and Rubin (1986) measures the degree of concern for others an individual exhibits, compared to concern for the self. Cooperation facilitates meeting the multiple needs of the individual while tacitly making concessions to the collective needs of the organization (Sullivan et al., 2006). The dual concern model is closely aligned with social motivation distinctions between being pro-social and being pro-self (Gelfand et al., 2011; Steinel & De Dreu, 2004). Pro-social negotiators make smaller demands and more concessions, perceive opponents as more fair and considerate, and exhibit more integrative and problem-solving behaviors (De Dreu & Van Lang, 1995). Pro-social negotiators are less likely to deceive their partners or misrepresent their motivation and preferences, have less fear of being exploited (Zhang & Han, 2007), are more satisfied in negotiation agreements, have higher trust in opponents (Brooks & Rose, 2008), and achieve higher joint gains (Van Kleef, De Dreu, & Manstead, 2006). Pro-social negotiators also tend to have less contention, more successful problem solving, and higher joint outcomes. However, pro-social negotiation is successful only when there is a high resistance to making concessions concerning the dual concern model (De Dreu, Weingart, & Kwon, 2000).

A word of caution: studies have found that typecasting an opponent yields compromised outcomes. That is, a negotiator who thinks he is facing a competitive opponent tends to behave less competitively and achieves lower outcomes. Similarly, when facing an opponent with a distributive reputation, he is likely be more distributive and to use fewer integrative tactics, which can lead to lower joint gains. Focusing too much on an opponent's reputation even prevents experienced negotiators from reaching higher individual outcomes (Tinsley, O'Connor, & Sullivan, 2002).

Resist Falling Victim to Stereotypes

Inconsistency has been the hallmark of research on gender and negotiation. A review of more than 65 studies by Rubin and Brown (1975) investigated the role of gender in negotiation and found men to be more cooperative in 21 studies, women to be more cooperative in 27 studies, and no difference between women and men in 20 studies. Twenty years later, Walters, Stuhlmacher, and Meyer (1998) conducted a meta-analysis that revealed modest differences in negotiation style. They determined that women bargained more cooperatively than men and less competitively than men, but they found that the magnitude of difference between the two genders was insignificant.

Social context is a critical moderator of gender effects, however. When women feel empowered they are more likely to initiate negotiation and exhibit less anxiety about negotiating (Gelfand et al., 2011; Small, Gelfand, Babcock, & Gettman, 2007). Female negotiators tend to negotiate differently from their male colleagues, and this difference in approach is sometimes typed as inferior, especially if salary is the lone measure of success (Barkacs & Standifird, 2008). Women frequently incorporate a broad spectrum of issues and interests (child care, peer mentoring, flexible work hours, diverse compensation) into negotiations, which builds in support for themselves as well as for colleagues, family, and community. Women retain a positive image (in the eyes of fellow negotiators) and dodge backlash ("pushy female" stereotype) by aggressively advocating for the needs of others—for fellow employees and disadvantaged groups—and the success of the outcomes helps meet their needs as well (Amanatullah & Morris, 2010; Kray, Galinsky, & Thompson, 2002). See Figure 10.1 and Figure 10.2.

Interestingly, *only those who believe themselves the target of negative stereotyping* fall victim to reactive behaviors associated with the stereotypes (Wout, Shih,

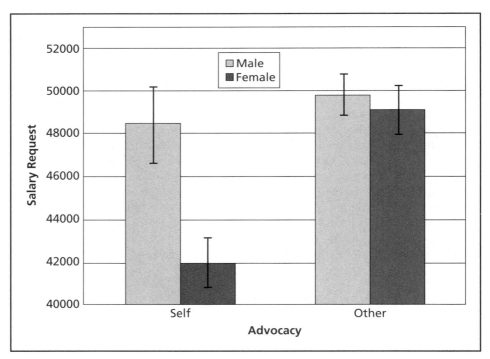

FIGURE 10.1   Female Negotiation, Self versus Others.

Concessionary negotiation behavior by gender and advocacy. Bars represent mean salary offers by gender and advocacy; vertical lines depict standard errors of the means.

Source: E. T. Amanatullah & M. W. Morris, 2010. Negotiating gender roles: Gender differences in assertive negotiating are mediated by women's fear of backlash and attenuated when negotiating on behalf of others. *Journal of Personality and Social Psychology, 98*(2), 261.

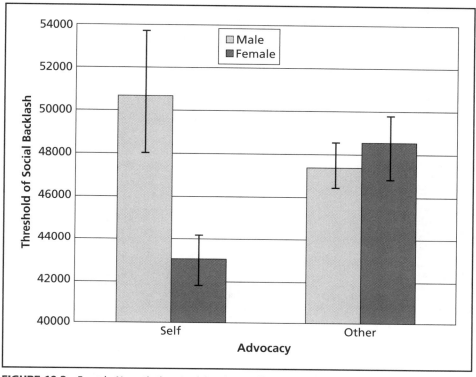

FIGURE 10.2   Female Negotiation Anticipation, Self versus Others—Pre-negotiation Reports of Anticipated Backlash by Gender and Advocacy.

Bars represent mean reports of how much salary negotiators can request before incurring negative consequences by gender and advocacy; vertical lines depict standard errors of the means.

Source: E. T. Amanatullah & M. W. Morris, 2010. Negotiating gender roles: Gender differences in assertive negotiating are mediated by women's fear of backlash and attenuated when negotiating on behalf of others. *Journal of Personality and Social Psychology, 98*(2), 262.

Jackson, & Sellers, 2009); individuals are able to dodge stereotypes or traps set by less well-intended negotiators by remaining proactive-minded.

Resist Power Plays with an Abundance Mind-set

Power is defined as the ability to influence decision making, and power takes on many forms, as indicated in Table 10-1. Two major orientations to power are "power over" and "power with" (Deutsch et al., 2006). Someone possessing a "power over" orientation seeks compliance and competitive advantage over others, believing it essential for successful negotiated outcomes. A "power over" orientation assumes that resources are limited or scarce in supply, thus fostering a scarcity or win/lose situation that fosters a mind-set in which "all spoils go to the winner," as described in the *Scarcity* column of Table 10-2. People who find themselves frequently on the receiving end of "power over" practices tend to feel dependent and powerless (Deutsch et al., 2006).

Personal Power	Moral Reasoning & Collective Thought	Information
TABLE 10-1 Powers We Bring to the Negotiation Table		
Intelligence, looks, personality; power of conviction	Reflective citizen/ professional	Knowledge, data
Association	**Legal Prerogatives**	**Rewards**
Political; connection with powerful people		Promotion, financial
Formal Authority	**Resources**	**Habitual**
As defined by role	Funding, scarce commodities	Status quo
Procedural Power	**Persuasion**	**Referent Power**
Control/ influence, decision making		Celebrity, public notoriety
Moral Power	**Expert**	**Perception of Power**
Force of truth, rightful cause	Professional experience	Do I consider myself powerful?
Definitional Power	**Normative**	**Environmental Power**
Define issues, insights	Shared beliefs, attitudes	Influence overall environment
Relationship Power	**Nuisance**	**Effective Power**
		Ability to make things happen
Friendliness	**Exchange Power**	**Legitimacy**

At the other end of the spectrum is the "power with" orientation that promotes power sharing and cooperation, which in turn inspires feelings of an abundant supply of resources as well as empowerment and optimism, as described in the *Abundance* column of Table 10-2.

Negotiators who considers themselves members of low power status (LPG) tend to blame their disadvantaged positions either on members of a higher or lower power status than their own, whereas people who align themselves with high power groups (HPG) defend their superior status by negatively stereotyping people in LPGs. LPGs are assumed inferior or lazy (Deutsch & Coleman, 2000; Deutsch et al., 2006). Negotiators who leave HPG/LPG assumptions unchallenged endure an environment of distrust and compromised communication. For example, Joanna avoids contact with her boss, Helena, whom she believes is indifferent to her well-being, but Helena thinks her employee, Joanna, is lazy and unmotivated because Joanna

TABLE 10-2	Scarcity versus Abundance Mind-set Guide	
Scarcity (Either/Or)	**Abundance (Both/And)**
1. Competitive	1. Collaborative
2. Win/Lose	2. Win/Win
3. Spoils to the Winner	3. Your Success Is My Success
4. Someone Must Lose	4. If Someone Loses, Everyone Loses
5. Get with the Program	5. Everyone Has Piece of the Truth
6. Analyze by Breaking into Parts	6. Synthesis: Integrate Parts into Whole
7. Usually Faster in the Short Run	7. Usually Faster in the Long Run
8. Survival of the Fittest	8. Interdependence of All Things

makes no attempts to better her station. From a systems perspective, Joanna and Helena are caught in negative triangulation, and the negative assumptions each one makes about the other have cut off meaningful dialogue and appreciation.

A wise negotiator takes a "power is as power does" attitude, knowing there are endless possibilities for influencing negotiated outcomes (refer to the list of powers in Table 10-1), and this kind of positive attitude, coupled with the belief that "everyone holds a piece of the truth," can help to hasten decision making, enhance problem solving, and increase innovative solutions around the negotiation table, ultimately producing satisfactory outcomes and dispute resolution (Gelfand et al., 2011; Mayer, 2000; Seligman, 1990; Turner & Reynolds, 2008).

Displaying Emotions in Negotiation

Using emotions to bring attention to and build support for an issue is a gamble—and the cards are stacked to favor those in higher power positions (Gelfand et al., 2011) because people with low power group (LPG) status almost always respond to emotional statements of someone from a high power group (HPG), whereas a person of HPG status responds positively to an LPG emotional statement only if the HPG person believes there is adequate justification for the negative emotions (Van Kleef & Côté, 2007). In addition, exposure to the LPG perspective increases HPG willingness to help (Bilewicz, 2009), especially if negotiations are taking place in a culture that models respect for leadership, inclusiveness, and self-disclosure (Schmid Mast, Jonas, & Hall, 2009).

Change of any kind is best embraced when placed in a positive frame or context. Projecting a positive outcome, such as "What will be my net profit from this transaction?" tends to inspire cooperation, more agreement, and satisfactory outcomes (Gelfand et al., 2011; Witte, Grunhagen, & Gentry, 2008). In contrast, negative framing, such as "What do I stand to lose?" yields lower concession making, more contentious behavior, the likelihood of impasse, and reduction in the number of agreements reached (Gelfand et al., 2011).

Multicultural Negotiation

Social interaction in our world society requires sensitivity to unique mixtures of cultural tendencies. This makes it imperative for organizations to do their homework before attempting negotiation in other countries as they expand globally. At the risk of using an oversimplified categorization (that can foster stereotyping), there are four important tendencies or differences that distinguish one culture from another, and these involove (1) the style of communication, (2) the process of relationship building, (3) orientation to power, and (4) identity source. If you are familiar with how these differences can manifest themselves in other cultures, you will avoid misunderstandings or unintended offenses to colleagues in an orientation that is different from your own.

Two broad categories distinguish cultural type: (1) high context/face/collectivist cultural dominance, often found in eastern nations such as China and Japan; and (2) low context/dignity/individualist dominance, which is more often found in western cultures such as those found in the United States, New Zealand, and Germany.

High context/low context cultural differences refer to communication practices. A person from a high context culture often relies heavily on nonverbal body language, gestures, and symbolism, leaving the listener to grasp meaning from the context of the situation. When a conflict arises, an individual from a high context culture may only make indirect references to the problem issue. A person from a low context culture, on the other hand, may be far less subtle, using carefully chosen words to communicate messages and relying on logic and rational strategies to make a point; such a person is direct in handling conflict management (Hall, 2000; Oetzel, Ting-Toomey, & Rinderle, 2006).

Face versus dignity cultural differences refer to how a person establishes his or her self-knowledge. That is, a man from a face culture draws his identity from his society, whereas a woman from a dignity culture defines herself in terms of self-reflection, with less dependence on her place in society as a whole (Kim, Cohen, & Au, 2010).

Collectivist versus individualist cultural differences refer to people's comfort with power distance and social approval. A person from a collectivist culture tends to prefer high power distance, which is often manifested as hierarchal-structured relations (Hofstede, 1980, 2001; Hofstede, Neuijen, Ohayv, & Sanders, 1990), and she places greater value on societal approval as opposed to personal autonomy. A person from an individualist culture is more comfortable with low power distance or a decentered power structure (Hofstede, 1980, 2001; Hofstede et al., 1990), while holding greater regard for self-approval than societal acceptance.

An analysis of conflict between western and eastern cohorts will likely reveal tension based on opposite tendencies, as each recognizes the vulnerability of the other—placing too much reliance on societal or individual opinion at the expense of the other—while ignoring its own vulnerability. From a systems perspective, people from a high context/face/collectivist culture place a high value on formality and relationships, put locus of control at the societal level, and defer to societal expectations because societal intactness is valued over personal stability (Rotter, 1966, 1990). A person from a collectivist culture often seeks the advice of societal elders to guide challenging decision making (Kim et al., 2010). Since people from a high context/face/collectiveness culture place great emphasis on relationship formality, conflict is managed indirectly with face-giving behaviors.

People from low context/dignity/individualist culture are less formal and more outcome focused (they want to see that signed contract) (Rotter, 1966, 1990), and for them, locus of control is centered at the personal level, because personal autonomy or stability is the societal expectation. This means that each individual is responsible for his or her own reasoning and good conscience when making decisions. Conflict is managed directly with face-saving behaviors.

Gelfand et al. (2011) explain that the preponderance of negotiation research has focused on the western culture, while very little study has been made to date of the negotiation tactics used by collectivist cultures. Logic suggests that a person from a high context/face culture would be inclined to exercise bias at the societal level, compared to a person from a low context/dignity culture, where bias is observed to occur at the individual level. Chapter 11 provides a more detailed review of biased tendencies (Heider, 1958; Isenhart & Spangle, 2000; Kelley, 1979).

Gelfand et al. (2011) believe cultural knowledge is instrumental in guiding information processing when challenged by situational factors, such as high cognitive load and/or high time pressure. The best way to avoid conflict is by establishing a learning environment in which diverse practices and perspectives are sought and channeled constructively, increasing competence and enlightenment in multicultural differences. An inclusive approach to decision making demonstrates goodwill toward multicultural competence and tends to produce more satisfactory outcomes (Mannix & Neale, 2005). Oetzel and Ting-Toomey (2006) recommend setting an ultimate goal of becoming "unconsciously competent," which means to possess the ability to spontaneously and naturally adjust to the culture of others when at the negotiation table.

Chapter Summary

In this chapter we explained how quality distributive negotiation and integrative negotiation produce good outcomes when appreciated for their strengths and limitations, while position-based negotiation threatens to compromise optimal gain because it does not build relations and it threatens to alienate participants. You should remember that a well-planned BATNA (best alternative to a negotiated agreement) can give parties the confidence to maximize gains during negotiation. The chapter also discussed situational and dispositional forces that complement or challenge quality organizational negotiation, such as orientation to power, stereotyping, comfort with delaying decision making, constructive use of emotion and positive framing, multicultural variance, and cultural competency.

Chapter References

Amanatullah, E. T., & Morris, M. W. (2010). Negotiating gender roles: Gender differences in assertive negotiating are mediated by women's fear of backlash and attenuated when negotiating on behalf of others. *Journal of Personality and Social Psychology, 98*(2), 256–267. doi:10.1037/a0017094

Argyris, C. (1999). *On organizational learning* (2nd ed.). Malden, MA: Blackwell Publishers, Inc.

Argyris, C., & Schön, D. A. (1978). *Organizational learning.* Reading, MA: Addison-Wesley.

Bar-Joseph, U., & Kruglanski, A. W. (2003). Intelligence failure and need for cognitive closure: On the psychology of the Yom Kippur surprise. *Political Psychology, 21,* 35–40.

Barkacs, L. L., & Standifird, S. (2008). Gender distinctions and empathy in negotiation. *Journal of Organizational Culture, Communications and Conflict, 12*(1), 83–92.

Barry, B., & Friedman, R. A. (1998). Bargainer characteristics in distributive and integrative negotiation. *Journal of Personality and Social Psychology, 74,* 345–359.

Bartel, C., Blader, S. L., & Wrzesniewski, A. (2007). *Identity and the modern organization.* Mahwah, NJ: Lawrence Erlbaum.

Bassler, B. L. (2002). Small talk: Cell-to-cell communication in bacteria. *Cell, 109*(4), 421–424.

Bies, R. J. (2001). Interactional (in)justice: The sacred and the profane. In J. Greenbery & R. Capanzano (Eds.), *Advances in organizational justice* (pp. 89–118). Stanford, CA: Stanford University Press.

Bilewicz, M. (2009). Perspective taking and intergroup helping intentions: The moderating role of power relations. *Journal of Applied Social Psychology, 39*(12), 2779–2786. doi:10.1111/j.1559-1816.2009.00548.x

Bohte, J., & Meier, K. J. (2000). Goal displacement: Assessing the motivation for organizational cheating. *Public Administration Review, 60,* 173–182.

Brooks, B. W., & Rose, R. L. (2008). The influences of matched versus mismatched negotiation orientations on megotiating processes and outcomes. *Journal of Marketing Theory and Practice, 16,* 199–218.

Cannon-Bowers, J. A., & Bowers, C. (2011). Team development and functioning. In S. Zedeck (Ed.), *APA handbook of industrial and organizational psychology* (Vol. 1, pp. 597–650). Washington, DC: American Psychological Association.

De Dreu, C. K. W., & Carnevale, P. J. (2003). Motivational bases of information processing and strategy in conflict and negoiation. *Advances in Experimental Social Psychology, 35,* 235–291.

De Dreu, C. K. W., & Van Lange, P. A. M. (1995). The impact of social value orientations on negotiator cognition and behavior. *Personality and Social Psychology, 21,* 1178–1188.

De Dreu, C. K. W., Weingart, L. R., & Kwon, S. (2000). Influence on social motives on integrative negotiation: A meta-analytic review and test of two theories. *Journal of Personality and Social Psychology, 78*(5), 889–905. doi:10.1037/0022-3514.78.5.889

Deutsch, M. (1949). A theory of cooperation and competition. *Human Relations, 2,* 199–231.

Deutsch, M. (1973). *The resolution of conflict: Constructive and destructive processes.* New Haven, CT: Yale University Press.

Deutsch, M. (1994). Constructive conflict resolution: Principles, training, and research. *Journal of Social Issues, 50,* 13–32.

Deutsch, M., & Coleman, P. T. (2000). *The handbook of conflict resolution theory and practice.* San Francisco: Jossey-Bass.

Deutsch, M., Coleman, P. T., & Marcus, E. C. (2006). *The handbook of conflict resolution: Theory and practice* (2nd ed.). San Francisco: Jossey-Bass.

Druckman, D., Druckman, J. N., & Arai, T. (2004). E-mediation: Evaluating the impacts of an electronic mediator on negotiating behavior. *Group Decision and Negotiation, 13,* 481–511.

Eisenhardt, K. M., & Martin, J. A. (2000). Dynamic capabilities: What are they? *The Strategic Management Journal, 21*(10–11), 1105–1121.

Eisenhardt, K. M., Schoonhoven, C. B., & Lyman, K. (2001). Effects of top management teams on the organization of innovation through alternative types of strategic alliances. In M. E. Turner (Ed.) *Groups at work: Theory and research.* Mahwah, NJ: Lawrence Erlbaum Associates.

Fisher, R., & Ury, W. L. (1981). *Getting to yes: Negotiating agreement without giving in.* New York: Penguin Publishing.

Galinsky, A. D., Maddux, W. W., Gilin, D., & White, J. B. (2008). Why it pays to get inside the head of your opponent: The differential effects of perspective taking and empathy in negotiations. *Psychological Science, 19*(4), 378–384.

Galinsky, A. D., Magee, J. C., Inesi, M. E., & Gruenfeld, D. H. (2006). Power and perspectives not taken. *Psychological Science, 17*(12), 1068–1074.

Gelfand, M. J., Fulmer, C. A., & Severance, L. (2011). The psychology of negotiation and mediation. In S. Zedeck (Ed.), *APA handbook of industrial and organizational psychology* (Vol. 3, pp. 495–554). Washington, DC: American Psychological Association.

Giacomantonio, M., De Dreu, C. K., & Mannetti, L. (2010). Now you see it, now you don't: Interests, issues, and psychological distance in integrative negotiation. *Journal of Personality & Social Psychology, 98*(5), 761–774.

Hall, E. T. (2000). Context and meaning. In L. A. Samovar & R. E. Porter (Eds.), *Intercultural communication: A reader* (9th ed., pp. 34–43). Belmont, CA: Wadsworth Publishing.

Harinck, F., & De Dreu, C. K. W. (2004). Negotiating interests or values and reaching integrative agreements: The importance of time pressure and temporary impasses. *European Journal of Social Psychology, 34*, 595–611.

Heider, F. (1958). *The psychology of interpersonal relations.* New York: Wiley.

Hofstede, G., Neuijen, B., Ohayv, D. D., & Sanders, G. (1990). Measuring organizational cultures: A qualitative and quantitative study across twenty cases. *Administrative Science Quarterly, 35*(2), 286–316.

Hofstede, G. H. (1980). *Culture's consequences: International differences in work-related values.* Beverly Hills, CA: Sage Publications.

Hofstede, G. H. (2001). *Culture's consequences: Comparing values, behaviors, institutions, and organizations across nations* (2nd ed.). Thousand Oaks, CA: Sage Publications.

Isenhart, M. W., & Spangle, M. (2000). *Collaborative approaches to resolving conflict.* Thousand Oaks, CA: Sage Publications.

Josvold, E. T., Wong, A. A., & Wan, P. M. K. (2010). Conflict management for justice, innovation, and strategic advantage in organizational relationships. *Journal of Applied Psychology, 40*(3), 636–665.

Katz, D., & Kahn, R. L. (1978). *The social psychology of organizations.* New York: Wiley.

Kelley, H. H. (1979). *Personal relationships: Their structures and processes.* Hillsdale, NJ: Lawrence Erlbaum.

Kim, Y. H., Cohen, D., & Au, W. T. (2010). The jury and abjury of my peers: The self in face and dignity cultures. *Journal of Personality and Social Psychology, 98*(6), 904–916.

Kohn, A. (1992). *No contest: The case against competition* (Rev. ed.). Boston: Houghton Mifflin.

Kohn, A. (1999). *Punished by rewards: The trouble with gold stars, incentive plans, A's, praise, and other bribes.* Boston: Houghton Mifflin.

Kray, L. K., Galinsky, A. D., & Thompson, L. (2002). Reversing the gender gap in negotiation: An exploration of stereotype regeneration. *Organizational Behavior and Human Decision Processes, 87*, 386–410.

Kruglanski, A. W., & Webster, D. M. (1996). Motivated closing of the mind: "Seizing" and "freezing." *Psychological Review, 103*, 263–283.

LeRoux, K., Brandenburger, P. W., & Pandey, S. K. (2010). Interlocal service cooperation in U.S. cities: A social network explanation. *Public Administration Review, 70*(2), 268–278.

Liberman, N., Trope, Y., McCrea, S. M., & Sherman, S. J. (2007). The effect of level of construal on the temporal distance of activiity enactment. *Journal of Experimental Social Psychology, 43*, 143–149.

Liberman, N., Trope, Y., & Stephan, E. (2007). Psychological distance. In A. W. Kruglanski & E. T. Higgins (Eds.), *Social psychology: Handbook of basic principles* (2nd ed.). New York: Guilford Press.

Mannix, E., & Neale, M. A. (2005). What differences make a difference? The promise and reality of diverse teams in organizations. *Psychological Science in the Public Interest, 6*(2), 31–55.

Mayer, B. S. (2000). *The dynamics of conflict resolution: A practitioner's guide* (1st ed.). San Francisco: Jossey-Bass.

Mayer, B. S. (2009). *Staying with conflict: A strategic approach to ongoing disputes* (1st ed.). San Francisco: Jossey-Bass.

Miller, M. B., & Bassler, B. L. (2001). Quorum sensing in bacteria. *Annual Review of Microbiology, 55*, 165–199. doi:10.1146/annurev.micro.55.1.165

Moran, S., & Ritov, I. (2002). Experience in integrative negotiation: What needs to be learned? *Journal of Experimental Social Psychology, 43*, 77–90. doi:10.1016/j.jesp2006.01.003

Naquin, C. E., & Kurtzberg, T. R. (2009). Team negotiation and perceptions of trustworthiness: The whole versus the sum of the parts.

Group Dynamics, 13(2), 133–150. doi:10.1037/a0013879.

Oetzel, J. G., Ting-Toomey, S., & Rinderle, S. (2006). Conflict communication in contexts: A societal ecological perspective. In J. G. Oetzel & S. Ting-Toomey (Eds.), *The SAGE handbook of conflict communication.* Thousand Oaks, CA: Sage.

Pruitt, D. G. (1983). Achieving integrative agreements. In M. H. Bazerman & R. J. Lewicki (Eds.), *Negotiation in orgnaizations* (pp. 35–50). Beverly Hills, CA: Sage.

Pruitt, D. G., & Rubin, J. Z. (1986). *Social conflict.* New York: Random House.

Putnam, R. D. (2000). *Bowling alone: The collapse and revival of American community.* New York: Simon & Schuster.

Rotter, J. B. (1966). Generalized expectancies of internal versus external control of reinforcements. *Psychological Monographs, 80,* 609.

Rotter, J. B. (1990). Internal versus external control of reinforcement: A case history of a variable. *American Psychologist, 45*(4), 489–493. doi:10.1037/0003-066X.45.4.489

Rubin, J. Z., & Brown, B. R. (1975). *The social psychology of bargaining and negotiation.* New York: Academic Press.

Schmid Mast, M., Jonas, K., & Hall, J. A. (2009). Give a person power and he or she will show interpersonal sensitivity: The phenomenon and its why and when. *Journal of Personality and Social Psychology, 97*(5), 835–850. doi:10.1037/a0016234

Seligman, M. (1990). *Learned optimism.* New York: Alfred A. Knopf.

Senge, P. M. (1994). *The fifth discipline fieldbook.* New York: Bantam Doubleday.

Small, D. L., Gelfand, M., Babcock, L., & Gettman, H. (2007). Who goes to the bargaining table? The influence of gender and framing on the initiation of negotiation. *Journal of Personality and Social Psychology, 93,* 600–613.

Spataro, S. E., & Chatman, J. A. (2007). Identity in the competitive market: The effects of inter-organizational competition on identity-based organizational commitment. In C. Bartel, S. Blader, & A. Wrzesniewski (Eds.), *Identity and the modern organization* (pp. 177–200). Mahwah, NJ: Lawrence Erlbaum.

Stephan, E., Liberman, N., & Trope, Y. (2010). Politeness and psychological distance: A construal level perspective. *Journal of Personality and Social Psychology, 98*(2), 268–280.

Steinel, W., & De Dreu, C. K. W. (2004). Social motives and strategic misrepresentation in social decision making. *Journal of Personality and Social Psychology, 86,* 419–434.

Sullivan, B. A., O'Connor, K. M., & Burris, E. (2006). Negotiator confidence: The impact of self-efficacy on tactics and outcomes. *Journal of Experimental Social Psychology, 42*(5), 567–581.

Tinsley, C. H., O'Connor, K. M., & Sullivan, B. A. (2002). Tough guys finish last: The perils of a distributive reputation. *Organizational Behavior and human Decision Processes, 88,* 621–642.

Trope, Y., & Liberman, N. (2003). Temporal construal. *Psychological Review, 110,* 403–421.

Turner, J. C., & Reynolds, K. J. (2008). The social identity perspective in intergroup relations: Theories, themes, and controversies. In R. Brown & S. L. Gaertner (Eds.), *Blackwell handbook of social psychology: Intergroup processes.* Oxford, UK: Blackwell Publishers Ltd.

Van Kleef, G. A., & Côté, S. (2007). Expressing anger in conflict: When it helps and when it hurts. *Journal of Applied Psychology, 92*(6), 1557–1569. doi:10.1037/0021-9010.92.6.1557

Van Kleef, G. A., De Dreu, C. K. W., & Manstead, A. S. R. (2006). Supplication and appeasement in conflict and negotiations: The interpersonal effects of disappointment, worry, guilt, and regret. *Journal of Personality and Social Psychology, 36,* 557–581.

Walters, A. E., Stuhlmacher, A. F., & Meyer, L. L. (1998). Gender and negotiator competiveness: A meta analysis. *Organizational Behavior and Human Decision Processes, 76,* 1–29.

Webster, D. M., Richter, L., & Kruglanski, A. W. (1996). On leaping to conclusions when feeling tired: Mental fatigue effects on impressional primacy. *Journal of Experimental Social Psychology, 32,* 181–195.

Weingart, L. R., Brett, J. M., Olekalns, M., & Smith, P. L. (2007). Conflict social motives in negotiating groups. *Journal of Personality and Social Psychology, 93,* 994–1010.

Witte, C. L., Grunhagen, M., & Gentry, J. W. (2008). An empirical investigation of framing effects in negotiations: A study of single-family home sales. *Psychology and Marketing, 25,* 465–484.

Wout, D. A., Shih, M. J., Jackson, J. S., & Sellers, R. M. (2009). "Targets as perceivers: How people determine when they will be negatively stereotyped." *Journal of Personality and Social Psychology, 96*(2), 349–362.

Zhang, Z., & Han, Y. (2007). The effects of reciprocation wariness on negotiation behavior and outcomes. *Group Decision and Negotiation, 16*, 507–525.

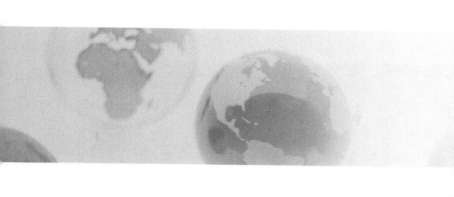

Organizational Conflict Management

CHAPTER OVERVIEW

In this chapter we present the dynamics that initiate and perpetuate conflict, and we explore ways to keep organizational conflict at a manageable level. Since conflict occurs at behavioral, emotional, and cognitive levels, it is important to address it at each level for full resolution.

Dimitri Vervits/Alamy

Well-managed conflict keeps communications open, builds trust, and strengthens relations between employees and management. Early conflict intervention prevents problem issues from spiraling beyond the source of their origins, thus minimizing damage to relations or systems. Emotional intelligence and conflict management skills are essential for employee and workplace resilience, and proactive work habits reinforce collective goal attainment while keeping competition at healthy levels.

This chapter provides a multidimensional approach to resolving conflict, including problem solving close to the source of implementation and deliberative dialogue geared toward retaining collective focus and organizational stability.

LEARNING OBJECTIVES

When you have finished reading this chapter, you will be prepared to do the following:

- Define conflict and discuss the three levels of conflict management
- Identify the signs of organizational conflict and how it is manifested in the workplace
- Explain conflict theory and describe how conflict is a systems phenomenon
- Explain how systems thinking guides organizational resilience or adaptability as well as conflict resolution
- Understand how organizational conflict reflects systems dysfunction and learn how to curb destructive or bad conflict while utilizing constructive or good conflict to strengthen relations, improve work outcomes, and retain organizational stability

Corbis/SuperStock

- Develop insight into the social system dynamics that precipitate and perpetuate organizational conflict
- Introduce intervention plans, tools, and skill sets essential for sustainable and effective conflict management

INTRODUCTION TO ORGANIZATIONAL CONFLICT

Unaddressed workplace conflict stresses employee relations, impedes communications, and threatens dysfunction within and outside the walls of the organization. Conflict is manifested as frequent work-related complaints, low morale, increased tardiness and absenteeism, lowered job commitment, compromised job performance, and increased employee turnover (Shirom, 2005).

Chronic conflict leads to employee burnout, as manifested by social withdrawal; feelings of isolation, hostility, anxiety; and physical breakdown, including reduced cellular immunity and higher incidence of cold and flu symptoms. Employees from lower socioeconomic status are at greater risk of emotional and physical burnout (Penner, Albrecht, Coleman, & Norton, 2007; Shirom, 2005). The price of unresolved conflict escalates if unsatisfied complaints become grievances, legal suits, and/or expensive severance packages. Employee turnover costs include high cost recruitment, new hire training, and temporarily compromised work production (Jamal, 2008; The Centre for Conflict Resolution International, 2012).

Workplace conflict disrupts the delicate balance essential for a cooperative work environment, predictable relations, and timeworn rituals on which organizational stability rests. Relationship conflict blocks communications and reinforces the perception of goal incompatibility between colleagues and management. Most importantly, conflict compromises organizational performance.

Cross-cultural studies conducted in the United States and the People's Republic of China indicate a negative relationship between relationship conflict and innovation and teambuilding and a positive relationship between relationship conflict and increased job turnover (Gelfand, Fulmer, & Severance, 2011).

Definition of Organizational Conflict

Organizational conflict is defined as perceived or actual incompatibility to meet needs or interests within an organization. Organizational conflict occurs at four levels: intrapersonal, interpersonal, intergroup, and interorganizational. *Intrapersonal* conflict arises from within an individual and usually involves choosing between real or perceived oppositional alternatives, such as when a person must choose to do something that has both negative and positive features—taking a promotion that includes a pay raise but which will lead to substantially more time at work, for example. *Interpersonal* conflict arises most frequently between two persons (dyadic conflict), although more persons can be involved, such as conflict among team members or clashes with members of other departments. *Intergroup* conflict can be very damaging to an organization, occurs quite frequently, and is best addressed immediately by bringing together the departments or units or representatives of each group and then moving quickly to address the conflict, with a manager serving as a third-party observer of mandated meetings between the parties. Intergroup conflict is usually limited to occurrences within a given organization, whereas *interorganizational* conflict arises between organizations, and may occur between business firms or between other entities, such as a governmental agency and an advocacy organization (Katz & Kahn, 1978; Lawson & Shen, 1998).

Conflict Theory

Conflict is broadly defined as perceived or actual incompatibility to meet the needs or interests of two or more interdependent parties or entities. There are a number of well-developed theories of conflict, including causal attribution theory, competition theory, and systems theory, each of which provides unique and mutually reinforcing perspectives on the origins and perpetuation of conflict. Causal attribution theory explains how conflict is brought about by personal bias and untested assumptions. Competition theory highlights the self-imposed limitations set regarding potential conflict resolution. Systems theory views conflict as a failure to appreciate the interdependence shared between disputing parties (Isenhart & Spangle, 2000; Mayer, 2000).

CAUSAL ATTRIBUTION THEORY According to *causal attribution theory*, biased thinking plays a major role in conflict experienced at home and at work. Causal attribution bias, put simply, causes an individual to assume that conflict derives from sources outside oneself—a flawed person, a flawed thing, or a flawed situation (Braiker & Kelley, 1979; Heider, 1958; Isenhart & Spangle, 2000; Kelley, 1973). The rationale behind such assumptions allows the person involved in the conflict to "pass the buck" to others rather than taking responsibility for the situation. For example, Mike blames his manager's ambiguous directions for his

TABLE 11-1 Causal Attribution Theory	
INTERNAL (person)	**EXTERNAL (situation)**
Positive consequences of actions are caused by me	*Negative* consequences of actions are caused by another person
I did well on the test because I am smart.	*I did poorly because the test was unfair.*
He is yelling at me because he cannot control himself.	*I am yelling because he is yelling at me.*
He is nervous because he was born that way.	*This situation is making me nervous.*

poor performance over the past few months rather than acknowledging that his frequent absences from training sessions and his resulting lack of preparation has influenced his performance. Table 11-1 shows how causal attribution theory assigns internal causes to positive actions and external causes to negative actions.

From a systems perspective, this type of personal bias serves as a kind of reflexive self-protection. It seems logical for someone to distance himself from the heat of conflict and the chaos it may incur. Unfortunately, denying your contribution to the conflict causes you to forfeit the opportunity to participate in resolving it, by taking positive action such as adjusting your practices to accommodate insights born of negative feedback. Failure to heed negative feedback perpetuates system imbalance, which can result in to self-elimination.

Bias, the human tendency to view oneself and close associates or an in-group in the best possible way, often and inadvertently makes others appear less impressive, less competent, and less valuable (Brewer, 2003; Brewer & Miller, 1996; Tajfel & Turner, 1979). Bias influences how a person interprets the behaviors of others. For example, an act of an ambiguous nature when performed by someone from one's in-group is usually deemed acceptable and well-intended, but the same act when performed by someone who is considered "out-group" will often be viewed negatively, with the out-group member suspected of wrongdoing (Haslam & Ellemers, 2005). The more isolated the individual or in-group, the less check there is on this personal bias (Brewer, 2003; Brewer & Miller, 1996), and the weaker the relationship between individuals or groups, the more vulnerable the "others" are to being typecast (Belschak & Den Hartog, 2009) or stereotyped by members of the in-group (Kaiser & Pratt-Hyatt, 2009). Empirical data reveals a reluctance to believe documented evidence of biased tendencies that lead to prejudiced behaviors (O'Brien et al., 2010) .

Status quo bias inspires a "don't rock the boat" orientation reflected by the proverb that says, "The devil we know is better than the devil we don't know." Eidelman, Crandall, and Pattershall (2009) identify the tendency to support the status quo as right and good. Surprisingly, status quo bias is supported by people on the losing side as well as those on the winning side of a conflict situation (Jost, Banaji, & Nosek, 2004). In fact, people tend to choose to continue current methods rather than alternative practices even when the consequences for the self (and the in-group) are extremely unfavorable (Eidelman et al., 2009; Jost et al., 2004; Kay et al., 2009).

Temptation to exercise status quo bias is reinforced by confirmatory bias, congeniality bias, and false-consensus bias. *Confirmatory bias* involves relying on pre-existing preferences and opinions by selectively attending to information that fits your attitudes and opinions (Hart et al., 2009), and *congeniality bias* refers to avoiding situations in which your beliefs will be challenged (Eagly & Chaiken, 1993). If you are prone to *false-consensus bias,* you are likely to overestimate how many other persons agree with your established attitudes and beliefs (Ross, Greene, & House, 1977). For example, Uvacsek et al. (2009) found that students who self-admitted to the use of performance-enhancing (versus psychoactive) illegal drugs overestimated the prevalence of drug use in a sample of 82 competitive athletes.

Interestingly, status quo bias is reinforced by people from both high power groups (HPG) and low power groups (LPG) (Deutsch & Coleman, 2000; Deutsch, Coleman, & Marcus, 2006). As discussed in Chapter 10, HPG individuals rationalize their advantaged status by stereotyping people from LPGs as inferior in intellect and/or ability, whereas people from an LPG blame both HPG individuals *and* people from even lower LPGs for their disadvantaged status. Strong emotions derived from the stereotyping and blame frequently block communication and perpetuate the power gap between HPG and LPG, locking them in negative triangulation.

Socially motivated bias or *self-enhancement bias* (Gelfand et al., 2011) is a tendency to see yourself as better than others in terms of fairness, competence, success, trustworthiness, cooperation, and social responsibility. Self-enhancement bias renders disputing parties vulnerable to believing that an arbitrator will favor their proposal over that of their opponent (Gelfand et al., 2011; Neale & Bazerman, 1983).

COMPETITION THEORY   Competition is good when kept in proportion. Low to moderate levels of interorganizational competition positively relate to employee goal commitment and performance, sharpen focus on goal achievement, and heighten morale for finding solutions that move more in an integrative than a compromise direction (Bartel, Blader, & Wrzesniewski, 2007; Katz & Kahn, 1978; Spataro & Chatman, 2007).

Competition theory takes a win/lose approach to finding resolution of a conflict situation; that is, it operates on the premise that for one party to win, the other must lose. The competitive orientation promotes enhancing your own power base by emphasizing differences and minimizing awareness of interest overlap between individuals and groups in competition with each other. People continuously exposed to a highly contentious environment become suspicious, hostile, and unwilling to cooperate, which can lead to polarization (Deutsch et al., 2006). Excessive competition leads to what is referred to as a *scarcity mindset* or self-imposed rigidity that leads to fear of being disadvantaged. This scarcity mind-set is self-perpetuating because it triggers hoarding, and hoarding creates a disproportionate resource distribution—thus confirming resource scarcity and inequitable distribution. Put simply, the imagined fears of one person become a reality for another. So powerful is this notion that the mere perception of an item's scarcity lends it greater value than items assumed to be in abundant supply (Mittone & Savadori, 2009).

CONFLICT SPIRAL THEORY   *Conflict spiral theory* explains how highly volatile problem situations, when inadequately addressed, spread beyond the point of the conflict origins. Spiraling conflict takes on a life of its own through solicitation of third-party support to gain momentum for sustained discord or negative triangulation (cutoff). Bystanders who may harbor grudges from a previous history of conflict with the targeted "enemy" allow perspectives to narrow, cause communications to cease, and encourage emotional volatility to peak. Longstanding conflict is in danger of infiltrating attitudes, behaviors, and organizational culture, which results in compromised services and/or production.

SYSTEM THEORY   *System theory* considers organizational conflict symptomatic of imbalance within the whole system. A source of imbalance is often overzealous attention to a primary stakeholder group while inadvertently ignoring the basic needs of another, or it may come from an incomplete information exchange that impedes self-organization or learning. Another cause of system dysfunction is inadequate sensitivity to boundary work between employees and management (Schein, 2004, 2010). Organizational conflict is frequently exacerbated by a failure to adequately respect personal *boundaries.* Boundary maintenance takes on three forms: spanning external boundaries to insure receptivity to vital information, boundary buffering to shield the inner system from outside distraction or harmful forces, and boundary reinforcement to retain internal integrity, stability, and resilience (Faraj & Yan, 2009; Gharajedaghi, 2006; Hackman, 2002).

SYSTEM DYSFUNCTION   System dysfunction is a product of unmanaged workplace conflict. Four common behaviors unique to system dysfunction are (1) transactional redundancy, or repeating the same behaviors expecting different results; (2) subsystem overfunctioning; (3) subsystem breakdown; and (4) negative triangulation or assumptions that block communication. From a systems perspective, workplace conflict at any level—intrapersonal, interpersonal, intergroup, or interorganizational—weakens relations and threatens cutoff or negative triangulation, as represented in Figure 11.1. And the greater the workplace interdependence, the greater the need to keep relations healthy and conflict free.

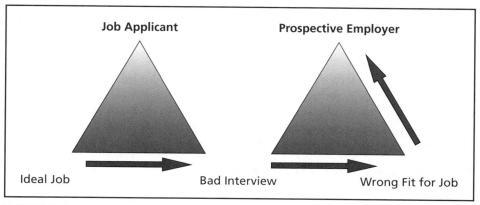

FIGURE 11.1   Negative Triangulation.

INTRODUCTION TO WORKPLACE CONFLICT MANAGEMENT

The first step in managing workplace conflict is to identify the type of conflict. There are two types of conflict: constructive and destructive. Destructive conflict is inherently damaging, but constructive conflict holds the potential for positive outcomes. Destructive conflict, which can be defined as deciding that another person is unworthy of rights otherwise afforded to members of a society, is commonly the product of prejudiced thinking and often leads to some level of moral exclusion (Deutsch & Coleman, 2000). Prejudice attaches negative attributes to individuals or groups and is identified by the "isms"—sexism, racism, ageism, or social status—rather than by evidence of wrongdoing. Negative profiling damages trust and sabotages collective efforts such as zero-tolerance non-discriminatory policies. To prevent negative profiling, practices containing well-articulated goals and actions must be openly reinforced at every level of the organization.

When group boundaries are closed to external forces and information, individual bias (e.g., narcissism) is at risk of becoming collective bias (e.g., collective narcissism) during group formation (Golec de Zavala, Cichocka, Eidelson, & Jayawickreme, 2009). If another group behaves in ways that insult or undermine its positive image, the group is likely to become aggressive towards the offenders (Dovidio, Glick, & Rudman, 2005). Similarly, Kaiser and Pratt-Hyatt (2009) find that high-visibility minority groups, when considered a threat to the status quo because they reject beliefs that legitimize the status hierarchy, generate stronger prejudiced behaviors by status-legitimizing individuals than do minorities from low-visibility groups.

The 2004 movie *Crash* demonstrates how unchecked biases and prejudices paralyze citizens and their community as growing distrust infiltrates every arena of their lives. In one fatal scene, a potential young ally is dead before the novice policeman realizes his fatal error: he shoots an ethnic minority young man who reached into his pocket for what the policeman assumes to be a gun; in fact, the object was a religious statue that matched one on the policeman's dashboard. Assumptions become reflexive thoughts that have been untested and practiced for so long that it is assumed true, so people tend to be unaware of their prejudices and allow them to taint personal perception (Bohm, 1994; Kay et al., 2009; O'Brien et al., 2010). Such was the case for that young policeman when in a tense moment, he drank from the jaundiced waters of his prejudiced society and could not undo the resultant destruction (Kaiser & Pratt-Hyatt, 2009), creating another victim of destructive conflict.

Constructive conflict, on the other hand, arises from tension that is born of diverse employee interests, needs, and talents that hold untapped opportunity. Constructive conflict can be properly channeled and supported by a learning culture to create incentives for change by challenging biases—including inertia or status quo bias—to generate innovative problem solving and creative production (Faraj & Yan, 2009; Mannix & Neale, 2005).

Behavioral Level Conflict Management

Conflict management style varies greatly from one employee to another. At one end of the spectrum are those people who deny the presence of conflict though avoidance or passive-aggressive behaviors. Others accommodate conflict by working around troubled relations or problem issues by justifying unhealthy attitudes or practices; they may say, for example, "Bosses and employees are always at odds, so why attempt improving relations?" Some employees encourage colleagues to compromise or meet in the middle; still others treat conflict as a competition—"For me to win this issue, you must lose." Successful assertive employees rally forces to identify the source of workplace conflict and then work together to find acceptable resolution to a problem issue.

Figure 11.2 describes response to conflict that accommodates the needs of self and others. The habits of conduct can model concern for only the self, concern for only the other, or concern for both self and other. The assertive approach to conflict management, addressing self-needs while remaining respectful of the needs of others, is the least likely to generate new conflict. An aggressive approach disregards the needs of others to accommodate self-needs, whereas a submissive approach accomplishes the opposite, sacrificing self-needs to accommodate the needs of others.

Emotional Level Conflict Management

Every practitioner who labors in emotion-laden work knows that emotion leads thought (Bohm, 1994; Mayer, 2000, 2009). Personal bias shields each of us until we are ready to let down that protective guard that renders us impermeable to new information and fresh perspectives. Whatever the profession or job, people at work—as mediators, doctors, lawyers, project managers, or brokers—know that wise decisions are possible only when emotions are in check.

Emotional intelligence or EI (Goleman, 1995) is crucial for maintaining resilience in highly charged workplace settings. Employees with high EI tend to foster well-being and healthy relations all around, allowing them

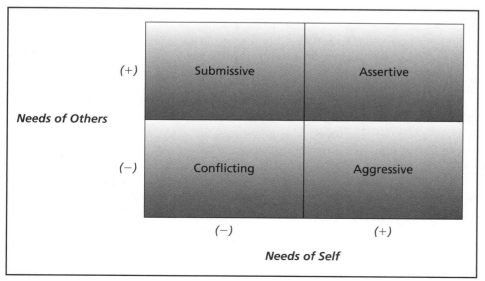

FIGURE 11.2   Response to Conflict: Accommodate the Needs of Self and Others.

to successfully accept and act on feedback from management, collaborate efficiently with colleagues, and be sensitive to the needs of clients/customers. The key components of emotional intelligence are the ability to manage feelings and utilize them appropriately in personal and professional settings and to possess self-awareness and adeptness at managing emotions in others.

For example, a recent college graduate is so fearful his inexperience will prevent him from getting his "dream job" that his anxious state prevents him from performing well in the job interview. Physical and emotional signs (often subconsciously acknowledged), such as rapid and shallow breathing, increased heart rate, sweating palms, and blurred eyesight, bring awareness that you are in a reactive state. In a reactive state, inner peace—physical and emotional calm—is lost, replaced by agitation that can easily lead to cognitive and behavioral dysfunction. Such is the case for the young job applicant who fumbles her way through the interview, forgetting to share relevant talents and accomplishments that qualify her as the ideal candidate for the job. Untested assumptions held by both parties, assumption on the applicant's part that her novice status disqualified her as a serious applicant, and impatience on the interviewer's part all preclude the interviewer asking questions and the applicant sharing information about talents and know-how that especially qualify the young woman for the vacant position. Unchecked emotional states lead to system dysfunction, also known as negative triangulation (see Figure 11.1). When negative triangulation occurs, both parties lose: the young woman failed to impress the prospective employer, and the prospective employer failed to recognize that the ideal candidate sat across the table.

Cognitive Level Conflict Management

Cognitive level resolution is to accept the realities that initiated and perpetuated a conflict situation, having found peace within the common ground that unites the disputing forces. To achieve this resolution at the cognitive level it is necessary to respect the perspectives of all disputing parties or entities, thus simultaneously validating at least two opinions or beliefs that on the surface appeared incompatible or inconsistent.

Troublesome workplace situations are often exacerbated by reductionist cause-and-effect thinking that lacks a long view of the situation surrounding conflict. Quick-fix solutions of this nature easily become a third-party "witch hunt" that intensifies unrest rather than resolve it (Churchman, 1979; Flood, 1999; Katz & Kahn, 1978; Mayer, 2000).

Conflict analysis, on the other hand, encourages "big picture" thinking that is essential for multidimensional analysis of the interdependent relationships initiating and perpetuating workplace turmoil. Workplace dysfunction is often indicative of unmet needs, poor system design, or an under-represented stakeholder group. You will find a resolution for the problem when you understand how to correct the system or make adjustments at the source of dysfunction (Katz & Kahn, 1978; Mayer, 2000).

ORGANIZATIONAL CONFLICT MANAGEMENT SYSTEMS

If you could buy a magic wand that would instantly produce a "can-do" workplace environment filled with healthy, happy, cooperative, and satisfied employees, you would witness practical, helpful, and friendly treatment of co-workers and customers (Diener & Seligman, 2004; Miles, Borman, Spector, & Fox, 2002). Your upbeat employees would produce quality work, maintain good morale (Diener & Seligman, 2004), and inspire customer satisfaction (Harter, Schmidt, & Hayes, 2002) even under difficult working conditions (Abbott, 2003; Karasek, 2001). Employee well-being even spills outside the workplace walls, as satisfaction with work positively impacts workers, helping to ensure a comfortable home life (Diener & Seligman, 2004; Judge & Hurst, 2007) and good physical health (Stinson et al., 2008) as well as bringing with it the benefits of higher income. The reality of a "can-do" workplace is populated with smart habits, deliberate practice, supportive management, and strategically designed in-house communications and conflict management practices.

Strengthen Relations

People tend to interpret the same behavior differently, depending on whether it is performed by an in-group or out-group member (Haslam & Ellemers, 2005).

A well-designed social infrastructure provides a venue to satisfy affiliation and closeness, which builds trust and affirms collective identity—that is, a sense of "who we are and who we are not as a group" (Lickel et al., 2000). In addition, a solid social infrastructure increases clarity and connectedness for effective boundary work (Faraj & Yan, 2009), information sharing (Messick & Mackie, 1989), and social identity (Tajfel & Turner, 1986; Turner & Reynolds, 2000, 2003).

As discussed in Chapter 6, early socialization of new hires hastens their adoption of the organizational identity and helps to build trust and commitment to shared goals more quickly, at the same time facilitating the new members' influence on the collective identity, reinforcing social cohesion and cooperation (Moreland, 1985; Moreland & Levine, 2001; Turner & Haslam, 2001). Structured socialization promotes inclusive practices and multicultural union through familiarization with the organization-wide diversity of talents and interests.

Open communication channels and active feedback loops, as discussed in Chapter 9, keep employee and management practices transparent and vital information accessible as it builds trust in the process and increases satisfaction for all concerned. In addition to these measures, periodic workshops for swapping stories, problem solving, and brainstorming innovative solutions builds commitment to collective work and can help employees find ways to turn annoyances into assets (Eisenhardt & Martin, 2000; Eisenhardt, Schoonhoven, & Lyman, 2001). For example, management can generate healthy competition among teams and inspire creative excellence by presenting a "Silver Lining Award" to the group that best redeems "efforts gone awry"—by turning failure into an asset.

In-House Conflict Management

Proactive early-onset conflict management preserves healthy relations and assists consistent quality work production. In-house conflict resolution resources and training accessibility also complements a learning culture and builds social capital, which translates into innovative problem solving, resilient systems, on-site peace-building support, and quality boundary management (Constantino & Merchant, 1996; Schein, 2004). Everyday resolution to problems experienced among an organization's leadership, management, and employees is best addressed close to the source of conflict origin, with the assistance of an on-site conflict resolution team (Constantino & Merchant, 1996; Follett, Fox, & Urwick, 1973; Stevens & Campion, 1994; Zhou & Shalley, 2011).

In-house conflict resolution takes a wider perspective to reflect on organizational problem issues, asking open-ended questions to identify signs of imbalance, and seeking complementary relationships to address self needs while remaining respectful of the needs of others. It is important to give equal weight to the perspective of each stakeholder by listening to that which may be difficult to hear, knowing that being able to relate to your opponent increases your appreciation for the challenges they face (Bilewicz, 2009). Partnering with your "opponent" in this way allows you to temporarily welcome him into your fold, thus rendering boundaries permeable to sending and receiving information vital to conflict resolution (Mayer, 2000; Messick & Mackie, 1989; Turner & Reynolds, 2003, 2008), and you are able to weigh the relevance of negative feedback from management or fellow employees who are not your team. The more disputing parties embrace overlapping interests and needs the more intrinsic their motivation to internalize shared identity all of which is essential for successful workplace resolution (Castano, Yzerbyt, & Bourguignon, 2003; Haslam & Ellemers, 2005; Lickel et al., 2000).

Critical thinking, the ability to remain curious about new information and utilize fresh perspectives to test preconceived assumptions, requires discipline and practice. Discovering collective wisdom entails respect for the feelings, thoughts, and perspectives of everyone physically and figuratively present. The use of neutral language—language that is free of prejudice, bias, or blame, and is agreed to be offensive to no one present—facilitates open exchange by relaxing (arbitrary) boundaries that otherwise block communication. Dialogue can occur at a personal level (self-reflection), or it can involve others who are party to the conflict or sympathetic to the conflict issue.

A reflective conflict management process asks, "What systems failed us? What did we not see coming? How can we better prepare ourselves to avert future conflict of this type? Which strengths work best to keep us on task and moving forward? Do we need to change some of our current practices so they are better aligned with the organizational needs (as identified by this conflict situation)? What did we learn here?"

Conflict Management Tools

CONFLICT ANALYSIS Conflict analysis is a multistep process that (1) identifies the parties impacted by conflict issues, (2) identifies the sources of conflict, (3) establishes the conflict theory that explains the dynamic origins, and

(4) frames the problem to assist in the resolution of conflict at affective, cognitive, and behavioral levels. Careful consideration of the perspective of every stakeholder—even that of a seemingly hostile dissenting voice—assists enlightenment and quality assessment of the problem situation.

Conflict resolution necessitates guiding the psyche away from negative triangulation (or cutoff) currently blocking communication between disputing parties, toward positive triangulation, which unites the parties in commonality and mutual benefit. Discovering collective wisdom requires respect for the feelings, thoughts, and perspectives of everyone involved in the conflict. Relaxing the boundaries that divide (management and employees) and the use of neutral language, free of prejudice, bias, or blame, facilitates the open exchange process.

Such dialogue can occur at a personal level (self-reflection) or it can involve others who are party to the conflict or sympathetic to the conflict issue. Diverse teams contribute to the higher pool of knowledge for information processing (Curşeu, Schalk, & Schruijer, 2010), which generates an electric, creative atmosphere, one that energizes and enhances group performance.

THE POWER OF TELLING ONE'S STORY   Stories are known in organizational cultures (see Chapter 3) to convey important values and beliefs, and storytelling can be utilized as a robust tool to resolve organizational conflict. Experiencing the stories of others is a way to witness how the nuisances of a specific time and a unique place influence the struggle for determining the right choice from the wrong choice. As the narrator walks the listener through a secondhand account of the trials and tribulations that led to victory or defeat, both gather insight from courage-backed actions that led to villains being conquered or survival of moments that held no victor. The stories include many choices made—some in the heat of the moment—that the narrator explains were fork-in-the-road decisions that made all the difference for subsequent choices.

In many ways each person's life is a mystery to every other person and will in many respects remain as such. However, when detailed accounts of highly charged situations ring true to an audience, the listeners are temporarily transported to a unique place and time, and in the intimacy of that moment, the choices made take on new meaning.

Conflict Management Intervention

Empirical evidence supports the positive effects of third-party intervention for achieving resolution. The mere presence of a third party generates pressure for agreement by reducing perceived differences between parties and helps to overcome reactive devaluation on the part of negotiating parties (Gelfand et al., 2011; Manzini & Mariotti, 2001).

When choosing intervention type, it is important to consider the degree of autonomy surrendered to third-party assistance for the decision outcome, ranging from full retention of autonomy in a negotiated agreement to the least amount of control over the decision outcome, with binding arbitration and litigation. As a word of caution, disputing parties should remember that personal bias (self-enhancement bias) tends to make the disputing party overly optimistic about benefiting from third-party (arbitrator or litigator) decisions because they falsely believe that their proposal will be favored over that of their opponent (Gelfand et al., 2011; Neale & Bazerman, 1983).

Mediation requires disputing parties that are at a comparable power level, and it lends support to negotiating parties that possess low self-efficacy (Arnold & O'Connor, 2006). Mediation is aided by close communication (Honeyman et al., 2004) and mediator credibility, and the ability to gain trust and confidence of negotiators is critical for success (Arnold & O'Connor, 2006). An employee from a high power distance culture tends to be more amenable to involving the boss in mediation than is an employee from a low power distance culture. In addition, members from an individualist culture make fewer apologies and acts of forgiveness during the mediation process than are observed between people from a collectivist culture (Gelfand et al., 2011).

Empirical evidence supports the positive effects of third-party intervention on reaching resolution, because the mere presence of a third party generates pressure for agreement by reducing perceived differences between parties and helps to overcome reactive devaluation on the part of negotiating parties (Gelfand et al., 2011; Manzini & Mariotti, 2001).

Chapter Summary

This chapter discussed how proactive practices preserve relations and correct system imbalances that otherwise initiate and perpetuate organizational conflict. We explained how being transparently accountable for mistakes opens opportunity for learning and continuous improvement on current practices. Since organizational and employee resilience rests on remaining in balance in an ever-changing environment, we advocated for removing barriers that block adaptation to change and/or internal integration. Lastly, we encouraged employees and management to constructively address disruptive behaviors and negative bias to preserve the healthy relations that are essential for collective decision making and sustaining a cooperative work environment.

Chapter References

Abbott, J. (2003). Does employee satisfaction matter? A study to determine whether low employee morale affects customer satisfaction and profits in the business-to-business sector. *Journal of Communication Management, 7*(4), 333–339. doi: 10.1108/13632540310807467

Arnold, J. A., & O'Connor, K. M. (2006). How negotiator self-efficacy drives decisions to pursue mediation. *Journal of Applied Social Psychology, 36*(11) 2649–2669.

Bartel, C., Blader, S. L., & Wrzesniewski, A. (2007). *Identity and the modern organization.* Mahwah, NJ: Lawrence Erlbaum.

Belschak, F. D., & Den Hartog, D. N. (2009). Consequences of positive and negative feedback: The impact on emotions and extra-role behaviors. *Applied Psychology, 58*(2), 274–303. doi:10.1111/j. 1464-0597.2008.00336.x

Bilewicz, M. (2009). Perspective taking and intergroup helping intentions: The moderating role of power relations. *Journal of Applied Social Psychology, 39*(12), 2779–2786. doi:10.1111/j. 1559-1816.2009.00548.x

Bohm, D. (1994). *Thought as a system.* New York: Routledge.

Braiker, H. B., & Kelley, H. H. (1979). Conflict in the development of close relationships. In R. L. Burgess & T. L. Huston (Eds.), *Social exchange in developing relationships* (pp. 135–168). New York: Academic Press.

Brewer, M. B. (2003). *Intergroup relations* (2nd ed.). Maidenhead, UK: Open University Press.

Brewer, M. B., & Miller, N. (1996). *Intergroup relations*. Buckingham, UK: Open University Press.

Castano, E., Yzerbyt, V., & Bourguignon, D. (2003). We are one and I like it: The impact of ingroup entitativity on ingroup identification. *European Journal of Social Psychology, 33*(6), 735–754. doi:10.1002/ejsp.175

Constantino, C., & Merchant, C. (1996). *Designing conflict management systems: A guide to creating healthy and productive organizations*. San Francisco: Jossey-Bass

Churchman, C. W. (1979). *The systems approach and its enemies*. New York: Basic Books.

Curşeu, P. L., Schalk, R., & Schruijer, S. (2010). The use of cognitive mapping in eliciting and evaluating group cognitions. *Journal of Applied Social Psychology, 40*(5), 1258–1291. doi:10.1111/j.1559-1816.2010.00618.x

Deutsch, M., & Coleman, P. T. (2000). *The handbook of conflict resolution theory and practice*. San Francisco: Jossey-Bass.

Deutsch, M., Coleman, P. T., & Marcus, E. C. (2006). *The handbook of conflict resolution: Theory and practice* (2nd ed.). San Francisco: Jossey-Bass.

Diener, E., & Seligman, M. E. P. (2004). Beyond money: Toward an economy of well-being. *Psychological Science in the Public Interest, 5*, 1–31.

Dovidio, J. F., Glick, P. S., & Rudman, L. A. (2005). *On the nature of prejudice: Fifty years after Allport*. Malden, MA: Blackwell.

Eagley, A. H., & Chaiken, S. (1993). *The psychology of attitudes*. Fort Worth, TX: Harcourt Brace Jovanovich College Publishers.

Eidelman, S., Crandall, C. S., & Pattershall, J. (2009). The existence bias. *Journal of Personality and Social Psychology, 97*(5), 765–775. doi:10.1037/a0017058

Eisenhardt, K. M., & Martin, J. A. (2000). Dynamic capabilities: What are they? *Strategic Management Journal, 21*(10–11), 1105–1121. doi:10.1002/1097-0266(200010/11)21:10/11<1105::AID-SMJ133>3.0.CO;2-E

Eisenhardt, K. M., Schoonhoven, C. B., & Lyman, K. (2001). Effects of top management teams on the organization of innovation through alternative types of strategic alliances. In M. E. Turner (Ed.), *Groups at work: Theory and research* (pp. 339–367). Mahwah, NJ: Lawrence Erlbaum.

Faraj, S., & Yan, A. (2009). Boundary work in knowledge teams. *Journal of Applied Psychology, 94*(3), 604–617. doi:10.1037/a0014367

Flood, R. L. (1999). *Rethinking the fifth discipline: Learning within the unknowable*. London: Routledge.

Follett, M. P., Fox, E. M., & Urwick, L. F. (1973). Dynamic administration: *The collected papers of Mary Parker Follett*. London: Pitman Publishing.

Gelfand, M. J., Fulmer, C. A., & Severance, L. (2011). The psychology of negotation and mediation. In S. Zedeck (Ed.), *APA handbook of industrial and organizational psychology* (Vol. 3, pp. 495–554). Washington, DC: American Psychological Association.

Gharajedaghi, J. (2006). *Systems thinking: Managing chaos and complexity: A platform for designing business architecture* (2nd ed.). New York: Elsevier.

Golec de Zavala, A., & Cichocka, A., Eidelson, R., & Jayawickreme, N. (2009). Collective narcissism and its social consequences. *Journal of Personality and Social Psychology, 97*(6), 1074–1096.

Goleman, D. (1995). *Emotional intelligence*. New York: Bantam Books.

Hackman, J. R. (2002). *Leading teams: Setting the stage for great performances*. Boston: Harvard Business School Press.

Hart, W., Albarracin, D., Eagly, A. H., Breachen, I., Lindberg, M. J., & Merrill, L. (2009). Feeling validated versus being correct: A meta-analysis of selective exposure to information. *Psychological Bulletin, 135*, 555–588.

Harter, J. K., Schmidt, F. L., & Hayes, T. L. (2002). Business-unit-level relationship between employee satisfaction, employee engagement, and business outcomes: A meta-analysis. *Journal of Applied Psychology, 87*(2), 268–279. doi:10.1037/0021-9010.87.2.268

Haslam, S. A., & Ellemers, N. (2005). Social identity in industrial and organizational psychology: Concepts, controversies and contributions. In G. P. Hodgkinson (Ed.), *International Review of Industrial and Organizational Psychology* (Vol. 20, pp. 39–118). Chichester, UK: Wiley.

Heider, F. (1958). *The psychology of interpersonal relations*. New York: Wiley.

Honeyman, C., Hudami, S., Tiruneh, A., Hierta, J., Chirayath, L., & Illiff, A. (2004). Establishing norms: Potential for participatory justice in Rwanda. *Peace and Conflict: Journal of Peace Psychology, 10,* 1–24.

Isenhart, M. W., & Spangle, M. (2000). *Collaborative approaches to resolving conflict.* Thousand Oaks, CA: Sage.

Jamal, M. (2008). Burnout among employees of a multinational corporation in Malaysia and Pakistan: An empirical examination. *International Management Review, 4*(1), 60–71.

Jost, J. T., Banaji, M. R., & Nosek, B. A. (2004). A decade of system justification theory: Accumulated evidence of conscious and unconscious bolstering of the status quo. *Political Psychology, 25*(6), 881–920.

Judge, T. A., & Hurst, C. (2007). Capitalizing on one's advantages: Role of core self-evaluations. *Journal of Applied Psychology, 92*(5), 1212–1227. doi:10.1037/0021-9010.92.5.1212

Kaiser, C. R., & Pratt-Hyatt, J. S. (2009). Distributing prejudice unequally: Do whites direct their prejudice toward strongly identified minorities? *Journal of Personality and Social Psychology, 96*(2), 432–445. doi:10.1037/a0012877

Karasek, R. (2001). Toward a psychosocially healthy work environment: Broader roles for psychologists and sociologists. In N. Schneiderman, M. Speers, J. Silva, H. Tomes, & J. H. Gentry (Eds.), *Integrating behavioral and social sciences with public health* (pp. 267–292). Washington, DC: American Psychological Association. doi:10.1037/10388-013.

Katz, D., & Kahn, R. L. (1978). *The social psychology of organizations.* New York: Wiley.

Kay, A. C., Gaucher, D., Peach, J. M., Laurin, K., Friesen, J., Zanna, M. P., et al. (2009). Inequality, discrimination, and the power of the status quo: Direct evidence for a motivation to see the way things are as the way they should be. *Journal of Personality and Social Psychology, 97*(3), 421–434. doi:10.1037/a0015997

Kelley, H. H. (1973). The processes of causal attribution. *American Psychologist, 28,* 107–128.

Lawson, R. B., & Shen, Z. (1998). *Organizational psychology: Foundations and applications.* New York: Oxford University Press.

Lickel, B., Hamilton, D. L., Wieczorkowska, G., Lewis, A., Sherman, S. J., & Uhles, A. N. (2000). Varieties of groups and the perception of group entitativity. *Journal of Personality and Social Psychology, 78*(2), 223–246. doi:10.1037/0022-3514.78.2.223

Mannix, E., & Neale, M. A. (2005). What differences make a difference? The promise and reality of diverse teams in organizations. *Psychological Science in the Public Interest, 6*(2), 31–55.

Manzini, P., & Mariotti, M. (2001). Perfect equilibria in a model of bargaining with arbitration. *Games and Economic Behavior, 37,* 170–195.

Mayer, B. S. (2000). *Staying with the dynamics of conflict resolution* (1st ed.). San Francisco: Jossey-Bass.

Mayer, B. S. (2009). *Staying with conflict: A strategic approach to ongoing disputes* (1st ed.). San Francisco: Jossey-Bass.

Messick, D. M., & Mackie, D. M. (1989). Intergroup relations. *Annual Review of Psychology, 40,* 45–81.

Miles, D. E., Borman, W. E., Spector, P. E., & Fox, S. (2002). Building an integrative model of extra role work behaviors: A comparison of counterproductive work behavior with organizational citizenship behavior. *International Journal of Selection and Assessment, 10,* 51–57.

Mittone, L., & Savadori, L. (2009). The scarcity bias. *Applied Psychology, 58*(3), 453–468. doi:10.1111/j.1464-0597.2009.00401.x

Moreland, R .L. (1985). Social categorization and the assimilation of "new" group members. *Journal of Personality and Social Psychology, 48*(5), 1173–1190.

Moreland, R. L., & Levine, J. M. (2001). Socialization in organizations and work groups. In M. E. Turner (Ed.), *Groups at work: Theory and research* (pp. 69–112). Mahwah, NJ: Lawrence Erlbaum.

Neale, M. A., & Bazerman, M. H. (1983). The role of perspective-taking ability in negotiating under different forms of arbitration. *Industrial & Labor Relations Review, 36,* 378–388.

O'Brien, L. T., Crandall, C. S., Horstman-Reser, A., Warner, R., Alsbrooks, A., & Blodorn, A. (2010). But I'm no bigot: How prejudiced white Americans maintain unprejudiced self-images. *Journal of Applied Social Psychology, 40*(4), 917–946.

Penner, L. A., Albrecht, T. L., Coleman, D. K., & Norton, W. E. (2007). Interpersonal perspectives on black-white health disparities: Social policy implications. *Social Issues and Policy Review, 1*(1), 63–98. doi:10.1111/j.1751-2409.2007.00004.x

Ross, L. D., Greene, D., & House, P. (1977). The false consensus effect: An egocentric bias in social perception and attributional processes. *Journal of Experimental Social Psychology, 13*(3), 279–301. doi:10.1016/0022-1031(77)90049-X,

Schein, E. H. (2004). *Organizational culture and leadership* (3rd ed.). San Francisco: Jossey-Bass.

Schein, E. H. (2010). *Organizational culture and leadership* (4th ed.). San Francisco: Jossey-Bass.

Shirom, A. (2005). Burnout and health: Expanding our knowledge. *Stress and Health: Journal of the International Society for the Investigation of Stress. Special Issue: Burnout and Health, 25*(4), 281–285.

Spataro, S. E., & Chatman, J. A. (2007). Identity in the competitive market: The effects of inter-organizational competition on identity-based organizational commitment. In C. Bartel, S. Blader, & A. Wrzesniewski (Eds.), *Identity and the modern organization* (pp. 177–200). Mahwah, NJ: Lawrence Erlbaum.

Stinson, D. A., Logel, C., Zanna, M. P., Holmes, J. G., Cameron, J. J., Wood, J. V., et al. (2008). The cost of lower self-esteem: Testing a self- and social-bonds model of health. *Journal of Personality and Social Psychology, 94*(3), 412–428. doi:10.1037/0022-3514.94.3.412

Tajfel, H., & Turner, J. C. (1979). An integrative theory of intergroup conflict. In W. G. Austin & S. Worchel (Eds), *Psychology of intergroup relations* (pp. 33–47). Monterey, CA: Brooks/Cole.

Tajfel, H., & Turner, J. C. (1986). The social identity theory of inter-group behavior. In S. Worchel & W. G. Austin (Eds.), *Psychology of intergroup relations.* (pp. 7–24). Monterey, CA: Brooks/Cole.

Turner, J. C., & Haslam, S. A. (2001). Social identity and organizations. In M. E. Turner (Ed.), *Groups at work: Theory and research* (pp. 25–65). Mahwah, NJ: Lawrence Erlbaum.

Turner, J. C., & Reynolds, K. J. (2003). Why social dominance theory has been falsified. *British Journal of Social Psychology, 42,* 199–206.

Turner, J. C., & Reynolds, K. J. (2008). The social identity perspective in intergroup relations: Theories, themes, and controversies. In R. Brown & S. L. Gaertner (Eds.), *Blackwell handbook of social psychology: Intergroup processes.* Oxford, UK: Blackwell Publishers Ltd.

Uvacsek, M., Nepusz, T., Naughton, D. P., Mazanov, J., Ranky, M. Z., & Petroczi, A. (2009). Self-admitted behavior and perceived use of performance-enhancing versus psychoactive drugs among competitive athletes. *Scandinavian Journal of Medicine & Science in Sports, 21*(2), 224–234. doi:10. 1111/j.1600-0838.2009.01041.x

Zhou, J., & Shalley, C. E. (2011). Deepening our understanding of creativity in the workplace: A review of different approaches to creativity research. In S. Zedeck (Ed.), *APA handbook of industrial and organizational psychology* (Vol. 2, pp. 275–302). Washington, DC: American Psychological Association.

Managing Change

Organizational Change and Learning

CHAPTER OVERVIEW

This chapter focuses on contemporary change management, which requires continuously enhancing quality production while remaining sensitive to altering landscapes and staying internally resilient. Change management has four elements: change as a person experiences it, change as it influences organizational life, change as it is conceptualized by industrial/organizational psychology, and change as it relates to organizational learning. A learning culture proactively manages change or

Steve Bloom Images/Alamy

self-organization by supporting innovative problem solving, learning
from mistakes, and celebrating successes. Learning theory and its
application in multiple workplace settings facilitates change management.
Aided by tools for processing information, it guides workplace change,
productivity, and well-being.

LEARNING OBJECTIVES

**When you have finished reading this chapter, you will be prepared to do the
following:**

- Define change management and explain how it is proactive to self-organization
- Explain the two orientations to organizational change, "to change" and
  "changing"
- Describe the advantages of a learning culture as a good venue for change
  management
- Define organizational learning and describe learning theory
- Explain the importance of a learning culture for balancing innovation with
  accountability

StockShot/Alamy

- Describe the multiple models and concepts that explain organizational learning
- Discuss how systems methodology instructs organizational learning and development
- Explain how inclusive practices facilitate cooperation and change management
- List the many tools and skills that facilitate organizational learning and development

INTRODUCTION TO CHANGE MANAGEMENT

> The question is not whether organizations will change, but how fast, and who will thrive? (Herold, Fedor, & Caldwell, 2007, p. 950)

Each of us manages change in our daily lives. In the workplace, successful change management involves capitalizing on trends and emerging opportunities through early awareness and participation, which facilitates riding the wave of change rather than being caught in its undertow. Proactive change or self-organization entails scanning the horizon for fluctuations in resource availability (e.g., recognizing early signs of a slowing economy) and expansion possibilities (e.g., identifying a budding growth market) and to be ready, willing, and able to accommodate the new dawn (Martins, 2011; Zhou & Shalley, 2011). To understand organizational change, it is critical to distinguish between two genres or types of change management, namely "change to" and "changing."

Receptivity to Change Management and Intervention Type

Workplace change can be considered from two perspectives: *"change to,"* which is a change that is imposed primarily from the top down, episodic, intentional, infrequent, planned, defined by relatively discrete start and end points, and discontinuous; and *"changing,"* coordinated change that is primarily inclusive and seeks participation from a wide variety of individuals within the organization, creating change that is ongoing, evolving, cumulative, and continuous.

"CHANGE TO"   A change that is imposed through a top-down hierarchy, in which power and decision making is concentrated at the top, comes from leadership that is directive. Employees—those people primarily impacted by the change—have minimal if any participation in the decision-making process that leads to this kind of change. Although the term "change to" implies a cause-and-effect relationship, organizational change is never a linear process. Organizationally imposed change requires self-organization (or adjustment) by every unit within the organization that is implementing the change, as well as by every individual or group affected by the change (Martins, 2011).

An example of an appropriate use of the "change to" intervention would be the implementation of an exit plan for guiding a frightened audience from a burning theater, because the normal habits associated with leaving the building do not accommodate the newly imposed time restraints (escaping the fire) and emotional volatility (fear of death by fire). Some everyday circumstances also call for "change to" intervention, such as rerouting traffic during road construction, or directing people to help retrieve a mischievous new puppy that has escaped its confines. More sophisticated examples of appropriate "change to" practices include imposing restrictions on access to a sterile field while conducting surgery, or adhering to rules and regulations that help protect the environment and people when removing toxic wastes.

A common workplace example of a "change to" intervention is a ban on all smoking privileges imposed as the result of an abuse of freedoms—that is, when smoking in designated locations has led to smoking in undesignated areas. The forced nature of a "change to" intervention risks counterintuitive outcomes (creating more problems than the intervention resolves) because compelling those most affected by a new rule to follow it without prior consultation may incite rebellion or passive resistance rather than compliance.

Leadership must adequately address resistance to "change to" interventions to ensure successful implementation. Tensions usually center on boundary issues or tension between disputing parties, leading to attitudes that can create us versus them anxiety—"these outsiders think they know better than *we* do what is good for us." The forced nature of the self-organization or integration of new ideas and practices is likely to incite ambiguity, frustration, or fear of unknown outcomes to existing structures and practices (Martins, 2011).

Tensions born of mandated change are felt at both ends of the hierarchy. Employees become nervous about how they can integrate the novel ideas and practices into their daily routine, while management is concerned about winning sufficient cooperation to successfully implement the change. Employee resistance to change is predictably passive-aggressive in nature. For example, newly imposed regulations may be criticized for unfairly targeting specific employee groups, or employee tensions may center around management/employee communications. Employees may complain that new directives lack clarity, asking, "Who is responsible for what?" Management may be perceived as lacking insight into nuisances that hinder forced-change practices, with employees wondering, for instance, "How can services remain constant when clientele needs and circumstances vary greatly?"

Edgar Schein (1990, 1999, 2004, 2010) warns that organizational change and development will be sabotaged by culturally reinforced resistance unless targeted adjustments or change are embraced by key players throughout the system. Katz and Kahn (1978) agree and suggest overcoming resistance by challenging the well-worn habits of established power relations (such as fear of losing ground in the relationship when resources are reallocated or a reward systems is revamped) that are inherent to change interventions. To understand the depths of resistance to change, it is wise to remember that "letting go the status quo" can be just as difficult for those who stand to gain from the change as it is for those people who perceive that they will lose ground when the change is implemented (Eidelman, Crandall, & Pattershall, 2009; Jost, Banaji, & Nosek, 2004; Kay et al., 2009).

"CHANGING"   The other major treatment of change is the "changing" or coordinated change approach. An intervention that promotes continuous change or "changing" is ongoing, evolving, and cumulative. Such a change intervention utilizes a process that wins cooperation: (1) it ensures that individuals at all levels are willing to "buy in" to the change (2) and it depends on built-in collective efficacy supported by (3) flexible practices that accommodate current needs while making room for evolving operations (Chen, Sharma, Edinger, Shapiro, & Farh, 2011; Schmid Mast, Jonas, & Hall, 2009).

To initiate a "changing" or coordinated change intervention, leadership encourages the parties most impacted by the change to be actively involved in inclusive decision making, constructing an intervention that is focused on optimizing performance and continuous learning (Martins, 2011; Orlikowski, 1996; Rindova & Kotha, 2001; Tsoukas & Chia, 2002). Tsoukas and Chia (2002) explain the philosophy behind the negotiated interaction experienced by affected parties, noting that "change must not be thought of as a property of the organization . . . rather, the organization must be understood as an emergent property of change" (p. 570).

Systemic change management has been a recurrent theme throughout I/O psychology history. As discussed in Chapter 1, Mary Parker Follett's 1924 work *Creative Experience* (as cited in Follett, Fox, & Urwick, 1973) recommends employee participation in the change process through *coordination* by direct contact of the responsible people concerned, *coordination* in the early stages of the change process, and *coordination* as a continuous process. Taking a similar approach, Argyris (1970) encourages the engagement of employees in change management and suggests that offering a choice of preferred intervention type to the employees who are most impacted by the change intervention is an effective way to ensure that the change is successfully implemented. Kurt Lewin (1951; Lewin & Lewin, 1948) a modern pioneer of social, organizational, and applied psychology, proposes one of the earliest foundational models of planned organizational change, which includes three phases: *unfreezing, moving,* and *refreezing.* To initiate planned organizational change, you must first unfreeze the status quo by introducing information that indicates a discrepancy between the organization's performances and aspirations (its goals and/or vision). In the next step, you alter the status quo by changing the organizational structures (such as divisions, departments, and teams) and processes (such as service to customers). In the final step, you will refreeze the status quo by reinforcing the new behaviors and values with policies and reward systems. Porras and Silvers (1991) and Porras and Robertson (1992) emphasize the importance of a well-designed infrastructure and hierarchy for retaining organizational health while achieving desired outcomes. They advise using change targets, designated employees who model, supervise, and support a flexible framework for implementing change throughout the organization.

Interventions that promote coordinated changing awaken the perennial student in everyone in welcoming participation in distinguishing between that which need be altered by the "new day and new time" and that which can hold constant (remain unchanged) to time and place (Ackoff, 1981, 1989; Flood, 1999; Katz & Kahn, 1978). "Changing" intervention plans acknowledge upfront the nonlinear nature of the change process. Coordinated change disperses the responsibility for its design and implementation, allowing a wide variety of people to participate in the change intervention (Katz & Kahn, 1978). Success or failure of the intervention reflects back on leadership *and* employees, and it will be incorporated in their annual collective and self-evaluations. Successes are jointly celebrated, and the analysis of failures guides continuous improvement. Adjustment to action plans capitalizes on employee strengths and provides support for individual and/or team challenge areas.

Although there are clearly many advantages to continuous change, the most obvious disadvantage to this kind of "change from within" intervention is the lengthy preparation for and process-intensive work during and following its implementation. In addition, self-designed change intervention plans may lack sufficient objectivity to curb possible overemphasis on the participants' specific roles and responsibilities in relation to the entirety of the organization (Katz & Kahn, 1978; Martins, 2011). To address these challenges, Orlikowski (1996) recommends flexible management of "changing" or coordinated change practices and suggests monitoring continuous improvement through an extensive interaction between employees and strategic partnerships, linking current to future projects through improvisation.

Organizational improvisation involves experimenting with everyday contingencies, breakdowns, exceptions, and opportunities as they arise. Some theorists compare the emergent property of workplace change—the adjustments to a unique time and space—to jazz improvisation (Hatch, 1999; Tsoukas & Chia, 2002; Weick, & Quinn, 1999). It is vitally important to remember that sacrifice at the individual level is sometimes necessary to protect the well-being of the whole system or organization. Refusal to respect this reality can seriously compromise system resilience (Flood, 1999; Katz & Kahn, 1978).

Capitalizing on Punctuated Equilibrium

Organizations utilize both "change to" and "changing" strategies to deal with a wide range of circumstances confronting daily practices and systems. Although some organizational modifications can be applied gradually ("changing"), others require immediate adjustment ("change to"). Best practice literature recommends timing workplace intervention to capitalize on change *patterns,* as enlightened by the *punctuated equilibrium model,* which is a framework that explains that organizational change involves uneven temporal sequences characterized by long periods of evolutionary or small incremental change and punctuated by shorter periods of revolutionary or radical change (Abernathy & Utterback, 1978; Gersick, 1989, 1991; Repetto, 2006).

The punctuated equilibrium model advocates gradual imposition of novel conditions on the work environment, thus allowing time for evolutionary change to occur. This enables everyone time to absorb the full force of the change throughout the organization. When the process of "changing" is initiated during the "calm before the storm," all levels of the organization will be prepared to ride the wave of radical change that—when left unmanaged—can threaten organizational stability and survival.

Maintaining Organizational Health in the Midst of Change

Change is *good* for organizations. Workplace change brings novel situations and new ideas for generating tension and lively debate, all of which keeps employees alert, ready to identify and solve focused operational problems as well as promote system-wide learning (Flood, 1999; Katz & Kahn, 1978). An organization that is closed to change risks self-elimination because organizational resilience requires negative entropy—taking action through hiring new people, pursuing novel perspectives, and making future plans (Martins, 2011; Porras & Robertson, 1992). Like a tortoise stalled at a busy intersection, an organization will self-eliminate if it loses its way or becomes stuck in the present. Doing too little too late to accommodate changing realities leads to waking up one day to bankruptcy or the reality of a takeover by a competitor.

Implementing change of any kind requires reflection on recent events to determine areas of success and failure. Organizations that refuse to manage change reflect poorly on everyone, indicating an imbalance of power or expertise, the presence of control issues between employees and management, or issues around status, prestige, or (perceived or real) lack of equity in distribution of key roles and jobs (Burke, 2008). Pacing the rate of organizational change helps ward off chronic or extreme workplace uncertainty that can have a deleterious effect on people (Herold et al., 2007; Hogg & Terry, 2001; Hogg, Sherman, Dierselhuis, Maither, & Moffitt, 2006), especially when the changes are extensive and roles that were once well-defined require revision (Wrzesniewski & Dutton, 2001). The greater the magnitude of the change (Boudreau & Robey, 2005) and the higher the change turbulence (Martins, 2011), the more likely employees with low change efficacy will exhibit reduced commitment to change (Boudreau & Robey, 2005).

Change Management Pioneers (Trailblazers)

Herold et al. (2007; Herold, Fedor, Caldwell, & Liu, 2008) recommend delegating "change target" employees to absorb the rapid exchange of information and day-to-day adjustments as a way to protect the entire organization from overload and disruption. Change threshold as measured by comfort with ambiguity, general orientation to change, and history of success or failure in change adaptation differ greatly from person to person and from organization to organization (Boudreau & Robey, 2005). People who possess high change efficacy understand the tenuous nature of organizational life and are aware that an organization's structures and processes need to be both dependable and changeable—an organization is, and should be, always in flux. *Change agents* or change targets—people comfortable with change—regularly span the boundaries, trying on new ideas, seeking new paths, and collecting possibilities to be ready for potentially leaner times (Herold et al., 2007). To retain good form, change agents deliberatively practice remaining emotionally calm, mentally objective, and open to new experiences and novel relations.

Change agents or change targets may be situated within management; they may hold strategic employee positions within the organization; or they may be outside consultants. Internal staff specialists or managers, when acting as change agents, are likely more thoughtful and cautious, because they often feel more accountable to colleagues for the consequences of their actions. Regardless of their station, however, change agents must know that they are backed by financial and social capital, receptive management, and flexible systems for accommodating new data and insight (Porras & Robertson, 1992; Cannon-Bowers & Bowers, 2011).

Change management is most attractive to *low uncertainty identity* individuals, because these people know their strengths and weaknesses, are unruffled by ambiguity, possess high self-efficacy, take calculated risks, learn from their mistakes, and capitalize on within reach opportunities (Fedor, Caldwell, & Herold, 2006; Herold et al., 2007; Hogg & Terry, 2001). At the other end of the spectrum, people with *high uncertainty identity* are uncomfortable with ambiguity and reluctant to change or are workers who strongly identity with targeted-for-change organizational values or practices (Bartel, Blader, & Wrzesniewski, 2007; Ellemers, 2003; Haslam & Ellemers, 2005; Hogg et al., 2006; Hogg & Terry, 2001).

Managing Risk Taking and Innovation

Survival in a fast-changing global economy is best supported by a learning culture that is open to new ideas, risk taking, and innovative practices (Schein, 2004; Schneider, Ehrhart, & Macey, 2011). *Innovation* is defined as an idea, practice, or object that is new and is adopted by an individual or team (Rogers, 2003); this idea, practice, or object is put into action to produce change (Bilewicz, 2009). The innovative process goes through predictable stages: enlightenment, adoption, implementation, and routinization (Rogers, 2003).

Challenges to innovative practices are twofold: first, the organization's leadership must make sure essential support measures are available, and second, everyone affected by the innovation must trust in the innovation process itself. Innovation is costly, risky, and difficult to achieve, and it requires synthesis of a variety of technologies and resources that even the wealthiest corporations find difficult to manage (Eisenhardt, Schoonhoven, & Lyman, 2001). Zhou and Shalley (2011) recommend setting the benchmark high and keeping the "kid gloves" handy, because high-level creativity thrives on four components: (1) possession of relevant knowledge and skills; (2) creativity-relevant skills and strategies; (3) positive challenge from the task itself; and (4) plenty of attentive support (Choi & Chang, 2009; Deci & Ryan, 1980, 1985, 2000; Zhou, 1998). The ambiguity and uncertainty inherent in the generation of new ideas and innovation are best overcome by raising the creative role identity to a unique status (differentiation from others in their team or organization) and supporting those individuals who take a creative role by providing a culture that celebrates and rewards the creative process as well as its end product (Thatcher & Greer, 2008; Tierney & Farmer, 2002, 2004).

Organizational slack is crucial to inspired risk taking and innovative problem solving (Argote & Greve, 2007). I/O literature traditionally refers to organizational slack as discretionary spending of unencumbered monetary resources. Organizational slack is actually manifested in three ways: as it relates to resource pool (financial or social capital); as the possession of an "abundance mindset," the belief that there are many ways to enlarge the pie; and as in the saying "to cut a person some slack"—giving those in the creative role the benefit of the doubt as they work, knowing how hardships endured can contribute to falling short of expected benchmark performance. Slack in any of these forms inspires generosity in brainstorming as well as relaxing cutthroat tendencies. Interestingly, slack of any type is more a matter of opinion than a reality, because "money to burn" today may be "barely meeting basics" tomorrow; circumstances change, often quickly, and sweet-spirited generosity can turn sour if exploitation is suspected. On the other hand, the absence of slack—a scarcity mind-set—can result in missed opportunities.

ORGANIZATIONAL LEARNING AND CHANGING

> The learning process is highly creative and adaptive, and eminently suitable to a systemic world . . . anyone thinking they have everything under control is badly mistaken . . . too much perceived certainty and agreement kills novelty and creativity, stifling adaptability, putting in doubt future survival in any guise. (Flood, 1999, pp. 90–91)

Organizational learning is more than a compilation of facts; it is a living and evolving "entity" that requires negotiated decision making, cooperation, patience, and tolerance for the attainment of a workable shared knowledge base. Organizational learning is never static or complete; it is ever-evolving and continuous. Adjustment to the new realities of a given moment builds awareness, and patterns within the changed environment emerge. If previously held opinions conflict significantly with new information, then collective efficacy is threatened; management and employees must step up to engage in reflective processing to challenge those old assumptions and allow new assumptions to be formed (Argyris, 1999; Argyris & Schön, 1978; Faraj & Yan, 2009).

Models of Organizational Learning

Several theoretical models describe the processes that facilitate the progression from individual to collective learning. As introduced in Chapters 1 and 3, classic organizational learning occurs when images that are created by individual employees inquiring about "how things are done around here" are discussed with other employees to form a map of shared descriptions that answers those questions about how things are done. The map, constructed jointly by the employees who will use it to guide future actions, is a manifestation of organizational learning. Figure 12.1 demonstrates the transition from individual image to shared map that is necessary for achieving organizational learning.

Organizational learning occurs when individual learning has been shared within the organization and is subsequently adopted by the group as "the correct way" to do things—the accepted practice for solving problems or completing tasks. Organizational learning shapes standard operating procedures as well as policy (Argyris & Schön, 1978; Schneider et al., 2011). *Single-loop learning* (individual learning) involves detection and correction of error to inspire change in the practices and procedures of one or more individuals, but it does not involve change in the fundamental norms or assumptions of the group or organization (Argyris, Putnam, & Smith, 1985). As a result of single-loop organizational learning, the organization gets better and better at doing the same thing. Organizational cultural change arises only when the change reflects a shift in basic organizational assumptions that result from double-loop learning. *Double-loop learning* (organizational learning) gives rise to cultural change because the basic norms or assumptions are changed as values are changed. In short, single-loop learning changes the way an organization manufactures or delivers a product or service, whereas double-loop learning results in changes in what the organization *does*. Successful organizational learning is enhanced when the organizational vision, organizational practice, and goals are all aligned.

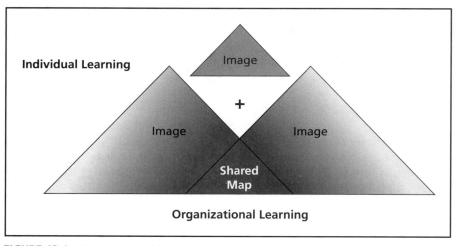

FIGURE 12.1 Organizational Learning.

Deutero learning (also called triple-loop learning) involves "learning about learning"; that is, it involves studying and learning from the context in which single-loop or double-loop learning occurred to discover what facilitated or inhibited the learning process. Deutero learning thus facilitates organizational learning capacity, particularly in relation to achievement of organizational goals (Argyris & Schön, 1978).

COMMUNITIES OF PRACTICE   Another model of organizational learning proposed by Etienne Wenger (Wenger, 1998; Wenger & Snyder, 2000) considers an organization (such as a school, municipality, or business) as a *community of practice* that provides structure for negotiating "meanings" to guide shared experience and learning. Wenger believes all change is a process of learning, and the learning centers around two interrelated components: reification and participation. The *reification* process, central to every practice, involves taking that which is abstract and turning it into a concrete form, creating documents (a policy or law), symbols (the American flag), and other tangible assets. The process of reification is essential to prevent fluid and informal group activity from getting in the way of co-ordination and mutual understanding in the group. Reification alone is not able to support the learning process, however.

Participation, the second element in the negotiation of meaning, requires active involvement in social processes centered on dialogue and reflection. Through "trying on" or "trying out" that which has been reified (enforcing legislation through procedural law, for example), participants gain new insight into that which "rings true"—or that which deserves supports—and that which does not hold up or work out when applied to the situation it was meant to improve. This reflective process is called *re-contextualizing meaning.* Wenger believes that organizational learning renders an organization capable of openness to utilize diverse perspectives by uniting them into a collective perspective, choosing a process that seeks outcomes and products acceptable to all. Leadership orchestrates identification of collective vision (reification), and leadership, management employees, and teams design action plans and practices that realize the shared vision constructed through participation of the all of the involved parties.

I-P-O MODEL   The input-process-output (I-P-O) model refers to a way of learning that is measured by *input,* or how information is taken in; *process,* or how information is analyzed and reorganized; and *output,* or how this processed information is shared with others (Ilgen, 1999). This learning model has been criticized for implying that learning follows a linear path (a straight line from inputs through outcomes), to which Ilgen, Hollenbeck, Johnson, and Jundt (2005) offered an alternative model, the input-mediator-output-input (IMOI), which acknowledges the influences of environment or culture and includes a cyclical feedback loop. IMOI research is organized around a two-dimensional system based on time and the nature of explanatory mechanisms that mediate between team inputs and outcomes. Recent theoretical and methodological works have advanced the understanding of teams as complex, multilevel systems that function over time, tasks, and contexts (Ilgen, Hollenbeck, Johnson, & Jundt 2005).

PROCESS MAPPING (COGNITIVE MAPPING)   Computer science has taught social scientists a lot about human mental processing, which is different from computer processing because it incorporates personal memory (with its emotion tags) as well as being similar to computers because it is constrained by limitations of information access (decisions are "best guesses" because they can include only the information available for processing). Process mapping benefits greatly from technological advancement (Cooke, Salas, Kiekel, & Bell, 2004; Van Knippenberg, De Dreu, & Homan, 2004), and cognition theorists advocate the use of process mapping for group learning to improve group performance (Hinsz, 1990; Hinsz, Tindale, & Vollrath, 1997). Conceptual mapping, developed at the group level, is used as a diagnostic tool for concrete representation of problem map construction. Process mapping assists the development of a shared problem model, which involves an explicit problem definition followed by articulation of plans, strategies, and decision rules associated with the problem, as well as overlapping knowledge and the roles and skills the group members bring to the process (Fiore & Schooler, 2004). Mapping the thought processes that go into collective decisions offers vital information for recipients who can use the information for future decision making.

Cognitive theorists believe that cognitive or process mapping is an effective tool for diagnosing and assessing group training needs (Smith-Jentsch, Campbell, Milanovich, & Reynolds, 2001). Its tools are "user friendly" and it takes a holistic approach to measure training effectiveness. The process mapping method compares knowledge and practices as measured before and after training, which makes it useful for evaluating training effectiveness (Curşeu, Schalk, & Schuijer 2010). Sutton (2006) describes cognitive maps or *exograms* as external memories for the group to encapsulate understanding of a particular matter at a particular moment in time. Sutton (2006) envisions these maps as serving three purposes: (1) they act as a reference point for the development of group cognition; (2) they facilitate the learning effectiveness of the group; and (3) the cognitive maps produced are artifacts or external memories or exograms that can be used to measure the future performance of the group.

Curşeu and colleagues (2010) conducted quantitative studies of group diversity with a disparity, variety, and separation taxonomy introduced by Harrison and Klein (2007). They found empirically based support for group variety contributing positively to the higher pool of knowledge within groups, whereas disparity had the opposite effect. Curşeu et al. (2010) espouse linking this taxonomy to the concept of collective cognitive representation to offer the possibility of pointing out the mechanisms that explain the differentiated effects of the three diversity types on group performance.

Methodology for Organizational Learning

Organizational learning is a dynamic and evolutionary process that is best understood by focusing on nonlinear relationships rather than linear ones, because it is manipulated by complex and dynamic systems that affect and are affected by a host of individual, task, situational, environmental, and organizational factors (Cannon-Bowers & Bowers, 2011).

The contemporary systems theorist Jamshid Gharajedaghi, a former student and colleague of renowned systems theorist Russell Ackoff (1919–2009), considers organizations purposeful systems with membership that intentionally and collectively formulates objectives and benefits from systems as "holistic" thinking. Gharajedaghi questions the wisdom of equating a multidisciplinary approach to a systems approach, because "the ability to synthesize separate findings into a coherent whole is far more critical than the ability to generate information from different perspectives" (Gharajedaghi, 2006, p. 108). He suggests understanding a system as a whole entity while examining the four elements that compose that whole entity (structure, function, process, and environment). These four elements are identified, tested, and fine-tuned to reveal the underlying assumptions about a social system's nature and functioning.

Gharajedaghi (2006) believes organizations learn and change via iteration (a coping mechanism) that allows them to examine what works and then modify the functional process accordingly. In other words, the members of an organization identify their realities in order to cope with them (Gharajedaghi, 2006). A system's structure, function, and process, along with its environment (organizational culture) or context, form an interdependent set of mutually exclusive and collectively exhausting variables. Together, these four perspectives define the "whole" and make possible the understanding of that whole. For example, the heart provides the *function* of a "pump" to circulate blood, while the *structure* of this pump consists of four chambers and a set of valves, arteries, and veins. The *process*, of pumping blood through the four chambers via contraction and expansion of the chambers, pushes the blood through the arteries and then pull it back into the chambers through the veins by suction.

Iterations of structure, function, and process in a given context allow the organization's members to examine assumptions and properties associated with each element in its own right, and then to examine assumptions and properties in relationship to the other members of the set. Subsequent iterations are used to establish the validity of the assumptions, and then compatibilities and conflicts are identified and dissolved. Resolving conflicts may require reconceptualization of the variables involved. Finally, successive iterations will produce an integrated design. Gharajedaghi explains how creative use of a screwdriver models production of different *functions* with a single *structure* in the same environment, because the screwdriver serves multiple purposes when used to gouge, chisel, and hammer a piece of wood.

The elastic nature of a community, which is a social system, renders it interchangeable in structure and function. An example of this elasticity is to juxtapose various forms of "community building." The first community structure can take the form of houses built in close proximity to one another (a city block, village, or town), or the community structure can be a series of apartments (single dwellings) within a large building, or the structure can be abstract in nature, such as a website where a virtual community with shared interests can meet via the Internet.

Each type of structure provides aspects of "community," such as networking and affiliation for psychological well-being. For example, the perfunctory habit (function) of regularly visiting an interactive workplace website may provide community (structure) for an otherwise reclusive person. Another individual has a habit of walking her dog on the same path every morning; this ritual eventually leads to her becoming acquainted with the other dog owners who routinely travel the same route. The dog walkers, in collectively choosing to traverse a common path, have built community (structure) while fulfilling the function of tending to their pets' needs.

As witnessed by these many examples, *complex systems* hold potential for great flexibility, as we find that multiple routes may achieve similar goals. (Gharajedaghi, 2006, p. 45). Von Bertalanffy (1968) introduced the concept of *equifinality* to define the final state that can be reached by any number of different developmental routes, and Buckley (2009) added the concept of *multifinality* as observed in sociocultural systems, in which similar initial conditions can lead to dissimilar end states.

Organizational Vision and Systems in Motion

The organization's vision reflects the comprehensive strategic plan, choice of organizational culture, and style of leadership and management (Schein, 1999, 2010) as implemented by the organizational structure and support systems (Porras & Robertson, 1992; Porras & Silvers, 1991). When frequent or radical change overwhelms employees, leadership is wise to transparently legitimize the employee tension by communicating to everyone involved that "things are moving at record speed here, and we know it's taking a toll on everyone." Adequate support measures ward off burnout and despair (Bartel et al., 2007; Hogg & Terry, 2001).

CHANGE MANAGEMENT AND DEVELOPMENT

Successful change management and organizational development benefit from participation at all levels of the organization, because the more fully integrated an intervention is, the better it can model a learning culture philosophy, and the greater the opportunity for all affected members to "own" the change when decisions are made collectively (Schneider et al., 2011). By engaging all factions early in the process, leadership averts the potential polarization of alienated factions that is typical in top-down change management (Schein, 2010). Well-honed efficacy in communication, conflict management, and related skills—often referred to as "people skills"—are crucial for facilitating successful change management.

Adjustment to change, even when parties are willing, requires work. Access to change management tools and skills is essential to a smooth transition. Organizational change management demands openness to the information relevant to the altered situation, thorough (unbiased) processing of new information and successful integration of that information so that individuals can effectively adjust behaviors to accommodate the now-altered situation. And even if this transition can be monitored by someone who remains emotionally calm, cognitively objective, and behaviorally open to possibilities, she may not know how to adjust actions to meet new demands—more effort may be required to implement the change successfully. For example, if a manager is told to do a better job meeting customer needs for an expensive product, he may need to seek more information, such as lists of the most popular alternatives and the benefits of the product the manager's staff is selling, to fulfill that task effectively.

Change Management Tools

Change management tools are in abundant supply, and marketing these "products" can be a lucrative business, but the marketing will probably tell you more about end results—what a particular tool promises to deliver—than information about how the tool can assist you in the change process. Change management tools facilitate group process at multiple levels; the simplest tool is a survey, and the most complex tool is the strategic planning process that has the potential to incorporate every change tool available.

Information Gathering and Processing Tools

Intervention models and tools that best orchestrate organizational development combine *"change to"* and *"changing"* practices.

Surveys are information-seeking tools. They usually employ either forced-choice questions (multiple choice or yes/no answers) or questions that request open-ended responses (essays). The feedback from surveys increases the learning of the organization's employees and may identify employees who need support, especially if their performance is not up to standard, to take corrective action and improve task performance. Surveys are useful for obtaining feedback quickly from a large number of employees and customers with minimal cost in terms of face-to-face interactions during the information-gathering activities; the information can be gathered from one source, from people in a specific category, or from a wide range of people in various categories. Interestingly, 360-degree evaluations, which involve feedback from an employee's peers, supervisors, and subordinates as well as a self-evaluation, invite a more diverse pool of people to participate in the evaluation process, rather just the employer or management.

Feedback loops serve many essential purposes, such as ensuring quality control during changing conditions inside and outside the organization. Exercising vigilant behind-the-scene information gathering and processing allows you to make timely adjustments within the organization and outside it to accommodate fluctuations in the economy and redesign of information technology. An inclusive feedback loop provides an opportunity for continuous improvement by enlightening membership in the loop about the perspectives of otherwise under-represented members to elicit their cooperation (Belschak & Den Hartog, 2008; Bilewicz, 2009). The most rigorous type of feedback loop is the 360-degree survey, a top-down, bottom-up, full employee evaluation that offers both the employee and management an opportunity to understand each other's perceptions of everyday performance, which is often used in conjunction with conflict and/or change management. The greatest advantage of this tool is the inclusiveness it affords the organization, and its greatest challenge is the subjective nature of the instrument.

Deliberative dialogue is a tool that is crucial for organizational health and membership well-being, and a structured dialogue format is perhaps the ideal environment for negotiating organizational or community shared identity, identifying the source of collective problems and means for their resolution and determining provisions for a self-sustaining environment. A deliberative or structured dialogue, also referred to as a strategic dialogue or study circle, unites forces to share information and to engage in meaningful dialogue with those with whom one shares interests or interdependence.

David Bohm (1994) encourages communities to engage in deliberative dialogue to identify habits of thought (aka reflexive thought) for the purpose of resolving long-standing conflict. Bohm distinguishes between coherent and incoherent thought, noting that incoherent thought conflicts with reason. Deliberative dialogue provides a venue to articulate the assumptions perpetuating collective incoherence or societal conflict, thereby making room for establishing workable solutions.

The strategic dialogue is built on the operating principle that the stakeholders in any system already have within them the wisdom and creativity to confront even the most difficult challenges. The roots of this tool are found in the work of Scandinavian study circles (Senge, 1994, pp. 508–509). The "community of inquiry" can extend beyond employees of an organization to include unions, customers, suppliers, and other stakeholders, making it a dynamic and reinforcing process that helps to create and strengthen the "communities of commitment" that Fred Kofman and Peter Senge emphasize lie at the heart of learning organizations capable of leading the way toward a sustainable future (Flood, 1999).

Social networks offer powerful bases for change implementation, as they can help build emotional commitment to champion on change projects and offer a way to monitor the emotions of those affected by the change. They are successful tools for gathering and disseminating information to manage transition even when implementing radical change (Martins, 2011).

Behavior modification ("change to") is classified as single-loop learning, which as you remember involves getting better and better at doing the same thing. This change management process focuses primarily on behavior and skips over the emotional and cognitive motives that have been influencing the old unacceptable behaviors. The behavioral approach encourages the employee to undertake new habits for personal management. Time management and stress management tools fit this approach to change management, and if these new habits are appropriate for the emotional and psychological needs of the individuals involved, the exercise can help refine time or stress management tools tailored to the unique needs of the employees.

The *SWOT analysis,* an acronym for Strengths-Weaknesses-Opportunities-Threats, is a "change to" process that can support "changing" when orchestrated in an open, inclusive, and supportive environment. A SWOT analysis is the process of identifying the strengths, weaknesses, opportunities, and threats or challenges that make up the everyday life of the organization.

You begin a SWOT analysis with a well-defined goal (or goals), ideally the product of a team that represents a broad range of perspectives. The SWOT analysis looks at external and internal factors that are important to achieve the goals of the organization. These may include the organizational systems in place, a competitive advantage, innovation activities, patents filed, morale, turnover, leadership, market demand, and insurmountable weaknesses.

A SWOT analysis can be very helpful if decisions and actions are well-documented (e.g., by keeping a detailed record of meeting minutes, process mapping goals, and clearly delineating role assignments), and it includes a mechanism for measuring quantitative progress toward the goals based on specific action plans. As discussed earlier in this chapter, process mapping, as you will recall, is a problem-solving tool that assists in the construction of a shared mental model of targeted problems by including the conceptualization process used to understand the problem, that is, by clarifying the issues surrounding the problem. Process mapping provides structure and discipline for the problem-solving process and ensures that each phase of the process is given adequate time. Without a structured process to guide people through problem solving, there is the likelihood of leaping to premature solution processing (Fiore & Schooler, 2004).

The *strategic planning process* (SPP) holds the greatest potential to orchestrate a "changing" process for the organization, because it welcomes the participation of employees from every level of responsibility in the change management process. A comprehensive strategic planning process gives vision clarity, tightens social bond, creates structure, and focuses support around production or services while shielding employees from disruptive forces within and outside of the workplace (Castano, Yzerbyt, & Bourguignon, 2003). By keeping members' attention aligned with the team's mission and tasks, boundary reinforcement in knowledge teams can enhance individual and collective learning and creativity (Faraj & Yan, 2009). The SPP is the most comprehensive of the change management interventions, because it engages employees from every organizational level in developing proactive systems, starting with the vision statement and ending with evaluation feedback.

Completing the initial strategic planning process is not the end of the action, however. Periodically revisiting of the SPP—on average at about three-year intervals—facilitates keeping a focus on relevant tasks and ensures sufficient financial and social capital to allow in-depth dialogue at each step of the SPP. It is important to set parameters for the decision-making authority and create firm timelines for completion of specific projects. The strategic planning process proceeds through multiple steps that serve to (1) identify the organizational vision, (2) articulate core organizational goals as determined by group consensus, (3) perform an assessment of the internal and external environments of the organization, (4) analyze conflict issues compromising performance quality, (5) design action plans and strategies for achieving goals, (6) choose best-practice evaluation tools for measuring organizational outcomes, (7) use 360-degree feedback loops throughout the organization whenever feasible, (8) celebrate successes, and (9) make periodic adjustments to action plans for continuous improvement.

Chapter Summary

In this chapter we presented the "change to" or imposed change and the "changing" or participatory change models of organizational development. We discussed how regularly scanning the horizon to gain insight into ways to advance worker relations and quality production puts an organization at the head of the line to take action when opportunity arises. People in a learning culture support the needs of their colleagues, and they embrace the idea of taking responsibility for change as they model transparent acknowledgment of falling short of goals and use insights gained from mistakes to do better next time. We described a proactive approach to organizational learning and development and explained the benefits of resolving conflict close to the site of its implementation. Leadership and management actively support the innovative work of employees, and the full organization practices a mantra of "one for all, and all for one." Guided by the laws of nature as well as by those of humankind, today's organizations use systems thinking to retain resilience in the exciting, fast-paced world of our 21st century.

Chapter References

Abernathy, W. J., & Utterback, J. (1978). Patterns of industrial innovation. *Technological Review, 80,* 41–47.

Ackoff, R. L. (1981). *Creating the corporate future.* New York: John Wiley & Sons.

Ackoff, R. L. (1989). The circular organization: An update. *Academy of Management Executive, 3,* 11–16.

Argote, L., & Greve, H. R. (2007). A behavioral theory of the firm: 40 years and counting. *Organization Science, 18*(3), 337–349.

Argyris, C. (1970). *Intervention theory and method: A behavioral science view.* Reading, MA: Addison-Wesley.

Argyris, C. (1999). *On organizational learning* (2nd ed.). Malden, MA: Blackwell.

Argyris, C., Putnam, R., & Smith, D. M. (1985). *Action science* (1st ed.). San Francisco: Jossey-Bass.

Argyris, C., & Schön, D. A. (1978). *Organizational learning.* Reading, MA: Addison-Wesley.

Bartel, C., Blader, S. L., & Wrzesniewski, A. (2007). *Identity and the modern organization.* Mahwah, NJ: Lawrence Erlbaum.

Belschak, F. D., & Den Hartog, D. N. (2009). Consequences of positive and negative feedback: The impact on emotions and extra-role behaviors. *Applied Psychology, 58*(2), 274–303. doi:10.1111/j.1464-0597.2008.00336.x

Bilewicz, M. (2009). Perspective taking and intergroup helping intentions: The moderating role of power relations. *Journal of Applied Social Psychology, 39*(12), 2779–2786. doi:10.1111/j.1559-1816.2009.00548.x

Bohm, D. (1994). *Thought as a system.* New York: Routledge.

Boudreau, M. C., & Robey, D. (2005). Enacting integrated information technology: A human agency perspective. *Organizational Science, 16,* 3–18.

Buckley, W. F. (2009). *Systems research for behavioral science: A sourcebook.* New Brunswick, NJ: AldineTransaction.

Burke, W. W. (2008). *Organization change: Theory and practice* (2nd ed.). Los Angeles: Sage.

Cannon-Bowers, J. A., & Bowers, C. (2011). Team development and functioning. In S. Zedeck (Ed.), *APA handbook of industrial and organizational psychology* (Vol. 1, pp. 597–650). Washington, DC: American Psychological Association.

Castano, E., Yzerbyt, V., & Bourguignon, D. (2003). We are one and I like it: The impact of ingroup entitativity on ingroup identification. *European Journal of Social Psychology, 33*(6), 735–754. doi:10.1002/ejsp.175

Chen, G., Sharma, P. N., Edinger, S. K., Shapiro, D. L., & Farh, J. L. (2011). Motivating and demotivating forces in teams: Cross-level influences of empowering leadership and relationship conflict. *Journal of Applied Psychology, 96*(3), 541–557.

Choi, J. N., & Chang, J. Y. (2009). Innovation implementation in the public sector: An integration of institutional and collective dynamics. *Journal of Applied Psychology, 94*(1), 245–253. doi:10.1037/a0012994

Cooke, N. J., Salas, E., Kiekel, P. A., & Bell, B. (2004). Advances in measuring team cognition. In E. Salas & S. M. Fiore (Eds.), *Team cognition: Understanding the factors that drive process and performance* (pp. 83–106). Washington, DC: American Psychological Association.

Curşeu, P. L., Schalk, R., & Schruijer, S. (2010). The use of cognitive mapping in eliciting and evaluating group cognitions. *Journal of Applied Social Psychology, 40*(5), 1258–1291. doi:10.1111/j.1559-1816.2010.00618.x

Deci, E. L., & Ryan, R. M. (1980). The empirical exploration of intrinsic motivational processes. In L. Berkowitz (Ed.), *Advances in experimental social psychology* (Vol. 13, pp. 39–80). New York: Academic Press.

Deci, E. L., & Ryan, R. M. (1985). *Intrinsic motivation and self-determination in human behavior.* New York: Plenum.

Deci, E. L., & Ryan, R. M. (2000). The "what" and "why" of goal pursuits: Human needs and the self-determination of behavior. *Psychological Inquiry, 11,* 227–268.

Eidelman, S., Crandall, C. S., & Pattershall, J. (2009). The existence bias. *Journal of Personality and Social Psychology, 97*(5), 765–775. doi:10.1037/a0017058

Eisenhardt, K. M., Schoonhoven, C. B., & Lyman, K. (2001). Effects of top management teams on the organization of innovation through alternative types of strategic alliances. In M. E. Turner (Ed.), *Groups at work: Theory and research* (pp. 339–367). Mahwah, NJ: Lawrence Erlbaum.

Ellemers, N. (2003). Identity, culture, and change in organizations: A social identity analysis and three illustrative cases. In S. A. Haslam, D. van Knippenberg, M. J. Platow, & N. Ellemers (Eds.), *Social identity at work: Developing theory for organizational practice* (pp. 191–203). Philadelphia: Psychology Press.

Faraj, S., & Yan, A. (2009). Boundary work in knowledge teams. *Journal of Applied Psychology, 94*(3), 604–617. doi:10.1037/a0014367

Fedor, D. B, Caldwell, S., & Herold, D. M. (2006). The effects of organizational changes on employee commitment: A multilevel investigation. *Personnel Psychology, 59,* 1–29.

Fiore, S. M., & Schooler, J. W. (2004). Process mapping and shared cognition: Teamwork and the development of shared problem models.

In E. Salas & S. M. Fiore (Eds.), *Team cognition: Understanding the factors that drive process and performance* (pp. 133–152). Washington, DC: American Psychological Association.

Flood, R. L. (1999). *Rethinking the fifth discipline: Learning within the unknowable.* London: Routledge.

Follett, M. P. (1924). *Creative experience.* New York: Longmans, Green and Co.

Follett, M. P., Fox, E. M., & Urwick, L. (1973). *Dynamic administration: The collected papers of Mary Parker Follett.* London: Pitman Publishing.

Gersick, C. J. G. (1989). Marking time: Predictable transitions in task groups. *Academy of Management Journal, 32,* 274–309.

Gersick, C. J. G. (1991). Revolutionary change theories: A multilevel exploration of the punctuated equilibrium paradigm. *Academy of Management Review, 16,* 10–36.

Gharajedaghi, J. (2006). *Systems thinking: Managing chaos and complexity: A platform for designing business architecture* (2nd ed.). Burlington, MA: Elsevier.

Harrison, D. A., & Klein, K. J. (2007). What's the difference? Diversity constructs as separation, variety, or disparity in organizations. *Academy of Management Review, 39,* 1199–1228.

Haslam, S. A., & Ellemers, N. (2005). Social identity in industrial and organizational psychology: Concepts, controversies and contributions. In G. P. Hodgkinson (Ed.), *International review of industrial and organizational psychology* (Vol. 20, pp. 39–118). Chichester: Wiley.

Hatch, M. J. (1999). Exploring the empty spaces of organizing: How improvisational jazz helps redescribe organizational structure. *Organization Studies, 20,* 75–100.

Herold, D. M., Fedor, D. B., & Caldwell, S. D. (2007). Beyond change management: A multilevel investigation of contextual and personal influences on employees' commitment to change. *Journal of Applied Psychology, 92*(4), 942–951. doi:10.1037/0021-9010.92.4.942

Herold, D. M., Fedor, D. B., Caldwell, S., & Liu, Y. (2008). The effects of transformational and change leadership on employees' commitment to a change: A multilevel study. *The Journal of Applied Psychology, 93*(2), 346–357. doi:10.1037/0021-9010.93.2.346

Hinsz, V. B. (1990). Cognitive and consensus processes in group recognition memory performance. *Journal of Personality and Social Psychology, 59*(4), 705–718. doi:10.1037/0022-3514.59.4.705

Hinsz, V. B., Tindale, R. S., & Vollrath, D. A. (1997). The emerging conceptualization of groups as information processors. *Psychological Bulletin, 121*(1), 43–64.

Hogg, M. A., & Terry, D. J. (2001). *Social identity processes in organizational contexts.* Philadelphia: Psychology Press.

Hogg, M. A., Sherman, D. K., Dierselhuis, J., Maitner, A. T., & Moffitt, G. (2006). Uncertainty, entitativity, and group identification. *Journal of Experimental Social Psychology, 43*(1), 135–142.

Ilgen, D. R. (1999). Teams embedded in organizations: Some implications. *American Psychologist, 54*(2), 129–139.

Ilgen, D. R., Hollenbeck, J. R., Johnson, M., & Jundt, D. (2005). Teams in organizations: From input-process-output models to IMOI models. *Annual Review of Psychology, 56,* 517–543.

Jost, J. T., Banaji, M. R., & Nosek, B. A. (2004). A decade of system justification theory: Accumulated evidence of conscious and unconscious bolstering of the status quo. *Political Psychology, 25*(6) 881–920.

Katz, D., & Kahn, R. L. (1978). *The social psychology of organizations.* New York: Wiley.

Kay, A. C., Gaucher, D., Peach, J. M., Laurin, K., Friesen, J., Zanna, M. P., et al. (2009). Inequality, discrimination, and the power of the status quo: Direct evidence for a motivation to see the way things are as the way they should be. *Journal of Personality and Social Psychology, 97*(3), 421–434. doi:10.1037/a0015997

Lewin, K., & Lewin, G. W. (1948). *Resolving social conflicts, selected papers on group dynamics [1935–1946]* (1st ed.). New York: Harper.

Lewin, K. (1951). *Field theory in social science.* New York: Harper & Row.

Martins, L. L. (2011). Organizational change and development. In S. Zedeck (Ed.), *APA handbook of industrial and organizational psychology* (Vol. 3, pp. 691–728). Washington, DC: American Psychological Association.

Orlikowski, W. J. (1996). Improvising organizational transformation over time: A situated change perspective. *Information Systems Research, 7,* 63–92.

Porras J. I., & Silvers R. C. (1991). Organization development and transformation. *Annual Review of Psychology, 42*(51), 78.

Porras, J., & Robertson, P. J. (1992). Organizational development: Theory, practice, and research. In M. D. Dunnette & L. M. Hough (Eds.), *Handbook of industrial/organizational psychology* (Vol. 3, 2nd ed., pp. 719–822). Palo Alto, CA: Consulting Psychologists Press.

Repetto, R. (2006). *Punctuated equilibrium and the dynamics of environmental policy.* New Haven, CT: Yale University Press.

Rindova, V. P., & Kotha, S. (2001). Continuous "morphing": Competing through dynamic capabilities, form, and function. *Academy of Management Journal, 44,* 1263–1280.

Rogers, E. M. (2003). *Diffusion of innovations* (5th ed.). New York: Free Press.

Schein, E. H. (1990). Organizational culture. *American Psychologist, 45*(2), 109–119. doi:10.1037/0003-066X.45.2.109

Schein, E. H. (1999). *The corporate culture survival guide: Sense and nonsense about culture change* (1st ed.). San Francisco: Jossey-Bass.

Schein, E. H. (2004). *Organizational culture and leadership* (3rd ed.). San Fancisco: Jossey-Bass.

Schein, E. H. (2010). *Organizational culture and leadership* (4th ed.). San Francisco: Jossey-Bass.

Schmid Mast, M., Jonas, K., & Hall, J. A. (2009). Give a person power and he or she will show interpersonal sensitivity: The phenomenon and its why and when. *Journal of Personality and Social Psychology, 97*(5), 835–850.

Schneider, B., Ehrhart, M. G., & Macey, W. H. (Eds.). (2011). Perspectives on organizational climate and culture. In S. Zedeck (Ed.), *APA handbook of industrial and organizational psychology* (Vol. 1, pp. 373–413). Washington, DC: American Psychological Association.

Senge, P. M. (1994). *The fifth discipline fieldbook.* New York: Bantam Doubleday.

Smith-Jentsch, K. A., Campbell, G. E., Milanovich, D. M., & Reynolds, A. M. (2001). Measuring teamwork mental models to support training needs assessment, development, and evaluation: Two empirical studies. *Journal of Organizational Behavior, 22*(2), 179–194.

Sutton, J. (2006). Distributed cognition: Domains and dimensions. *Pragmatics & Cognition, 14*(2), 235–247.

Thatcher, S. M. B., & Greer, L. L. (2008). Does it really matter if you recognize who I am? The implications of identity comprehension for individuals in work teams. *Journal of Management, 45,* 1137–1148.

Tierney, P., & Farmer, S. M. (2002). Creative self-efficacy: Potential antecedents and relationship to creative performance. *Academy of Management Journal, 45,* 1137–1148.

Tierney, P., & Farmer, S. M. (2004). The Pygmalion process and employee creativity. *Journal of Management, 30,* 413–432.

Tsoukas, H., & Chia, R. (2002). On organizational becoming: Rethinking organizational change. *Organization Science, 13,* 567–582.

van Knippenberg, D., De Dreu, C. K. W., & Homan, A. C. (2004). Work group diversity and group performance: An integrative model and research agenda. *Journal of Applied Psychology, 89,* 1008–1022.

von Bertalanffy, L. (1968). *General system theory: Foundations, development, applications.* New York: George Braziller.

Weick, K. E., & Quinn, R. E. (1999). Organizational change and development. *Annual Review of Psychology, 50,* 361–386.

Wenger, E. C. (1998). *Communities of practice: Learning, meaning, and identity.* New York: Cambridge University Press.

Wenger, E. C., & Snyder, W. M. (2000). Communities of practice: The organizational frontier. *Harvard Business Review, 78*(1), 139–145.

Wrzesniewski, A., & Dutton, J. E. (2001). Crafting a job: Revisioning employees as active crafters of their work. *The Academy of Management Review, 26*(2), 179–201.

Zhou, J. (1998). Feedback valence, feedback style, task autonomy, and acheivement orientation: Interactive effects on creative performance. *Journal of Applied Psychology, 83,* 261–276.

Zhou, J., & Shalley, C. E. (2011). Deepening our understanding of creativity in the workplace: A review of different approaches to creativity research. In S. Zedeck (Ed.), *APA handbook of industrial and organizational psychology* (Vol. 1, pp. 275–302). Washington, DC: American Psychological Association.

NAME INDEX

SUBJECT INDEX